How to Make Your Airplane Last Forever

Other books of interest

How to Make Your Airplane Last Forever

Mary Woodhouse

Scott Gifford

TAB Books
An imprint of McGraw-Hill

New York   San Francisco   Washington, D.C.   Auckland   Bogotá
Caracas   Lisbon   London   Madrid   Mexico City   Milan
Montreal   New Delhi   San Juan   Singapore
Sydney   Tokyo   Toronto

McGraw-Hill

A Division of The McGraw·Hill Companies

pbk   1 2 3 4 5 6 7 8 9 FGR/FGR 9 0 0 9 8 7 6 5

Library of Congress Cataloging-in-Publication Data
Woodhouse, Mary.
    How to make your airplane last forever / by Mary Woodhouse & Scott
Gifford.
      p.   cm.
    Includes index.
    ISBN 0-07-071704-4
    1. Private planes—Maintenance and repair.   I. Gifford, Scott.
    II. Title.
    TL671.9.W66   1995
    629.134'6—dc20   95-25670
                                                                  CIP

McGraw-Hill books are available at special quantity discounts to use as premiums and
sales promotions, or for use in corporate training programs. For more information, please
write to the Director of Special Sales, McGraw-Hill, 11 West 19th Street, New York, NY
10011. Or contact your local bookstore.

Acquisitions editor: Shelley IC. Chevalier
Editorial team: Robert E. Ostrander, Executive Editor
                Sally Anne Glover, Book Editor
Production team: Katherine G. Brown, Director
                Ollie Harmon, Coding
                Wanda S. Ditch, Desktop Operator
                Toya B. Warner, Computer Artist
                Jeffrey Miles Hall, Computer Artist
                Jodi L. Tyler, Indexer
Design team: Jaclyn J. Boone, Designer   0717044
                Katherine Lukaszewicz, Associate Designer   AV1

Contents

Acknowledgments

WE WOULD LIKE TO TAKE THIS OPPORTUNITY TO THANK THE PEOPLE and organizations who have helped on this project: Malcolm Barrett; Ray Crumley; Steve Crumley; Dave Baron; Mile High Avionics and Magnum Aero, both of Prescott, Arizona; Tom Hood; Bill Helm; Marcy Rogers; and Ed Seibling of Aviation Laboratories, Houston, Texas.

Introduction

FEW THINGS ARE MORE REWARDING IN LIFE THAN TAKING OFF IN YOUR airplane, cruising through the skies, and returning safely to Mother Earth. And few things can disrupt that experience faster than mechanical problems. To prevent or at least minimize the risk of mechanical problems interrupting your flying, it's important that you become familiar with the various aircraft systems, their functions and foibles, and how to guard against or repair them. From break-in to overhaul, there are many things you as an owner/operator can do to extend the life of your plane. You made a major investment when you purchased your plane, and the information in this book will help you protect that investment.

As you are no doubt aware, the FAA limits the work that an owner/operator may perform on an aircraft. It's very tempting for the person who is used to tinkering with cars and lawn mowers to crawl under the cowling of a plane and see what's there. Unfortunately, you will quickly run afoul of the FAA for doing so. You are permitted to perform only simple, largely cosmetic repairs and maintenance, while the majority of the work must be performed by an appropriately rated aircraft mechanic. But even though there is much work you cannot do, it is the truly prudent pilot who at least performs regular, detailed inspections. Not only can these inspections alert you to potential problems before they become costly, but they also will familiarize you with the unique characteristics of your aircraft. Airplanes vary widely, even among the same make and model. The more effort you put into understanding your particular aircraft, the more likely it is that you will have years of trouble-free flying.

In 1982, TAB Books published *Make Your Airplane Last Forever*, a guide to preventive maintenance for the owner/operator. Much has changed in the aviation world since then, and this book updates the original manual and provides you with the most current technology and information available.

We begin with the ever-popular regulations involving maintenance and preventive maintenance. From the mysterious FAR Part 43 through service bulletins, airworthiness directives, and type certificate data sheets, we try not to bore you with too much legal mumbo-jumbo—just enough to try to keep you out of trouble with your friends at the FAA. The 1995 edition of the FAR/AIM incorporates Part

43, but for those of you who have been flying since just after Orville and Wilbur, we have provided you with the full text of that part. You can't say we didn't warn you.

Not only is an owner/operator restricted as to what work is permitted to be done, but also there are tight reins placed on how that work can be accomplished. This is also true of certificated mechanics, who are not permitted to deviate from a compendium of directions that would boggle the mind. Since it is you who are primarily responsible for the airworthiness of your aircraft, however, we discuss these things so that you can ensure that only the right person with the right equipment and manuals works on your airplane.

Whether your plane is hangared, shaded, or on tiedowns, there is much you can do to protect it and ensure that it is ready to fly when you are. We discuss various methods of securing the aircraft after flight and methods of covering it for further protection. And since cleanliness is next to airworthiness (you may embroider that on a pillow), we offer tips on materials and procedures for cleaning the plane.

Next we proceed with a discussion of the various systems of an aircraft, such as hydraulics, pneumatics, avionics, etc. We discuss their form and function in sufficient detail to give you a basic understanding of the systems without bogging you down with a lot of techno-babble. Sprinkled throughout the section are some operating tips we have picked up or stolen from someone else over the years that might help you increase the longevity of your airplane.

Your instructor surely taught you the value of a proper preflight inspection, but if you are like most of us humanoids, you start cutting corners after awhile. We'll jar you back to reality by discussing the importance of a preflight that can keep you from crashing and save you money, and we offer a few additional tips on looking for things you might not have thought about.

Our next section deals with troubleshooting problems with your airplane. Why aren't you getting full power? What is making all those noises in your headset that are preventing you from hearing the tower? How do you describe to your mechanic what is going on? Being able to isolate the problem is half the battle and possibly half the cost when it comes to repairs and maintenance.

Believe it or not, there are ways to cut down on the cost of an annual, and one section deals solely with this subject. We give you tips on how to find a maintenance shop that will perform work legally and properly.

And finally, we get into preventive maintenance—those things you are permitted to do and should do if you have the time. These procedures will keep your airplane running at its peak, giving you many hours of flying pleasure. The more of these items you tackle, the more you will know your plane and its characteristics, and that can only make you a safer pilot.

We have tried to provide as much useful information as possible without being brand-specific. Every aircraft manufacturer does things just a little bit differently, and to attempt to discuss variances among aircraft would take volumes. Learn your aircraft and ask questions of your mechanic when applying the information provided here.

We also have stayed away from making recommendations about specific types of items to use when working on your plane. For every person who likes one thing, there is one who dislikes it. If you want brand recommendations, check with the mechanic who regularly maintains your plane. That way, at least there will be consistency.

We have made a few basic assumptions in putting together this guide. We have assumed that your plane is U.S. certificated and has an air-cooled, horizontally opposed engine. You don't have to be a professional mechanic to use this book, but we do assume you know a wrench from a screwdriver and how to use each one. We have attempted to find a balance between explaining things to the neophyte and describing things to the pilot who is more knowledgeable about aircraft systems.

We highly recommend that you obtain a copy of the maintenance manual for your airplane, if one exists. In it are the procedures and time intervals recommended by the manufacturer to work on an airplane, engine, prop, or accessory. A mechanic is required to have access to the appropriate manuals, and so should you.

If your airplane is a "Wichita Spam Can," your mechanic most likely has the manual in his or her library. However, if your pride and joy is unique (i.e., antique, foreign built, etc.), your mechanic probably won't have a manual. By having your own copy, you will ensure that the maintenance performed is correct and appropriate.

You should use this book the same way we recommend that you use the maintenance manuals. First read it through completely. Depending on what information you are looking for, you could find the answer in "Understanding your bird" (chapter 3), "Preventive maintenance," (chapter 5), or "Troubleshooting" (chapter 7). Likely, though, you will gain the best understanding through a combination of all the sections.

This manual is not intended as a substitute for advice from your mechanic, the manufacturer, or the FAA. The book is simply intended as a collection of tips and hints that should help those who are most familiar with your aircraft.

We realize that this subject matter, particularly regulations, can be very dry, stiff reading, so we have attempted to make it easier for you to plow through all this with some lighthearted humor and a casual style. This is not to downplay the importance of what we are trying to teach you. We hope that if you enjoy reading this book once, you will read it again and use it as a reference. So sit back, grab your favorite beverage and a bag of munchies, and enjoy.

1

The regulations

WE KNOW WHAT YOU'RE THINKING. YOU BOUGHT THIS BOOK TO LEARN more about your aircraft, not to study FARs. But bear with us. Like your mother, we are doing this for your own good.

The 1995 issue of FAR/AIM has finally included a copy of a mysterious FAR that you might never have heard about—until the FAA pulled a ramp check and started citing you for all sorts of things. It's Part 43—"Maintenance, preventive maintenance, rebuilding, and alteration"—and it forms the basis for determining what work an owner/operator may perform and what work must be done by a certificated maintenance technician. It also details how the paperwork is to be handled, what constitutes major repairs and alterations, how paperwork is to be maintained, and how work is to be signed off.

Pilots have innocently run afoul of this regulation and paid the price with certificate suspension or civil penalties. Remember, ignorance of the law is no defense. If you have a pilot certificate, you are expected to know all about this.

Since regulations aren't the most stimulating of reading, we have tucked the text of Part 43 in the back of this book for your late-night reading enjoyment, and we will use this chapter to discuss Part 43 in language that we hope is a little easier to read and understand. And just relax. In a few minutes, the regulations part will be all over, and you can get to the stuff you really bought this book for.

APPLICABILITY

Except for the exception, Part 43 applies to all aircraft having U.S. airworthiness certificate, Part 121, 127, or 135 foreign-registered civil aircraft used in common carriage or carriage of mail, and components of such aircraft. The exception is experimental aircraft, unless a different kind of airworthiness certificate had previously been issued for that aircraft. More on that later. It's rather dense and official sounding verbiage, but, essentially, any plane manufactured in this country or being used in general aviation here probably meets the requirement.

MAINTENANCE, PREVENTIVE MAINTENANCE, REPAIRS, ALTERATIONS

You won't be too surprised to know the FAA has developed very detailed definitions, including lists, of each of these topics. The detailed lists are included in the copy of Part 43 at the back of the book but, since there is the potential of getting into big trouble if you don't understand this, and since the regulation is written as regulations are wont to be, we will go into some detail here.

Anyone who takes on any sort of work on an aircraft must follow all the prescribed methods, practices, and techniques that the FAA and the manufacturer of the aircraft or component have determined are the best way to accomplish that work. In addition to the maintenance and parts manuals issued by the manufacturer, Advisory Circulars 43.13-1A and 43.13-2A issued by the FAA provide more details for maintenance of aircraft. But be careful. Just because you have a copy of this AC doesn't grant you permission to do the work. Much of the procedures and practices listed in it are for work that must be done by an A&P or IA. FAR 43 requires that any work you or your mechanic do is done using the specified tools, equipment, and testing gear that are in compliance with the FAA and manufacturer's requirements.

Regulations require that any work that is done by anyone on an airplane must be done in such a manner that the plane is returned to its originally manufactured or properly altered condition. This means aerodynamics or operations cannot be changed. Strength characteristics and functions must be borne in mind when making any repairs, as well as weight and balance.

That bit about "originally manufactured or properly altered condition" refers to what the basic standard is for determining airworthiness. If you have a major alteration done on your airplane, that becomes the new standard, not the way the plane was built. In most cases, you cannot interchange the standards. An exception might be if your plane was altered to use skis. You can interchange skis and wheels without altering airworthiness. (Thank heaven. Skis on tarmac don't last long.)

There is, of course, considerable debate about whether the FAA or the manufacturer chose the "best" way. If you are an accomplished mechanic in other areas, you might have developed techniques or procedures for doing things that you consider to be better, faster, stronger, or more economical. Forget them. If they are not approved by the FAA or the manufacturer or are not part of standard aircraft industry practices, you cannot use them.

When push comes to shove, the FAA assumes the manufacturer knows best about how its aircraft should be maintained. Given a choice between what you think is stronger and what the manufacturer thinks is, odds are the manufacturer is going to win. After all, the company has spent big bucks designing and building its plane. And since the FAA approved those designs and construction, they are going to go with the manufacturer almost every time.

So if you take on any work on your plane, get the manufacturer's maintenance and parts manuals and do exactly as you are told. You might have the best argument in the world about stresses, aerodynamics, part substitution or the technique you used, but odds are the FAA isn't going to go for it unless a lot of people have done it before you.

AUTHORIZED PERSONNEL

There are a number of categories of maintenance technician that are described more fully in Part 65, but we will touch on it here for the sake of clarity. Aircraft mechanics are required to be at least 18 years of age, be able to read, write, speak, and understand English, and pass prescribed tests, both oral and practical, before a certificate is issued.

At this writing, they are also required to have at least 18 months of experience performing the work for which they have sought certification. However, the FAA is considering changing that requirement to an hourly requirement rather than 18 months. Mechanics can also obtain a graduation certificate from an appropriate educational facility that the FAA has approved for training mechanics. Certifications are available for airframe and for powerplant ratings—the well-known A&Ps. These ratings permit the mechanic to perform 100-hour inspections for the parts they have been approved for.

A person holding an inspection authorization certification (IA) must first have airframe and powerplant ratings, have worked in the field for at least two years, have all the equipment and data necessary to do the work, and pass a written test. The person also must work from a fixed base of operations—not out of the trunk of a car. An IA certificate must be renewed annually. The IA can do anything other A&P mechanics can do, as well as supervise and train. The IA is also the only person authorized to perform annual inspections and approve major repairs and alterations.

There is another designation called repairman, which is seen less frequently but which is used for avionics and less complicated aircraft such as gliders and hot air balloons. Then there is the category you probably fall into—that of owner/operator. When you bury yourself in reading Part 43, you will find that the regulation does not say a pilot may perform preventive maintenance; it says the owner/operator. There is a big difference.

In order to perform preventive maintenance on an aircraft, you must be an owner/operator, which the courts have determined means you have an interest in the plane you are working on. That means it has to be a plane you own or fly regularly and, therefore, care about maintaining. You may not work on your buddy's plane or the one you share a hangar with or anyone else's. If you don't fly the plane on some sort of a regular basis, you can't work on it. And sorry, students; you also must hold at least a private pilot's certificate to approve the aircraft for return to service.

If you are the owner of an experimental aircraft, you might be in a unique situation. The person who builds such a plane is authorized by the FAA to perform all the maintenance and inspections on the craft, as long as the builder can show he or she built more than 51 percent of the plane. If the plane is sold, it must then be maintained by authorized IAs or A&Ps.

Another nuance of the regulations that gives people a lot of grief is the difference between being able to perform the work and being able to approve the plane for return to service. Sounds confusing, but it is another thing that can come back to bite you.

Almost anyone can work on a plane, provided the right supervision is available. The big worry to the FAA is who inspects the work and determines the plane can go back into service. Uncertificated people can and do work on airplanes legally. After all, that is how they meet their experience requirement for an A&P or IA rating. But before the airplane can be flown again, someone must inspect the work to be sure it meets all requirements and must sign the maintenance records, approving the aircraft for return to service. For work that must be done by an A&P or IA, someone without a certificate may do the work, but inspection must be done by an appropriately rated person. That is why you or someone you know might be doing work on a plane that is not approved by an owner/operator. An IA might trust the person doing the work enough to be comfortable inspecting it later and approving it for return to service.

The signoff in the maintenance records is the approval for return to service and is mandatory for all work, even preventive maintenance, before the airplane can be legally flown again. Maintenance instructions also take the form of service bulletins, service instructions, and airworthiness directives. Service bulletins (SBs) are issued by the manufacturer of the airplane, engine, propeller, or accessory and might advise you of some difficulty that has been discovered in the field. Service instructions (SIs) are a clarification of how a particular maintenance item is to be handled. Airworthiness directives (ADs) are issued by the FAA and are for correcting a potential problem.

There has been some confusion about SBs and ADs in terms of which ones are mandatory and which ones are not. ADs are mandatory. Some manufacturers have started putting out what they call mandatory service bulletins. The manufacturer considers them mandatory merely because the company attorney says so. The FAA does not consider them mandatory. If you get a mandatory service bulletin, pay close attention because they have a tendency to become ADs.

So you get a service bulletin from the manufacturer. It would be advisable to stick your copy in with the maintenance records and talk to your favorite mechanic about it. If everyone agrees that the corrective action is a good idea, then everyone can start planning on when to have it done, and you can start saving your pennies. Sometimes the service bulletins will have special prices on parts and labor allowances that are only good for a limited time. This is another way the manufacturer has of encouraging people to modify the airplanes. There is an advantage to taking care of the service bulletin when it first comes out. Usually the manufacturer will have all the parts available that are necessary to make the fix called for. When the service bulletin becomes an airworthiness directive, the stock disappears because everyone now needs it. There have been instances of a delay of as much as three months for parts for various ADs. By completing the service bulletin before it becomes an AD, you get a jump on everyone else. When the service bulletin become an AD, the AD usually references the SB for instructions about how the work is to be done. If you have already performed the service bulletin, then the AD becomes very simple paperwork. All that is required is a maintenance record entry stating that the AD is already complied with in accordance with service bulletin no. X on a given date.

MAJOR ALTERATIONS

Those items that the FAA considers to be major alterations are listed in appendix A of Part 43. This is fairly clear but it is worth discussing simply because of its importance. Essentially, you cannot make any changes to any of the aircraft systems that the manufacturer and the FAA have not already approved. That means substituting parts, rerouting lines, or using unapproved methods for accomplishing this work.

It's very tempting to run down to the local hardware store and pick up some parts or to take shortcuts in the way you do the work when you are anxious to fly. Doing so not only jeopardizes the integrity of the airplane, but it also presents safety questions and might well invalidate your insurance. Not to mention having to answer a lot of pesky questions from the FAA inspector when he or she pulls a ramp check and sees your handiwork. So don't even think about getting creative in your work.

The requirement not to make any major alterations applies to all parts of the plane—the airframe, the powerplant, the propeller, and accessories such as the radio and the navigational equipment. If you wish to change your plane in any way, talk to an aviation technician or the manufacturer first.

MAJOR REPAIRS

You might not have any lofty ambitions about altering your plane, but the FAA doesn't want you even repairing things that are too involved or require special training or instructions. You may not work on anything structural or do most riveting or welding unless you are an approved repair technician. You cannot reroute hydraulic lines or even replace them. Appendix A delineates those things that you may not work on. The list is not complete, since technology changes so much and the FARs do not, but the list is a good guideline. And if you wonder whether or not you can work on something, the safest route is to leave it to the professionals.

PREVENTIVE MAINTENANCE

And just in case there is still a question about what work you can perform, appendix A tells you exactly what the FAA considers to be preventive maintenance. It is pretty much all cosmetic and minor stuff that even the most unskilled can handle—things you have probably done before like changing batteries, putting air in the tires, adding fluids, etc.

PRIMARY CATEGORY AIRCRAFT

In 1990, the FAA established a category of aircraft called "primary." Those owning aircraft with this designation are permitted to do much more of their own work—including some inspections—after they have received training from the manufacturer or some other entity that the FAA recognizes.

The rule was designed, in part, to make it more affordable to own small aircraft and, it was hoped, give a shot in the arm to the light aircraft industry. At this writing, the category was still new, and implementation of the rule was still being studied.

A primary category certificate can be issued for aircraft that are built under a production certificate by an aircraft manufacturer or for kit planes. Under certain conditions, foreign-built craft are also eligible. It is not necessary to obtain the certificate at the time the craft is new. If your plane has a standard airworthiness certificate, you can switch it to primary category by applying through your local Flight Standards District Office.

Some limitations have been put on planes in the primary category. You may not carry persons or property for hire. Those designated as primary category light (having a maximum certificated gross weight of 1000 pounds or less) may not operate in controlled airspace without prior approval of the air traffic facility that has jurisdiction of that controlled airspace. Also, for the light craft, you must operate with visual reference to the surface (i.e., no high-altitude flying or flying above clouds).

THE DREADED PAPERWORK

If you haven't learned anything else at this stage in your flying, you have learned the importance of paperwork. It is said that a plane cannot legally fly unless the paperwork weighs at least as much as the plane.

Everything that is done to an airplane must be recorded in the maintenance records and becomes a permanent part of the aircraft's paperwork. All these records must be transferred to the new owner when the plane is sold.

Notice we use the term "maintenance record," not logbook. It has become standard practice and very convenient to put maintenance data in the aircraft log, but it is not necessary. If the logbook isn't available, you can get the appropriate signoff from the person performing maintenance—including work you perform—on a separate sheet of paper. Better that than no record at all. And we trust you won't be too surprised to learn that falsifying, altering, or reproducing records is a definite no-no.

RECORDING MAINTENANCE WORK

You are not only responsible for recording any work you do, but also for being sure that maintenance personnel record their work. As mentioned earlier, it doesn't necessarily have to be in the logbook, though that is probably the easiest way to keep track of everything.

Major repairs and alterations

It will come as no surprise that the FAA has a special form for recording major repairs or major alterations. It's called Form 337 and a copy of one is shown in Fig. 1-1.

US Department of Transportation **Federal Aviation Administration**	**MAJOR REPAIR AND ALTERATION** **(Airframe, Powerplant, Propeller, or Appliance)**	Form Approved OMB No. 2120-0020 **For FAA Use Only** Office Identification

INSTRUCTIONS: Print or type all entries. See FAR 43.9, FAR 43 Appendix B, and AC 43.9-1 (or subsequent revision thereof) for instructions and disposition of this form. This report is required by law (49 U.S.C. 1421). Failure to report can result in a civil penalty not to exceed $1,000 for each such violation (Section 901 Federal Aviation Act of 1958).

1. Aircraft	Make		Model	
	Serial No.		Nationality and Registration Mark	
2. Owner	Name (As shown on registration certificate)		Address (As shown on registration certificate)	

3. For FAA Use Only

4. Unit Identification — **5. Type**

Unit	Make	Model	Serial No.	Repair	Alteration
AIRFRAME	~~~~~~~~~~~~~ (As described in Item 1 above) ~~~~~~~~~~~~~				
POWERPLANT					
PROPELLER					
APPLIANCE	Type				
	Manufacturer				

6. Conformity Statement

A. Agency's Name and Address	B. Kind of Agency	C. Certificate No.
	U.S. Certificated Mechanic	
	Foreign Certificated Mechanic	
	Certificated Repair Station	
	Manufacturer	

D. I certify that the repair and/or alteration made to the unit(s) identified in item 4 above and described on the reverse or attachments hereto have been made in accordance with the requirements of Part 43 of the U.S. Federal Aviation Regulations and that the information furnished herein is true and correct to the best of my knowledge.

Date	Signature of Authorized Individual

7. Approval for Return To Service

Pursuant to the authority given persons specified below, the unit identified in item 4 was inspected in the manner prescribed by the Administrator of the Federal Aviation Administration and is ☐ APPROVED ☐ REJECTED

BY	FAA Flt. Standards Inspector	Manufacturer	Inspection Authorization	Other (Specify)
	FAA Designee	Repair Station	Person Approved by Transport Canada Airworthiness Group	
Date of Approval or Rejection	Certificate or Designation No.	Signature of Authorized Individual		

FAA Form 337 (12-88)

Fig. 1-1. Form 337 is used to get approval of major repairs and alterations. A copy is kept on file at the FAA office in Oklahoma City, and another remains part of the permanent maintenance records kept with the aircraft.

NOTICE

Weight and balance or operating limitation changes shall be entered in the appropriate aircraft record. An alteration must be compatible with all previous alterations to assure continued conformity with the applicable airworthiness requirements.

8. Description of Work Accomplished
(If more space is required, attach additional sheets. Identify with aircraft nationality and registration mark and date work completed.)

☐ Additional Sheets Are Attached

★U.S.GPO:1990-0-568-012/40004

Fig. 1-1. Continued.

The 337 is issued in duplicate by the person who has performed the work and details exactly what work was done. It is then sent to the FAA, who approves it, and the owner gets a copy. The 337s become a permanent part of the maintenance records and must be transferred if the plane is sold.

If a major repair is done by a certificated repair station that follows directions in a repair manual or other generally accepted industry procedures, the maintenance person can opt to use the work order instead of a 337. The FAA still gets a copy and so does the aircraft owner.

Part 43 in appendix B of this book details the wording the FAA likes to see when major repairs are done. The work order and/or the 337 should also include exact details to identify the parts repaired or replaced, as well as registration number, serial number, make, and model of the aircraft.

If the FAA has some occasion to check your maintenance records, these are the things they will want to see in there:

- A description of the work performed.

- Date of completion.

- Signature and certificate number of the person performing the work. That includes you, not just the maintenance guys. When you do the work, you sign your name, and for certificate number you use your pilot license type (private, commercial) and the certificate number. That way you are signing the airplane off approving it for return to service.

For inspections of the aircraft they will look for:

- Type of inspection (annual, 100 hour, periodic).

- Brief description of the extent of the inspection.

- Date of the inspection.

- Total time in service for the aircraft.

- Signature, certificate number, and type of certificate held by the person who performed the inspection.

- A statement certifying the airworthiness status of the aircraft.

Other records they might look for are:

- Total time in service for the airframe, each engine, and each propeller.

- The current status of life-limited parts of each airframe, engine, propeller, rotor, and appliance.

- Total time since last overhaul for those items installed on the aircraft that are required to be overhauled on a specified time basis.

- Current inspection status of the aircraft, including time since last inspection, as required by the program under which the aircraft is maintained.

- Copies of FAA Form 337 for each major alteration to airframe, engine, rotos, propellers, and appliances.

And for any airworthiness directives that have been issued:

- The method of compliance.
- The airworthiness directive number and revision date.
- The time and date of any recurring actions required by the airworthiness directive.

If you are maintaining separate records for the airframe, powerplant, propellers, appliances, and other components, you can have the person performing annual or 100 hour inspections make one entry, and you can copy that entry into the individual records. Speaking of record keeping, here is a test question: When is an annual not an annual? When it has not been recorded in the maintenance records. (See FAR 91.417)

That is why we mentioned earlier that the maintenance entries do not have to be in the logbook. If the logbook disappears, first blame the maintenance facility because, being the good customer you are, you delivered it when you delivered your plane. Then get them to put the signoff on some other piece of paper, like the work order. Then when you get caught in a ramp check, as you most assuredly will if you don't have the right paperwork, you will be home free.

SOMETHING YOU MIGHT NOT HAVE KNOWN IF YOU HADN'T SPENT THE MONEY ON THIS BOOK

Repair stations are only required to keep paperwork for two years. Although you are not required to, you would be wise to get a copy of every work order and be sure it spells out any model, serial, batch, or other identifying numbers of any parts replaced, no matter how inconsequential. You should also ask for the source of all those parts (manufacturer, distributor, etc.). That way, if you have problems down the road or hear about a recall, you can easily determine if your parts (well, your plane's parts) are affected. Repair stations get sold or close down, pilots move, and records get destroyed. It's best to have your own copies of work orders and keep them with the rest of your aircraft's documents.

There is another reason for being able to trace the genesis of any parts in your plane. Bogus parts—those not approved for use in aircraft—are an endemic problem in the aviation industry. Many parts have been found that look and smell like proper parts but might be made of inferior materials. FAA inspectors are constantly on the lookout for such parts. If they find some on your plane and you can prove you purchased them from a supposedly reliable source, you might not be left holding the bag for the installation of those parts.

THE FAA INSPECTOR'S HANDBOOK

In an effort to bring you all the information you need to know to stay out of trouble with the FAA, we have spent countless, sleepless nights plowing through a book called the *FAA Inspector's Handbook*. While the book is available to the public, there is really no earthly reason why anyone would want to buy it except to help out our fellow aviators and aviatrixes (that was a word they used to use for female pilots back in the days when you were allowed to use separate words for men and women).

This book is used by employees of the FAA as a guide for how to do their jobs. It is constantly being updated as FAA personnel develop new and more cunning methods for finding out what pilots and maintenance personnel are really doing and stopping it. But we are bringing you the most current information we can get.

Definition of airworthiness

Nowhere in the FARs is the term "airworthy" defined—much to the chagrin of lawyers. But the FAA has come up with its own private meaning, which they will tell you about after they cite you for violating some rule or other.

Actually, the definition is printed on the certificate of airworthiness (Fig. 1-2), a document we trust you all have committed to memory. In order to be airworthy, an aircraft must meet its type design and be in condition for safe operation. There you have it, clear as mud. What does it mean?

TYPE CERTIFICATE DATA SHEET

When an aircraft is manufactured, the builder obtains (through a lengthy and costly process) a type certificate data sheet (see Fig. 1-3). The TCDS, as we in the

---

UNITED STATES OF AMERICA
DEPARTMENT OF TRANSPORTATION–FEDERAL AVIATION ADMINISTRATION
STANDARD AIRWORTHINESS CERTIFICATE

1. NATIONALITY AND REGISTRATION MARKS	2. MANUFACTURER AND MODEL	3. AIRCRAFT SERIAL NUMBER	4. CATEGORY
N72507	CESSNA 140	9677	NORMAL

5. AUTHORITY AND BASIS FOR ISSUANCE
This airworthiness certificate is issued pursuant to the Federal Aviation Act of 1958 and certifies that, as of the date of issuance, the aircraft to which issued has been inspected and found to conform to the type certificate therefor, to be in condition for safe operation, and has been shown to meet the requirements of the applicable comprehensive and detailed airworthiness code as provided by Annex 8 to the Convention on International Civil Aviation, except as noted herein.
Exceptions:

NONE

6. TERMS AND CONDITIONS
Unless sooner surrendered, suspended, revoked, or a termination date is otherwise established by the Administrator, this airworthiness certificate is effective as long as the maintenance, preventative maintenance, and alterations are performed in accordance with Part 21, 43, and 91 of the Federal Aviation Regulations, as appropriate, and the aircraft is registered in the United States.

DATE OF ISSUANCE	FAA REPRESENTATIVE	DESIGNATION NUMBER
12-19-55 replacement	Edward J. Prentice	WP–FSDO–07

Any alteration, reproduction, or misuse of this certificate may be punishable by a fine not exceeding $1,000, or imprisonment not exceeding 3 years, or both. THIS CERTIFICATE MUST BE DISPLAYED IN THE AIRCRAFT IN ACCORDANCE WITH APPLICABLE FEDERAL AVIATION REGULATIONS.

FAA Form 8100-2 (7-67) FORMERLY FAA FORM 1362   ☆ U.S. Government Printing Office — 1976-675-526

Fig. 1-2. The airworthiness certificate is the only place where the FAA defines airworthiness. An aircraft is considered airworthy when it meets its original type certificate data sheet or properly altered condition and is in condition for safe flying.

Revision 30
CESSNA
120
140

February 29, 1956

AIRCRAFT SPECIFICATION No. A-768

Manufacturer	Cessna Aircraft Company
	Wichita, Kansas

I — Model 140, 2 PCL-SM, Approved March 21, 1946 (see NOTE 5 for 1948 version)

| **Engine**	Continental C-85-12 or C-85-12F (see items 105, 107 and 109 for
|	optional engines)

Fuel	73 min. octane aviation gasoline

Engine Limits	For all operations, 2575 rpm (85 hp)

Airspeed Limits

Landplane	: Level flight or climb 115 mph (100 knots) True Ind.
	Glide or dive 140 mph (122 knots) True Ind.
	Flaps extended 82 mph (71 knots) True Ind.
Seaplane	: Level flight or climb 105 mph (91 knots) True Ind.
	Glide or dive 140 mph (122 knots) True Ind.
	Flaps extended 82 mph (71 knots) True Ind.

C.G. range	Landplane : (+13.5) to (+17.7)
	Seaplane : (+13.7) to (+17.5)

Empty weight	Landplane : (+12.3) 50 (+14.7) Item 402 not installed.
C.G. range	(+12.3) to (+14.1) when Item 402 is installed.
	Seaplane : (+12.7) to (+14.7) Item 402 not installed.
	(+12.7) to (+14.2) when Item 402 is installed.
	Ranges are not valid when Item 606, C.G. shifter,
	is installed or for any non-standard arrangement
	except as noted. When empty weight C.G. falls within
	the proper range, computation of critical fore and
	aft C.G. positions is unnecessary.

Maximum weight	Landplane or skiplane: 1450 lbs.
	Seaplane (with item 206a): 1556 lbs.

No. seats	2 (+19.5) See Item 402 for jump seat.

Maximum baggage	80 lbs. (+37.5)

Fuel capacity	25 gals. (Two 12.5 gal. tanks) (+23)

Oil capacity	4.5 or 5 qts. (–31.5)

Fig. 1-3. The type certificate data sheet details those items that are necessary for any aircraft to meet the airworthiness standards. Among the information to be found here is the type of fuel to be used, load limits, required equipment, and approved engine and propeller designs.

Control surface movements	Elevator	Up	20 deg.	Down	20 deg.
	Elevator tab	Up	6 deg.	Down	33 deg.
	Rudder	Left	16 deg.	Right	16 deg.
	Aileron	Up	22 deg.	Down	14 deg.
	Flaps			Down	40 deg.
	Stabilizer	Fixed.			

Serial Nos. eligible   8001 and up

Required equipment In addition to the pertinent required basic equipment specified in CAR 4a, the following items of equipment must be installed:
(Landplane) : Items 1, 201(a), 202(a), 403, 601
(Seaplane) : Items 2, 206(a), 403, 601
(Skiplane) : Items 1, 202, 204, 403, 601

CESSNA 120, 140
AIRCRAFT SPECIFICATION No. A-768 FEBRUARY 29, 1956, REVISION 30 SHEET 1 (BACK)

II — Model 120, 2 PCL-SM, Approved March 28, 1956 (See Note 5 for 1948 version)
  (Same as Model 140 except for equipment installation; wing flaps not installed)
| **Engine**   Continental C-85-12 or C-85-12F (see items 105, 107 and
| 109 for optional engines)

Fuel   73 min. octane aviation gasoline

Engine Limits   For all operations, 2575 rpm (85 hp)

Airspeed Limits Landplane : Level flight or climb 115 mph (100 knots) True Ind.
               Glide or dive   140 mph (122 knots) True Ind.
         Seaplane : Level flight or climb 105 mph (91 knots) True Ind.
               Glide or dive   140 mph (122 knots) True Ind.

C.G. range   Landplane : (+13.5) to (+17.7)
         Seaplane : (+13.7) to (+17.5)

Empty weight   Landplane : (+12.3) 50 (+14.7)   Item 402 not installed.
  C.G. range   (+12.3) to (+14.1)   when Item 402 is installed.
         Seaplane : (+12.7) to (+14.7)   Item 402 not installed.
             (+12.7) to (+14.2) when Item 402 is installed.
             Ranges are not valid when Item 606, C.G. shifter, is
             installed or for any non-standard arrangement except as
             noted. When empty weight C.G. falls within the proper
             range, computation of critical fore and aft C.G. positions is
             unnecessary.

Maximum weight Landplane or skiplane: 1450 lbs.
         Seaplane (with item 206a): 1556 lbs.

No. seats   2 (+19.5) See Item 402 for jump seat.

Maximum baggage 80 lbs. (+37.5)

Fuel capacity 25 gals. (Two 12.5 gal. tanks) (+23)

Oil capacity 4.5 or 5 qts. (–31.5)

Control surface	Elevator	Up	20 deg. Down	20 deg.
movements	Elevator tab	Up	6 deg. Down	33 deg.
	Rudder	Left	16 deg. Right	16 deg.
	Aileron	Up	22 deg. Down	14 deg.
	Flaps		Down	40 deg.
	Stabilizer	Fixed.		

Serial Nos. eligible 8003 and up

Required equipment In addition to the pertinent required basic equipment specified in CAR 4a, the following items of equipment must be installed:
(Landplane) : Items 1, 201(a), 202(a), 403, 601
(Seaplane) : Items 2, 206(a), 403, 601
(Skiplane) : Items 1, 202, 204, 403, 601

Specifications Pertinent to All Models

Datum Leading edge of wing
Leveling means Top edge of sheet along fuselage side aft of doors
Certification basis Type Certificate No. 768 (CAR 4a)
Production basis Production Certificate No. 4
Export eligibility Eligible for export to all countries subject to the provisions of MOP 2–4 except as follows:
(a) Canada – Landplane, seaplane and skiplane eligible

CESSNA 120, 140
AIRCRAFT SPECIFICATION NO. A-768 SEPTEMBER 24, 1958, REVISION 33 SHEET 2 (FRONT)

Equipment: A plus (+) or minus (–) sign preceding the weight of an item indicates net weight change when that item is installed.

Approval for the installation of all items of equipment listed herein has been obtained by the aircraft manufacturer except those items preceded by an asterisk(*). The asterisk denotes that approval has been obtained by other than the aircraft manufacturer. An item marked with an asterisk may not have been manufactured under a CAA monitored or approved quality control system, and therefore attention should be paid to workmanship and conformity with pertinent data called for in this specification.

Propellers and Propeller Accessories

For C-85 Engine Installation

1. Propeller – Sensenich 74FC-47, 74FC-49, 74FK-47 or 74FK-49 or   11 lbs. (–50)
    any other approved fixed pitch wood propeller which is eligible
    for the engine power speed and which meets the following limits:
    Static rpm at max. permissible throttle setting: Not over 2160,
      not under 1885. No additional tolerance permitted.
    Diameter: Not over 74 in., not under 72 in.
    Not eligible on seaplane models.
2. Propeller – fixed pitch metal – McCauley 1A90-CF, 1A90-CH or   22 lbs. (–50)
    1B90-CM
    Static rpm at max permissible throttle settings:
      (a) Landplane: Not over 2300 not under 2100 rpm.
      (b) Seaplane: Not over 2225 not under 2200 rpm.

Fig. 1-3. Continued.

No additional tolerance permitted. Diameter: Not over 71 in., not under 69.5 in.	
3. Propeller – controllable – Beech R002-101 or R003-100 hub with R003-201-75 to -72; R003-225-75 to -72; R003-231-75 to -72; or R003-232-75 to -72 blades. (Eligible on landplane only) Static rpm at max permissible throttle settings: Not over 2325 not under 2250. No additional tolerance permitted. Pitch settings at 27 in. sta.: Low 13 deg., High 19 deg. Includes Beech mechanical propeller pitch control. When this item is installed on 1947 version (See note 3 for description), trailing edge of engine cowling must be flared and metal roll attached to bottom of firewall per Cessna Dwg. 0450103 or equivalent.	30 lbs. (–50)
*4. Propeller – ground adjustable – Hartzell HA-12U with 7414, 7214, or 7214M blades. Static rpm and diameter limits same as for fixed pitch wood propeller.	18 lbs. (–50)
*5. Propeller – automatic – Koppers Aeromatic F200 with 00-73E or 00-73F blades. (Eligible on landplane only.) Parts List Assembly No. 4312. Low pitch setting 11 deg. at 24 in. sta. Static rpm at max. permissible throttle setting: Not over 2575, not under 2475. No additional tolerance permitted. Diameter: Not over 73 in., not under 71.5 in. When this item is installed, installation and operation must be accomplished in accordance with Koppers' "Installation Procedure and Operating Limitations" No. 2B. Cooling flap, Koppers' Dwg. No. 3323 or equivalent, must be installed on 1947 version 120 and 140 airplanes when this item is installed.	30 lbs. (–50)
*6. Propeller – fixed pitch metal – Sensenich M76AK-2 Static rpm at max. permissible throttle setting: Not over 2290, not under 2190. No additional tolerance permitted. Diameter: Not over 74 in., not under 72.5 in.	23 lbs. (–50)
*7. Propeller – fixed pitch metal – Sensenich M74CK-2 (Eligible on landplane only.) Static rpm at max permissible throttle setting: Not over 2250, not under 2150. No additional tolerance permitted. Diameter: Not over 72 in., not under 70.5 in.	21 lbs. (–50)
*8. Propeller – Sensenich Hydraulic Controllable C2FB1 with PC-276A7 blades. Pitch settings at 27 in. sta.: Low 8.5 deg., High 14.5 deg. Diameter: Not over 76 in., not under 74.5 in.	27 lbs. (–50)

CESSNA 120, 140
AIRCRAFT SPECIFICATION NO. A-768 SEPTEMBER 24, 1958, REVISION 33 SHEET 2 (BACK)
For C-90 Engine Installations:

| 11. Propeller – Sensenich 72RK-56, 74FK-51 or any other fixed pitch wood propeller which is eligible for the engine power and speed and which meets the following limits: Static rpm at max. permissible throttle setting: Not over 2160, not under 1835. No additional tolerance permitted. Diameter: Not over 74 in., not under 70.5 in. (Eligible on landplane only.) | 11 lbs. (–50) |
| 12. Propeller – fixed pitch metal – McCauley 1A90-CF, 1A90-CH or 1B90-CM | 21 lbs. (–50) |

Static rpm at max. permissible throttle settings:
    (a) Landplane: Not over 2350 not under 2050
    (b) Seaplane: Not over 2350 not under 2150
No additional tolerance permitted.
Diameter:
    Landplane : Not over 71 in., not under 69.5 in.
    Seaplane   : Not over 73 in., not under 69.5 in.

  *13.   Propeller – automatic – Koppers Aeromatic F200 with 00-73E   30 lbs. (–50)
       blades.
       Parts List Assembly No. 4340. Low pitch setting 12.5 deg. at
         24 in. sta.
       Static rpm at max. permissible throttle setting: Not over 2475,
         not under 2425. No additional tolerance permitted.
       Diameter: Not over 73 in., not under 71.5 in.
       When this item is installed, installation and operation must
         be accomplished in accordance with Koppers' "Installation
         Procedure and Operating Limitations" No. 32.
       (Eligible on landplane only.)

  *14.   Propeller – Flottorp-Beach controllable metal hub R003-100   30 lbs. (–50)
        with R003-232-72T blades (For interchangeable blade
        models see Propeller Specification No. P-804 (NOTE 6))
       Static rpm at max. permissible throttle setting:
        Not over 2400, Not under 2300. No additional
         tolerance permitted.
       Pitch settings at 27 in. sta.: Low 13 deg., High 19 deg.
       Diameter: Not over 72 in., Not under 70.5 in.
       (Eligible on landplane only.)
       With this installation the following engine limits are applicable:
        Maximum continuous: 2475 rpm (90 hp)
        Take-off (Five Minutes):   2625 rpm (95 hp)

For either C-85 or C-90 Engine Installation:

  *15.   Propeller spinner, Aviaid Metal Products Model 100140   2 lbs. (–50)
       (Eligible with items 2 or 12)

CESSNA 120, 140
AIRCRAFT SPECIFICATION NO. A-768 SEPTEMBER 28, 1956 REVISION 32 SHEET 3
(FRONT)

Engine and Engine Accessories – Fuel and Oil System

  101.   Starter (Delco-Remy 1109656)   16 lbs. (–25)
  102.   Carburetor air cleaner   3 lbs. (–45)
  104.   Winterization equipment   2 lbs. (–35)
  105.   Continental C-90-12F or –14F engine   Use actual Weight
       See NOTE 5 for limits and installation data
 *106.   Oil filter – Fram PB-5 installed in accordance with Fram Corp. Dwg.   4 lbs. (–21.5)
       61528. Eligible on only those aircraft equipped with exhaust
       manifolds incorporating muffler assemblies.
  107.   Continental C85-14F engine
       Limits same as for C-85-12F engine
       New engine mount, Cessna Dwg. 0451111, necessary when this engine
       installed.

Fig. 1-3. Continued.

*108. Controllable cowl flaps
    (a) SerVair Accessories, Model SAC-100, installed in accordance with installation instructions dated November 8, 1950, supplied by SerVair Accessories, P. O. Box 557, Williston, North Dakota. Eligible on Serial Nos. 11843 through 14364 unless Item 3, 5, or 105 installed.
    (b) SerVair Accessories, Model SAC-100A, installed in accordance with installation instructions dated November 8, 1950, Amendment No. 1, dated January 24, 1951, supplied by SerVair Accessories, P. O. Box 557, Williston, North Dakota. Eligible on Serial Nos. 14365 and up unless Item 3 or 5 installed.

*109. Lycoming 0-235-C1 engine   Use actual weight
Eligible on 120 and 140 landplanes with the following limits:

Fuel	80 min. octane aviation gasoline
Engine Limits	For all operations, 2600 rpm (108 hp)
Propeller	Sensenich M76AM-2 with the following limits:

            Static rpm at max. permissible throttle setting:
                Not over 2340, not under 2240
                No additional tolerance permitted
            Diameter: Not over 74 in., not under 72.5 in.

Oil capacity	6 quarts (–29.5)

Installation must be accomplished in accordance with McKenzie Aircraft Repair, 1300 North 27th, Springfield, Oregon. Installation Instructions and Drawing L149-0600-244, Sheet 2, dated September 10, 1955; utilizing components listed in Parts List dated September 10, 1955. CAA Approved Airplane Flight Manual Supplement dated October 18, 1955 for Cessna 120–140 landplane required when this engine is installed.

Landing Gear

201. Two main wheel-brake assemblies, 6.00-6, Type III: (See NOTE 4 re variation in arms) (+2)
    (a) Goodyear Model L6HBD
        Wheel Assembly No. 511413-M, Brake Assembly No. 9520292

(1) with 6.00-6 4 ply rating tires & tubes	34 lbs.
(2) with 7.00-6 4 ply rating tires & tubes	36 lbs.
(3) with 8.00-6 4 ply rating tires & tubes	44 lbs.

    (b) Goodyear Model LF6HBD
        Wheel Assembly No. 511960-M, Brake Assembly No. 9520517

(1) with 6.00-6 4 ply rating tires & tubes	31 lbs.
(2) with 7.00-6 4 ply rating tires & tubes	33 lbs.
(3) with 8.00-6 4 ply rating tires & tubes	41 lbs.

    (d) Goodyear Model CL6HBM (Castering)
        (Wheel Brake Assembly No. 9540234 and 5)
        Wheel Assembly No. 9530242 and 3, Brake Assembly No. 9530368 and 9
        Installed in accordance with Cessna Dwg. No. 0441150

(1) with 6.00-6 4 ply rating tires & tubes	48 lbs.
(2) with 7.00-6 4 ply rating tires & tubes	50 lbs.
(3) with 8.00-6 4 ply rating tires & tubes	58 lbs.

202. Tail wheel and tire

(a) Scott 3-24B	5 lbs.(+201)
(b) Scott non-steerable, full swiveling	4 lbs.(+201)
*(c) Lang (formerly Decker) D-501 steerable	7 lbs.(+201)
(Pacific Coast Aircraft Dwg. A-550)	
*(d) Scott 3200, steerable, swiveling	8 lbs.(+201)
(Installed in accordance with Scott Bulleting No. I-168)	
*(e) Maule SFS-1-2-P8	7 lbs.(+201)
(f) Goodyear Model 95-0843 8-inch wheel with pneumatic tire in accordance with Cessna Dwg. No. 0542110	6 lbs.(+201)

203. Tail wheel and tire, Maule SFS-1-2   6 lbs. (+201)

204. Two skis (See NOTE 4 re variation of arms)
    (a) Federal A-1500 according to Cessna Dwg. 0441102 or   32 lbs. (–1)
         Federal Instal. Dwg. 11R245
   *(b) Woychik R-1 according to Woychik Aircraft Equipment   42 lbs. (–1.5)
         (Middleton, Wisc.) Dwg. 1, 2, 3, (22 psi tire pressure required.)
   *(c) Federal A-1500A, Federal Installation Dwg. 11R245   Use actual wt. change
   *(d) Federal A-1850, Federal Installation Dwg. 11R245   Use actual wt. change
   *(e) Federal A-2000, Federal Installation Dwg. 11R245   Use actual wt. change
   *(f) Federal A-200A, Federal Installation Dwg. 11R245   Use actual wt. change
   *(g) Federal CA1850-6, Federal Installation Dwg. 11R245   Use actual wt. change
   *(h) Federal AWA-1500 Wheel-Ski, Federal Instl. Dwg. 11R395   +35 lbs.

	Retracted	Extended
	(0)	(+3.5)

         Eligible with mechanical conversion on ground only.
         Not eligible with Item 201(a)(3) or 201(b)(3) installed.
         Note: Weight and balance of aircraft shall be checked with
         ski in retracted and extended position.
   *(i) Call S2, S6 or S7 according to Call Dwgs. 1004 and 1014   Use actual wt. change
   *(j) Federal AWB-1500 Wheel-Ski, Federal Instl. Dwg. 11R549   76 lbs.

	Retracted	Extended
	(-4.5)	(–2)

         Eligible with hydraulic conversion on ground and in flight.
         Not eligible with Item 201(a)(3) or 201 (b)(3) installed,
         Note: Weight and balance of aircraft shall be checked with
         ski in retracted and extended position.
         Placard required: "Do Not Extend or Retract Skis While in
         Motion on the Ground."
   *(k) Federal AWB-1500A Wheel-Ski, Federal Instl. Dwg. 11R896   84 lbs.

	Retracted	Extended
	(-4.5)	(-2)

         Eligible with hydraulic conversion on ground and in flight.
         Not eligible with Item 201(a)(3) or 201(b)(3) installed
         Note: Weight and balance of aircraft shall be checked with ski
         in retracted and extended position.
         Placard required: "Do Not Extend or Retract Skis While in Motion
         on the Ground."
   *(l) Woychik R-1A, Woychik Dwgs. 1 through 5 (32 psi tire   58 lbs.   (–3)
         pressure required)
 *(m) Federal AWB-2100 Wheel-Ski, Federal Instl.   93 lbs.
         Dwg. 11R1100

	Retracted	Extended
	(–5)	(–1.5)

         Eligible with hydraulic conversion on ground and in flight.
         Not eligible with Item 200(a)(3), 201(b)(3) or 201(d)(3)
         installed.
         Note: Weight and balance of aircraft shall be checked with
         ski in retracted and extended positions.
         Placard required: "Do Not Extend or Retract Skis While in
         Motion on the Ground."
   *(n) Wesco Skis, Western Aircraft Equipment Co. Dwgs. 11 and 48.

(1) A-15	46 lbs.	(–4)
(2) A-20	48 lbs.	(–4)
(3) A-25	69 lbs.	(–4)
(4) AS-2	50 lbs.	(–4)
(5) AS-2A	62 lbs.	(–5)
(6) AS-2B	64 lbs.	(–5)

205. Tail Ski, Federal AT-1500   3 lbs.   (+198)
206. Float installation
    (a) Two Edo 88-1650 according to Cessna Dwg. No. 0440111   208 lbs.   (+13)

Fig. 1-3. Continued.

*(b) Two Edo 92-1400 according to Edo Dwgs. 06704 and 06822   174 lbs.   (+14)
        This item eligible for approval for a maximum weight of
        1474 lbs. only and with propeller Item 12 and engine
        Item 105 only.

207.	Two main wheel streamlines per Cessna Dwg. 0441143 (Kit No. 52-3-102). See NOTE 4 re eligibility and arms.	6 lbs.	(+2)
208.	Landing gear adaptor plate, Cessna Parts 0441147, 52-3-115 or 52-3-116. See NOTE 4 re eligibility and arms.	5 lbs.	(+1.5)
*209.	Two Decker C-200 wheel pants per Decker installation instructions and Dwg. 2A. See NOTE 4 re eligibility and arms.	9 lbs	(+3)
*210.	Two Consolidair model 16 wheel fenders per Consolidair Dwg. No. 0026. See NOTE 4 re eligibility and arms.	8 lbs.	(+2)
*212.	Geisse Safety Gear installed according to St. Louis Machine Co. Dwgs. 1 and 2 and instructions dated May 5, 1953 (revised October 8, 1953).	12 lbs.	(0)

        With 1948 Landing gear springs, Cessna Dwg. 0441149, arm
        is (–3).
        This item not eligible with items 201(d), 204, 205, 206, 207, 208,
        209, or 210 installed.

CESSNA 120, 140
AIRCRAFT SPECIFICATION NO. A-768 APRIL 25, 1956, REVISION 31 SHEET 4 (FRONT)

*213.	Two "no drag" wheel fenders per Liquid Tool Co., Box 299, Morrow, Ohio, Dwg. 105.	8 lbs.	(+3)

Electrical Equipment

301.	Generator (Delco-Remy 1101876)	10 lbs.	(–25)
302.	Battery – 12 Volt 14 amp. hr.	24 lbs.	(+56)
303.	Landing Light – Grimes G3602 and installation	6 lbs.	(+15)
304.	Omitted		

Interior Equipment

401.	Cabin heater	3 lbs.	(–26)
402.	Jump seat installation, Cessna Dwg. 0413202	6 lbs.	(+44)

        When this item is installed, the compartment must be placarded
        for the weight of passenger or baggage as determined by weight
        and balance computations except that the total weight shall not
        exceed 80 lbs. C.G. of passenger in jump seat is at (+44)

403.	CAA Approved Airplane Flight Manual (optional nomenclature: "Approved Operating Limitations") and pertinent revisions applicable to the particular model and serial number. Tentatively approved Airplane Flight Manuals in use up to and including the 1947 version aircraft are acceptable without replacement.		
404.	Blind flight cover, Cessna Dwg. 0413267	4 lbs.	(+5)

Miscellaneous (Not listed above)

601.	Wing flaps (Model 140 only)	6 lbs.	(+55)
602.	International flares, 3 Mark I – 1.5 minute	18 lbs.	(+48)
603.	Airspeed static outlet installation on fuselage		
604.	Auxiliary seaplane fin, Cessna Dwg. 0431144	3 lbs.	(+101)
605.	Omitted		
* 606.	Weight shifter, Aircraft Devices Model CGS-7 per Campbell Dwg. Nos. 4042, 355 and 356	FWD. 19 lbs. (+57.1)	(AFT.) (+144.5)

Rear C.G. limit with weight shifter in aft position is (+18.4) and with weight shifter in fwd. position is (+17.7) Maximum allowable baggage** is limited for each aircraft as determined by weight and balance check with the weight shifter in either the fwd. or aft position whichever is critical. The following placards shall be installed:
   (1) "Maximum Baggage** lbs." (on baggage compartment).
   (2) "Intentional Spins Prohibited with Shifter Weight in Rear Position as Indicated by Red Cable." (In full view of pilot).

*607.	Y-1 sprayer installed in accordance with Yingling Aircraft Inc., Wichita, Kansas, Dwg. No. Y-1 and installation instructions.	82 lbs.	(+10)
*608.	Installation of dorsal fin in accordance with Consolidated Aircraft Repair, Inc., Ft. Wayne, Indiana, drawing entitled "Dorsal Fin, Increased Effective Area of Fin is 0.61 Sq. Ft., Aircraft Modification to Improve Directional Stability."	2 lbs.	(+149)
*609.	Blister windows are eligible when in conformance to the Don L. Meyers Company, P.O. Box 993, San Mateo,l California, installation instructions and either Dwg. No. 70-10-50 or No. 122953.	Use actual weight change	
*610.	Woychik retractable lifting handles, Woychik Aircraft Equipment, Middleton, Wisc., Dwgs. 50 & 50A.	13 ozs.	(+118)
*611.	Metal Plating of Wings Models 120 and 140 are eligible for certification when wings are covered with metal skin per Technical Instruction Report No. 1401 by Birtcraft Engineering Co., 11836 Cherry Ave., Inglewood, California.	Use actual weight change	
*612.	Metal wing skin installed in accordance with Ruleto Industries Inc., 4823 Rosecrans Ave., Hawthorne, California, Dwgs. Nos. R-1013, R-1014 and R-1015 and Installation Instructions CKW-1 and CKW-2.		
l*613. l	Metal skin installed in accordance with Met-Co-Aire, Fullerton, California, Drawing No. 6108.	Use actual weight change	

CESSNA 120, 140
AIRCRAFT SPECIFICATION NO. A-768 APRIL 25, 1956, REVISION 31 SHEET 4 (BACK)

Note 1. Current weight and balance report including list of equipment included in certificated weight empty, and loading instructions when necessary, must be in each aircraft at the time of original certification and at all times thereafter (except in the case of air carrier operators having an approved weight control system).

Note 2. The following placards must be displayed in full view of the pilot:
   (a) Model 140 – "Intentional Spins with Flaps Extended Prohibited."
   (b) Seaplane if Item 604 is installed – "Intentional Spins Prohibited."
   (c) "This Airplane to Be Operated in Accordance with the Flight Limitations of the Operations Manual." (Refers to Item 403, "Airplane Flight Manual.")
   (d) For aircraft with Item 204(j) or (k) installed – "Do Not Extend or Retract Skis While in Motion on the Ground."

Note 3. The 1947 Version (Model 140 – Serial Nos. 11843 through 14364; Model 120 – Serial Nos. 11843 and up) has revised cowling; instrument panel, exhaust manifold which incorporates silencer, relocated engine primer and primer lines. When Beech

Fig. 1-3. Continued.

controllable propeller (Item 3) is installed on the 1947 version, the trailing edge of engine cowling must be flared and a metal roll attached to the bottom portion of the firewall. The flared cowling trailing edge and roll on firewall are optional with fixed pitch wood and metal propellers.

Note 4. When Item 208 or 1948 version landing gear spring, Cessna Dwg. 0441149, is installed, the main wheels are moved 3 inches forward, changing the arms of Items 201, 207 and 210 from (+2) to (–1); the arm of Item 204(a) from (–1) to (–4); the arm of Item 204(b) from (–1.5) to (–4.5); the arm of Item 204(h) form (0) to (–3) for retracted position and from (+3.5) to (+0.5) for extended position; the arms of 204(j) and (k) from (–4.5) to (–7.5) for the retracted position and from (–2) to (–5) for the extended position; the arm of Items 209 and 213 from (+3) to (0).

Item 207, 209 or 210 is not eligible when Item 201(a)(2) or (3), 201(b)(2) or (3), or 208 is installed. Item 204(h), (j) or (k) is not eligible when Item 201(a)(3) or 201(b)(3) is installed. Item 201(d) is not eligible with Item 204(either), 207, 208, 209 or 210. Item 208 is not eligible with Item 204(either) or with revised landing gear spring, Cessna Dwg. 0441149.

Note 5. The C-90-12F or C-90-14F engine is eligible for installation on the Models 120 and 140 landplanes and seaplanes with the following special limitations which are standard for the 1948 version:

Engine	Continental C-90-12F or C-90-14F (Item 105)
Fuel	80 min. octane aviation gasoline
Engine limits	For all operations, 2475 rpm (90 hp)
Oil capacity	5 or 6 quarts (Integral) (–31.5)
Required equipment:	
(Landplane)	Items 11, 201, 202(a), 403, 601 (Model 140 only)
(Seaplane)	Items 12, 206, 403, 601 (Model 140 only)

When the Continental C-90-12F engine is installed, it is necessary for Cessna 0450240 blast tube assembly and Cessna 0452183 lower cowl assembly with Cessna 0452208 lower cowl bottom doubler or the equivalent to be installed. In addition, when the C-90-14F engine is installed, new engine mount, Cessna Dwg. 0451111, is required:

. . . END. . .

biz call it, details how that aircraft was approved to receive its certificate of airworthiness. It will tell you how many wings there are, what kind of fuel to use, what avionics are approved for it, etc. In short, pretty much everything but what color it was painted. At the time an airplane is certified by the manufacturer, this document is prepared and published by the FAA. It details the standards to which maintenance, preventive maintenance, repairs, and alterations must adhere.

A TCDS can range from one small paragraph for a simple, older airplane to several volumes for the more complex craft. Combined with the engineering drawings on file with the FAA, this forms the basis for how a given plane is to be maintained. Besides what the FARs dictate, the aviation mechanic and the owner/operator must meet standards set forth in the TCDS for each aircraft.

By referring to this document, the mechanic can determine if work is a repair or an alteration. As an example, the TCDS provides such details as what type of fuel is to be used in the aircraft. If you wish to use something else that is not prescribed in this document, it would be considered a major alteration and must be handled appropriately, which means more paperwork.

Type certificate data sheets are published in two volumes: one for large aircraft and one for small. A&Ps, IAs, and repair stations are required to subscribe to these volumes and receive regular monthly updates to them. If you find someone who is friendly at the FAA, you might be able to persuade him or her to give you a copy of the TCDS for your airplane. More likely, you will have to go to a federal library (there is one in most large cities) and ask for it. Alternatively, you can ask your mechanic for a copy.

The second part of the definition of airworthiness—"in condition for safe operation"—is the one the lawyers make their money over. Safe in whose opinion, we hear you (and the lawyers) cry. Much of that is obvious. A plane might have all the appropriate parts and pieces but have gaping holes in the fuselage, no windscreen, or broken avionics. Obviously, it cannot be operated safely. You might have your own opinion about what is safe and what is not but, in a dispute between you and the manufacturer, odds are you'll lose. The FAA will almost invariably side with the manufacturer's opinion.

THOSE PESKY RAMP CHECKS

You know how it goes. The day is perfect and you have arranged to meet your best friend at the beautiful little spot 200 miles away for breakfast. You arrive at the airport only to find you-know-who pulling a ramp check.

You feel like everything is in order, but you never know what they might be looking for. You get nervous, your palms start sweating, you know this is going to ruin your whole day.

Well, relax. Just like with your checkride, the FAA has developed a list of the kinds of things they will look for on a ramp check, and most of it is pretty routine. In special circumstances, like looking for a drug smuggler, they can change this list but, by and large, the ramp checks are routine. Forewarned is forearmed, as they say. Mostly, the FAA is interested in paperwork. They will look for any obvious problems with your plane, but if your paperwork is in order, you have made them very happy.

According to the *FAA Inspector's Handbook*, these are what they are interested in:

Determination of currency of annual/100-hour inspection. For your review, an annual inspection is due by the end of the twelfth calendar month following the last inspection. One-hundred-hour inspections are due if an aircraft is operated for compensation or hire or for flight instruction for hire, if furnished by the instructor. Note: When a flight instructor is not included in the rental agreement, a 100-hour inspection is not required on an aircraft when it is rented out.

According to the *Handbook*, computer programs designed to track maintenance records do not have prior approval of the FAA. If you wish to use one, talk to your local inspector and get approval. And you'll like this so much we will quote it directly: "FAA approval of one of these computerized programs for one owner/operator does not constitute approval for use of the same program by all operators." You might have known.

Status of airworthiness directives, service bulletins, and service letters. You must keep track of any of these correction notices issued for your aircraft. The record must include the AD, service bulletin or service letter number, revision dates, method of compliance, and time when the next action is required. All this data must be transferred at the time of sale of the aircraft.

Total time in service records. This may include separate records for components such as engine, propeller, or avionics. (By now you are surely swimming in paperwork.)

Current status of life limited parts. They like to get tricky with this one. If you have an engine, propeller, rotor, or appliance that must be removed from service after a given amount of time, your records must show the amount of time remaining on that part. We know it should be easy enough to look at the time in service and subtract it from the limited-life time, but make it easy on yourself and do it the way they want it.

The record you keep must also contain any modification of the part according to ADs, service bulletins, or product improvements by the manufacturer or by an owner/operator. Some records are not acceptable for this record. Work orders, purchase requests, sales receipts, manufacturers' documentation of original certification, or other historical data are nice to have and important for tracing the parts, but you must be keeping track of the hours in service remaining.

And if you'd rather set your hair on fire than keep detailed records, here's motivation: If the life-limited status of the part cannot be established, you will be required to take it out of service.

Approval for return to service. Remember all those signoffs of repairs, alterations, and inspections we told you about earlier? We really meant it.

Overhaul records. The records for this type of work are essentially the same as all other records. It must contain a description of the work performed, date of completion, and the name, signature, and certificate number of the person who did it. A return to service tag does not constitute an overhaul record.

Major repair and major alteration records. That's all that Form 337 stuff we told you about a few pages back. If your friendly FAA person wants to see your records, remember you are not required to have them with the aircraft. In fact, it is suggested that they not be carried in the plane since a crash would wipe out the history of the plane and give the FAA and the lawyers a lot of headaches—which could be a plus, but don't be tempted. When you deliver the records to the FAA, they will give you a receipt for them.

Ramp inspections will, of course, include visual inspections of the plane, but if you follow all the valuable advice we give you here and use only approved parts, you should have no problem with that. According to the *Inspector's Handbook*, computer programs designed to track maintenance records do not have prior approval of the FAA. If you wish to use one, talk to your local inspector and get approval.

2

When the airplane isn't flying

WOULDN'T IT BE GRAND IF HANGARS RENTED FOR $50 A MONTH AND we all could afford to store our planes out of the weather? Not only would the plane be better off, but think of all the hours you could kill hanging around the hangar talking about flying if the weather isn't suitable to fly. If wishes were horses . . . But with a little attention to detail, planes can be well cared for on tiedowns. After all, they were made to be out in the weather.

KEEPING IT IN ONE PLACE

Don't you hate seeing those pictures the media loves to show after a storm where planes were blown upside down or sideways? While they're dramatic pictures, your heart probably sinks when you see them. Those shots ought to encourage you to check your tiedowns, even if you don't live in Florida where they get hurricanes biweekly.

A three-point tiedown will provide the most security in almost any wind. If possible, tiedown with two points downwind and one upwind. Using the tiedown rings on the aircraft, secure at both wings and the tail. If your plane doesn't have any attachment rings, talk to your mechanic about having some installed. Some manufacturers such as Piper and Taylorcraft have kits available to modify planes for tiedowns.

Those struts hanging right out where you can reach them look tempting as tiedown points, but don't use them. Struts are designed to carry diagonal loads. Tying straight down could bend them. In addition, the ropes can slide along the struts and damage the wing or other points of attachment.

If you are tying to a ground attach cable, move the attachment point so it is directly under the plane's attachment points and pull the rope or chain tight enough that it pulls the cable slightly off the ground.

Tiedown kits are available for most planes from pilot shops such as Sporty's. They might include augur bits, which screw into the ground and can be helpful in tying down in soft ground. If you are more mechanically inclined, you can make your own tiedown kit. Something as simple as three pieces of scrap steel rod or construction rebar can be utilized to make a usable tiedown system.

There are several ways to make them. Start with three pieces of rebar either ½-inch or ¾-inch diameter. For the wing tiedown stakes, around 18 inches long seems to be a workable length. For the tail tiedown stake, you can probably get by with a slightly shorter piece. You have two choices: you can use either rope or chain for tying down the airplane. If you want to use rope, take a scrap piece of re-bar, heat it hot enough to bend, and form three loops or half circles. After the metal cools, weld them or have them welded to the tiedown stakes. Don't weld them to the very top of the stake; leave a short stub of the stake sticking above them. That way when you take your hammer to drive them into the ground, you will be able to pound directly on the stake as opposed to pounding on the formed piece, thus breaking it off, eventually. If you are going to use chain instead of rope, weld the last link of each section to the stakes in the same manner as the loop, for the same reason. As for the end of the stake that gets driven into the ground, you really don't have to do anything fancy. If you want, you could grind a kind of pointed end, but it's not going to stay very sharp anyway since it's going to be shoving rocks out of the way. You also might not want a sharp point on it since it will be in your baggage compartment poking holes in your airplane. Simply cutting the stake at an angle works. Just leaving it square will work.

As far as the length of the rope or chain, give yourself plenty to work with. If you are using rope, make sure you have lots of rope to go through the tiedown ring and make whatever knots you like. If you wish to use rope rather than chains, se-lect one that will stand up to the weather. Hemp, though less expensive, tends to rot from the inside, and you might not know the rope is no good till your plane goes cruising across the field on its own. Polypropylene is resistant to damage by ultraviolet rays and does not absorb water like hemp does.

Figures 2-1 and 2-2 offer some comparisons. Several knots can be used on the ropes. If you are not the macrame queen from the 1970s, learn one or two from those suggested here (see Figs. 2-3 through 2-6).

Rope and fiber comparison chart

	Hemp	Nylon
Relative strength	Very low	Very high
Relative weight	Low	High
Elongation	Very low	Very high
Resistance to impact or shock loads	Very low	Very high
Mildew and rot resistance	Very low	Very high
Acid resistance	Very low	Low
Alkali resistance	Very low	Very high
Sunlight resistance	High	High

Fig. 2-1. Rope can be used to tie your plane down. Ropes made of different materials have different strengths and resistance to moisture.

Weights and minimum breaking strengths

Size (inches)		Hemp			Nylon		
Dia.	Cir.	Net Wt. 100 ft.	Ft. per pound	Breaking strength	Net Wt. 100 ft.	Ft. per pound	Breaking strength
³⁄₁₆	⅝	1.47	68	450	1	100	1,000
¼	¾	1.96	51	600	1.5	66.6	1,700
⁵⁄₁₆	1	2.84	35	1,000	2.5	40	2,650
⅜	1⅛	4.02	25	1,350	3.6	28	3,650
⁷⁄₁₆	1¼	5.15	19.4	1,750	5	20	5,100
½	1½	7.35	13.6	2,650	6.6	15	6,650
⁹⁄₁₆	1¾	10.2	9.8	3,450	8.4	11.4	8,500
⅝	2	13.1	7.6	4,400	10.4	9.5	10,300
¾	2¼	16.3	6.1	5,400	14.5	6.9	14,600
⅞	2¾	22	4.55	7,700	20	5	19,600
1	3	26.5	3.77	9,000	26	3.84	25,000

Fig. 2-2. The strength of the rope will vary according to its size. While you can buy a large-diameter rope to give maximum security for a tiedown, consideration must be given to the weight and storage requirements of the rope.

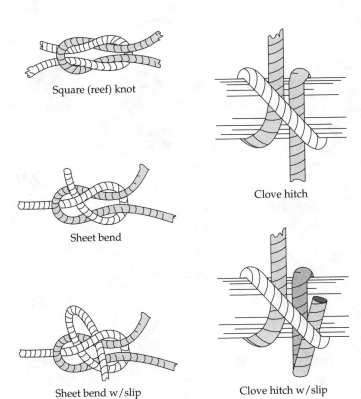

Square (reef) knot

Sheet bend

Sheet bend w/slip

Clove hitch

Clove hitch w/slip

Fig. 2-3. A number of knots are appropriate for tying your aircraft in place. Choose one you are comfortable using. These are some you might want to try.

Fig 2-4. This knot has worked well in the past, along with several others. Start with a half-hitch after pulling the rope snug.

Fig 2-5. Loop the rope behind the half-hitch as shown.

Fig 2-6. Slide the knot down the tiedown rope and tighten as shown. This is what it looks like when you are all done. You can secure the loose end of the rope with a bowline.

If you are using chain, you can get by with a shorter length and put an S-hook in the end link. Purchase the S-hook in a small enough size so it will fit through the tiedown. Choose a chain that will slide through the tiedown ring and with loops large enough so you can insert a link 90 degrees through another link. Crimp one end so the hook stays with the chain. When you are tying the airplane down with chain, you are not using the S-hook to hold the airplane down. These S-hooks are not very strong in tension, in fact, they can straighten out very easily. After pounding the stake in the ground, take the end of the chain with the S-hook, slide it through the tiedown ring, and pull the chain so it is fairly snug. Then take one of the links, insert it back through another link, and then hook the S-hook. This way, the hook is just keeping the links in position, and the load is being taken by the links, not the S-hook (Figs. 2-7 through 2-10).

It is best not to put the stakes directly underneath the tiedowns. Place them two to three paces away for better stabilization.

Fig. 2-7. You can tie your airplane down using rope or chain. If you select chain, run it through the tiedown ring, then take one link on the side with the S-hook and insert it into a link on the other side, as shown here.

Fig. 2-8. Insert the second link through the first one as shown.

When the airplane isn't flying

Fig. 2-9. Insert the S-hook into the second link.

Fig. 2-10. If you are unable to insert the S-hook through the tiedown ring, modify the tiedown sequence as shown here.

When you pound the stakes into the ground, make sure you pound them in at an angle back towards the airplane to keep them in the ground. They should be approximately three-quarters of the way in the ground. This will also give you something to grab onto when it's time to remove the stake.

A trick for removing the stake is to take your hammer and rap the stake on the side just above the ground in several directions. You will work the stake back and forth, loosening the ground's hold, and you can then pull the stake straight out with little or no effort. If no tiedowns are available, try to park in the lee of a building and use chocks to minimize rolling.

Now that you have prevented your airplane from moving, prevent your controls from moving. For aircraft with built-in locking systems, lock the aileron and elevator systems. If your plane does not have a built-in system, tie the control yoke or stick back with the seat belts.

External locks, like the tiedowns, can be made or purchased. These external locks will slide between the aileron and wing, stabilizers, and elevator and rudder to prevent movement during strong wind (Figs. 2-11 and 2-12). An external lock

Fig. 2-11. External control locks come in all shapes and sizes and can be easily homemade. This Cessna 180 uses external control locks on the rudder, elevator, and ailerons.

Fig. 2-12. This photograph shows a closeup of external control locks on an aircraft made of two-by-four lumber with carpeting on one side to protect the plane. A bolt in the control lock runs through the hinge areas of the control surface. The board on the other side has a nut to hold it all together.

can be as simple as 2 two-by-fours, padded with carpet, bolted together. They could be real exotic. The lock should be large enough to hold the control stationary. Too small a lock would concentrate stresses in a small area and cause damage. Be sure to cover the locks with something soft so you don't scratch the paint when you install them. A bungee cord can also be used to fasten the two control yokes together.

COVERING IT ALL UP

Anyone who lives in the desert southwest or has ever flown there knows firsthand what sun and sand can do to a plane. The unrelenting sun not only makes most of the plane too hot to touch, but it also fades upholstery and carpeting and can burn out the LED crystals on instruments. Blowing dust will pit the exterior of the plane, especially Plexiglas windows, as surely as if you turned a sand blaster on it.

No matter where you live, creepy, crawly things as well as birds can find a home pretty quickly in all the little hiding places on your plane, plugging up places that should be open.

Even winter weather can wreak havoc with your plane. Heavy accumulations of snow and ice can cause corrosion, and the winter sun can be as harsh as any in

Fig. 2-13. External cabin covers can be attached in two ways. The aircraft in the foreground shows the wrap-on method. In the background, you can see an aircraft with a snap-on cover. The wrap-on cover has small fasteners on the cover that hold the cover together and hold it on the aircraft. The snap-on cover requires snap hardware attached to the aircraft.

the summer. Just the weight of the snow can damage wings, struts, and other parts of your plane. Covers are a bother to put on and take off, but the more covers you use, the better protected your plane will be (Fig. 2-13).

Many materials are available for covers. Reflective silver sun shields and fabrics made especially for outdoor use are some of the more popular and durable materials. Be wary of using vinyl, however, especially if you will be covering metal portions of the plane. Vinyl does not breathe. Moisture will build up under the vinyl and cause corrosion. Make sure the edgings on the covers are not made of something that will scratch, particularly on the window covers. Plexiglas scratches if you breathe too heavily on it.

Cover the pitot and fit covers over the windows. If the coverings are on the inside of the windows, you have added protection from prying eyes (Figs. 2-14 through 2-19). You might also want to cover the prop, whether metal or wood, to protect it from Mother Nature. Wheels without fenders will deteriorate more quickly due to exposure to ultraviolet rays. Even a simple cloth cover over them will extend their lives.

And if you haven't been able to fly lately, drive out and check on your plane periodically to double-check the security of tiedowns and covers. (Like we needed to tell you to visit your plane.)

Fig. 2-14. Interior covers can be as simple as automobile cardboard screens.

Fig. 2-15. Old sectionals can be recycled as interior covers.

Fig. 2-16. Aluminized bubble plastic also works well for keeping out the sun and prying eyes.

Fig. 2-17. Covers should be used to keep the critters out of places they like to build homes. They show up in all kinds of shapes and sizes. This cover protects holes in the cowling from invasion.

Fig. 2-18. Wrap an exterior cover over the cowl for additional protection.

Fig. 2-19. Pitot tube covers will depend on what kind of statement you want to make. You can be very formal and use the cover the manufacturer makes, or you can create your own—like a rubber chicken stuck on the end of the tube, or in this case, tennis balls. Be creative.

CLEANING

Of all the things you as an owner/operator can do to keep your plane in its best condition, cleaning it often is probably the most important. Not only will the plane look good and operate better, but cleaning it will make you aware of any changing conditions in the plane. Small problems can often be found while you're cleaning—like oil or fluid leaks, worn parts, corrosion, or other telltale indications of future problems. You can then resolve the problem while it is still small and, possibly, inexpensive. Well, less expensive.

Where to start

Cleaning your plane isn't anything like cleaning your car unless you count getting wet and grubby in the process. To take best advantage of this chance to know your plane, do a walkaround before you get started. Carefully check for any oil leaks or evidence of other fluid leaks. Carry a notepad with you as you go, and jot down anything you find that you want to check later or want to let Ace, your star aviation mechanic, know about.

Also look for any indications of corrosion or other damage. Rust, loose fasteners, chipped paint, or dents and scratches in the surface of the plane all deserve further inspection. Note any missing fasteners, grease around the wheel bearings, cracks in cowlings or Plexiglas, or anything else that you wouldn't see on a brand new plane.

What products to use

If you were paying attention in the first chapter, we struck fear in your heart over using anything on your plane that hasn't been approved by the FAA or the manufacturer. While cleaners and solvents don't pose as big a hazard as, say, using the wrong rivets, there is the potential of doing damage to your plane if you use certain products. Some products might only dull the paint, but some could do more harm. Your Plexiglas could develop all the transparency of waxed paper, or you could turn the composite material into mush. Some household products might be good for use on the plane, particularly degreasers, but some of these products caution against use on aluminum. And some polyurethane paint manufacturers recommend only mild soaps, not detergents. Some Plexiglas cleaners leave a residue behind that attracts dust. You didn't think this was going to be easy, did you?

Products approved for use on an airplane will have MIL-Spec, Douglas, Boeing, or other test criteria numbers. Many are sold in concentrated form, which you must dilute first. Diluting not only saves you money but also avoids unduly heavy concentrations of the product, which could cause damage. Be sure to follow the instructions for dilution. If you aren't sure about a product, swallow your pride and ask someone.

Washing and waxing

Before you begin, prepare the plane so water and solvents don't get in the wrong places. Using black electrical tape or a colored vinyl tape, tape off the pitot tube and static ports. (The colored tape will show up readily, and you won't end up taking off on your next flight with the tape still in place.)

Spot clean any particularly disgusting places first—like oil, bugs, or the place where your passenger got sick out the window. Be careful about using any abrasives like steel wool or scrapers, which could damage the surface. One of those plastic scrubbie things that were made for use on Teflon pots and pans is good for tough spots. And of course, fingernails work well.

Wheels and landing gear pose a special problem because of all the grease and hydraulic fluid that accumulates around them. Use a degreaser and a cloth to take it off if you get to it before it gets too bad. Hydraulic fluid that has become stuck on can be cleaned with a small amount of gasoline or solvent made for the specific use.

Check the dust caps or lubricaps and replace any that are missing or damaged. These little guys will keep grease and fluids off your shiny, clean plane, as well as keeping dust out of the orifice they cover.

Whether you use a pressure washer or just a bucket of water and a sponge, you need to be careful of where you wash. Obviously, you want to get the dirt and crud off, but certain places can be damaged by water.

Keep water out of cowling openings and away from the spinner or hub of a constant speed propeller. Water in the magneto, air pump openings, or prop hub bearings could make your next flight a real thriller.

And you won't spray water or cleaners on a hot engine but once, will you? There are less expensive ways of learning about thermal shock than having to replace major portions of the engine.

Again, keep water and solvents away from the magnetos, dry vacuum, or pressure pump associated with the instrument air system. It might be helpful to cover or wrap these parts with plastic just for safety. Also, avoid direct water pressure on the place where the blade comes out of the hub. It could force water into the bearings. Dry the places you can reach, and go find a ladder for the places you cannot reach.

Doing windows is a requirement when cleaning the plane, particularly if you have an affinity for seeing where you are going. Plexiglas is a relatively soft plastic and can be easily damaged. If you can find anyone who has used real baby diapers instead of disposables, try to snag a few or at least find out where they got them. They make the best cloths for cleaning Plexiglas. If there are a lot of bugs on the windows, it's best to keep putting water on them and rubbing gently until they loosen. It'll take a while, but you won't damage the Plexiglas.

Use a cleaner specifically made for Plexiglas, but don't use too much. It can cause clouding and possibly damage the window. Some pilots dilute the cleaner to prevent using too much. Several products are on the market for removing scratches in Plexiglas, both small and deep. Ask around the airport, at a pilot shop, or ask your mechanic.

If you decide to wax the plane, again, use a product that is approved for use on aircraft. (Where have you heard that before?) Be careful not to gum up the works by getting wax buildup in seams and panels or parts that are supposed to move.

If you cleaned fluid off the landing-gear shock strut, recoat it with a light film of approved fluid. Dry off the exhaust pipe and muffler to prevent rusting. Some pilots like to apply a thin film of WD-40 to them as a rust preventative. And after all that hard work, go for a flight, even once around the pattern. It'll reward you for a job well done and dry everything off thoroughly.

Now for the interior

If the seats come out of your plane, removing them will make this job easier. On most Cessna aircraft, there are two horizontal stop pins, fore and aft, which are held in place by cotter pins or screws. Many Pipers have a special piece that fits over the top of the seat rail, fore and aft, and is held in place by a screw. If you aren't sure how your seats are secured, check the aircraft manual or ask someone who owns the same kind.

Dirt, paper, peanut butter sandwiches, even small children have been known to work their way under the carpeting, so periodically remove it and vacuum underneath. If the carpeting is loose, you might want to fasten it in place with Velcro to prevent it from slipping or curling. Be careful about using anything more permanent like screws, though. Check with Ace, your star mechanic, before adding more screws to hold the carpeting down. Aircraft manufacturers have a tendency to hide things under the floor, such as fuel lines, bundles of electrical wires, and control cables with assorted pulleys. Inserting screws into such items is definitely not in your best interest. Also, the carpeting might need to come out during annual inspection, and removing and re-installing all those screws are just going to run up your bill.

Standard cleaners used to clean cars will usually work fine in your plane, with one or two exceptions. Before cleaning the face of instruments, determine if it is glass or plastic. Some glass cleaners can damage plastic and, over time, will create a haze. Use products that are specifically made for cleaning plastic or Plexiglas. Also, some cleaners will react with residue from cigarette smoke and turn surfaces yellow or brown. If you smoke, or fly with someone who does, check for cleaners specifically made for the purpose.

It's not a good idea to open the door and spray everything in sight, no matter what cleaner you are using. The cleaner could seep into instruments or controls and cause corrosion or gumming. Spray the cleaner on a clean, soft cloth then clean the surface. Use extra common sense when cleaning the oxygen equipment so nothing seeps in and contaminates the oxygen or closes up any openings.

Different types of metal cleaners are available for removing surface rust or corrosion, but if fasteners have deteriorated, you might want to replace them. (Remember that part about using approved parts?) Many trim pieces are made of plastic and can be damaged by overtightening, so don't use this occasion to demonstrate what weight training has done for you. Just tight enough to hold the strip is all that is necessary.

We are sure you are not the clumsy type who spills coffee and ketchup and lemon pie on your precious plane, but if you sometimes carry passengers who are so thoughtless, you might want to apply a protectant on the seats to protect them (the seats, not the passengers). Some of these products also inhibit deterioration from ultraviolet rays, but some also destroy the chemicals in the fabric that give it the flame resistance the FAA loves. We don't need to tell you to put the seats back in and fasten them in place, do we?

And now, just as when you finished cleaning the outside, go for a flight. It doesn't help the cleaning process any, but you've been such a good little "do-be" by doing all this work, you deserve it.

3

Understanding and operating your bird

THE DESIGN OF YOUR AIRPLANE IS AN INTRICATE ARRANGEMENT OF A number of systems that work in harmony with each other to keep the airplane aloft and running efficiently. A basic understanding of the form and function of these systems will not only help you keep your plane operating at peak efficiency, but it will also help you troubleshoot problems.

AVIONICS

As you know if you have recently purchased new radios for your aircraft, the systems have become so technologically advanced that they all but defy understanding. Mysterious signals are telegraphed through the air and picked up by all sorts of even more mysterious components, providing you with important information such as where you are and where other airplanes are. (For those of us who don't believe in electricity because we can't see it, avionics is even more mysterious.)

The avionics industry is one that is best left to those who have the extensive training (and might we add, patience) for understanding, designing, and maintaining avionics. Even if you are an electronics whiz kid, you would be better off leaving these systems to the experts. However, there are one or two operating techniques that will aid the longevity of these very expensive items.

One of the worst things you can do to your radio is fail to turn it off when you shut down, then start up with the radios on. On initial start-up and shutdown, the alternator might have a temporary voltage spike. While this voltage spike isn't strong enough to damage light bulbs or motors, it is death to the delicate equipment in the radio. Shut the radios off before you shut the engine down, and don't turn them on till after start-up. You might want to have an avionic master switch installed that will shut everything off and turn it on with one switch rather than flipping several switches.

Heat or extreme cold will cause your radios to meet an early demise. Pilots have come into the repair station saying the radio has quit operating only to have the technician find the radio is so hot, he or she can't touch it. After it is on the bench and cools a bit, it tests fine. And it continues to test fine once it is re-installed in the airplane. You can partially prevent this embarassment by proper use of airplane covers. Some manufacturers have designed their planes in such a manner that cool air is directed on the radios to prevent problems. In more complex aircraft, which are likely to have a number of radios, the manufacturer might have also added an additional cooling fan for the radios. These fans can be retrofitted to most aircraft.

COOLING SYSTEM

Most general aviation aircraft use air-cooled engines. The more efficiently the airflow cools the engine, the longer the engine will last. The engineer who designed your plane used as many tricks of the trade as he or she knew to achieve this. In some of the older aircraft, cylinders and other parts are out in the open. The Piper J-3 Cub is an example of this. Later, aircraft designers perfected the fully enclosed cowling, called the pressure cowl, which pressurizes air. Air entering the cowl is pressurized due to being rammed in. The air is then carefully directed around the cylinders through the use of strategically placed baffles, carrying away heat generated by the combustion process. This air then circulates around the exhaust and the rear of the engine carrying away more heat as it leaves the cowl. As long as the air flows the way it was intended, the engine will keep its cool.

Unfortunately, the best airplane designs in terms of aerodynamics are the least desirable in terms of introducing air into the engine compartment. Large air inlet ports simply do not lend themselves to optimum airspeed. This makes it especially important that you be sure you do everything possible to ensure that air circulates around the engine. The cooler you can run the engine, the better chance your engine will have of reaching or exceeding the manufacturer's recommended time between overhaul (TBO).

The general theory, then, is to keep the air moving in order to keep engine parts cool. This is accomplished through operating methods and regular inspections of the system to be sure there are no obstructions to airflow.

Depending on your plane and finances, you have either two or three gauges that will help you keep track of how hot or cool your engine is running. The cylinder head temperature (CHT) gauge might have a probe to sense the temperature in each cylinder, or it might be a less expensive single-probe unit. The multiprobe system could indicate a variation of as much as 150 degrees between cylinders, but this is not unusual. Variations such as the location of the cylinder relative to baffles or the cowling account for such differences.

If your plane is not equipped with a CHT gauge, you should watch the oil temperature gauge and to a lesser extent, the exhaust gas temperature gauge, if so equipped, for indications of an overheating engine.

During such operations as taxi and runup, the engine is producing the most heat with the least amount of air flowing around it. It is important that you do everything possible to encourage the air to flow.

Whenever the engine is running but the plane is still, turn the plane into the wind to get more airflow. Avoid prolonged taxi and idle time whenever possible. If operating out of a controlled airport and the temperatures are edging toward the red, advise the controller so he or she can try to expedite your departure.

While performing maintenance, avoid running the engine for a prolonged period of time or under high power settings with the cowling removed. The cowling is an important part of the system that forces air into the far reaches of the engine. Keep cowl flaps open during ground operations.

Unless ambient conditions require otherwise, always run the engine at full rich mixture during takeoff and climb. And follow carefully the directions in the *Pilot's Operating Handbook* (POH). The manufacturer has already calculated the best combination of rate of climb, cooling, and optimum handling.

Avoid shifting quickly from cruise to idle power during descent, which can cause inconsistent cooling of the engine. Larger engines, which are more difficult to cool, come equipped with cowl flaps that the pilot can open during times when the engine is least efficiently cooled by ram air pressure. Follow instructions in the POH carefully for the best cooling of these engines.

During shutdown, allow the engine to cool as much as possible rather than simply shutting down. Nose the plane into the wind and allow the engine to idle a few minutes before shutdown, particularly on hot days.

LUBRICATING SYSTEMS

Whether the oil flows through the engine or is mixed with the fuel, the lubricating system serves several functions. First, the lubricating system reduces friction between components, but there is always some friction occurring, so eventually parts will wear out. Nothing will completely eliminate friction.

The second function of the lubricating system is to clean the inside of the engine. The oil collects small particles such as metal flakes and specks of carbon and holds them in suspension until they are circulated through and caught in the oil filter and/or screens. If the particles are small enough to pass through the screens and filters (especially the screens), they will create a sludge buildup. This is one reason engine manufacturers recommend more frequent oil changes when the engine has only screens.

The third thing the oil does is help keep the engine cool. The oil will absorb heat from the engine components, then flow to the sump and through a cooler (if so equipped) where the heat is then transferred to the air flowing past. Should the oil capacity get too low, this cooling is greatly reduced, resulting in higher engine temperatures.

Ask 15 aircraft owners what is the best oil to use, and you're likely to get 20 answers. It's like asking who builds the best airplanes; it's a matter of personal opinion. The best thing to do is listen, try them, and find out what your airplane likes.

Formal and informal studies have been made as to whether multigrade or single-grade oils are the best. In simple terms, oil viscosity—that number or numbers such as 10W40, or 30W—indicates whether oil will change its characteristics as the temperature changes. As a rule, oil with a range of numbers (i.e., 10W40) indicates that the oil has been formulated to do its job at a wider range of temperatures than oils with a single viscosity number.

Since the beginning of aviation, mineral oil has been used, particularly for break-in. While it has many good properties, there can be a problem with sludge buildup. Then came ashless-dispersant oil, sometimes called detergent oil, which is mineral oil with additives to prevent the formation of carbon sludge. Use of mineral oil for break-in of a new or rebuilt engine is no longer necessary, due to improved metallurgy and oil compositions. Mineral oils are single-viscosity.

In terms of cleanliness and wear of the engine, there appears to be no difference between single-grade or multigrade oils. However, other differences have been observed on individual engines. Some engines running on multigrade oil in extreme temperatures, i.e., the southwest desert in summer, can have a very low oil pressure at idle rpms but at higher rpms pressure is fine. Some engines might also change oil consumption rate with the change in oil. As we said earlier, try it for a while and find out how your engine reacts.

Oil filters and screens are used to trap contaminants that could clog passages in the lubricating system. As the filter or screen captures more and more contaminants, it becomes clogged itself, and metal filings, dirt, and other particles remain in the oil. Regular and frequent changes of these components is imperative to protect the engine from damage these contaminants can cause.

Oil should be changed at least as often as the manufacturer recommends, but if you fly in dirty, dusty climates, you might want to change it more often. And if you are not a frequent flier, at least start the engine every few weeks and run it for some time. This keeps seals softened, prevents condensation from forming, and in general, keeps all the systems ready to go when you are.

An oil analysis is part of routine maintenance. Having this analysis done at each oil change will show any trends of deterioration or wear, which can help you prevent any major problems. An analysis done infrequently is next to useless since it doesn't help you to determine at what rate and to what extent there are any changes in the engine.

A word of caution, however: this analysis is designed to pick up minute particles in the oil. There have been cases in which the engine has just had a catastrophic failure but the oil analysis has come back reading okay. So don't rely on this as the sole indicator of the condition of the engine. Oil analysis is a tool; use it as such.

Oil additives are available that are said to improve the functions of the lubricating system. Not everyone agrees that they perform as advertised, but the FAA does approve these additives for use, so if it makes you feel good, go ahead and use them.

COLD WEATHER STARTS

Cold weather starts can be taxing on the engine—and your nerves. Attention to a few details can make the process easier. As the temperature drops, oil thickens, preventing it from moving through the system as efficiently. The battery is also affected by low temperatures, resulting in less cranking power. In extreme cases, it might not put out enough power to crank at all. So the key is getting heat to these systems.

If the battery is easily accessible, you might want to remove it and store it in a warm room between flights. If it is not that accessible, or if you aren't fond of installing it with numbed fingers, a blanket wrapped around it could help some.

Oil-heating devices are in widespread use and might provide some advantage, depending on how they're used. Some models are a heating element probe that is put into the oil by way of the dipstick tube, and others are a heating pad that is glued to the bottom or side of the oil sump. Both styles not only warm the oil, but, if left on long enough, will warm the engine itself to some degree. If the unit has been properly installed, you can safely leave it on overnight without worrying about starting a fire. A third style of heater uses electrical heating elements that are screwed into the cylinder heads. This style is sometimes installed in conjunction with the heating pad style heater. The major disadvantage of these units is the necessity of having an electrical outlet close by.

We will break our rule against mentioning brands here simply because there is an item on the market that will help with cold starts and is only manufactured by one company. Tanis makes a sort of electric blanket for engines and lubrication systems, and these blankets have met with considerable success in frigid climates. Look for the company's ads in aviation publications.

Starting your airplane during cold weather requires special techniques if you hope to get it running before the battery goes flat. If you are lucky enough to have a hangar to put your plane in, most of your problems during cold weather are over. But planes left outdoors in cold weather have cold oil, fuel, batteries and spark plugs—everything necessary to get the engine running and keep it going. And trying to start during extremely cold temperatures can cause scoring of the cylinders and other unpleasantries.

First, prime exactly as instructed in the POH. Don't think because it's cold you should give it a couple of extra shots. The manufacturer has already figured all this out. Leave the throttle closed while the engine cranks. An open throttle not only won't get more fuel into the cylinder (assuming you have properly primed), it might actually make starting more difficult by making the mix leaner. While cranking, keep your hand on the primer so you can give it a quick shot as the cylinders fire.

Extremely cold temperatures—lower than, say, 15°F—might require extra efforts such as preheating. Special preheating equipment is available but can put a major dent in your checkbook. Something as simple as a 100-watt bulb placed in the engine compartment overnight can provide quite a bit of heat. Another technique is using the hot-air-blast preheaters. But be careful. They put out a lot of heat and can turn your cowling and other engine components into a molten mass, so don't leave them running unless you are standing there watching.

THE ENGINE

Here are some real basics that you probably learned during your driver's training class in high school. An internal combustion engine works on the suck-squeeze-bang-blow principle. As the piston inside a cylinder is pulled down to the bottom of the cylinder, fuel and air are pulled in (suck). The piston then pushes the mixture up to the top of the cylinder, compressing it (squeeze). As the piston reaches the top of the cylinder, the spark from the spark plugs ignite the mixture (bang). The piston is pushed back to the bottom of the cylinder and the gases produced from this process are pushed out the exhaust system (blow).

All this requires perfect timing so that the ignition of the fuel/air mixture occurs as the piston reaches the top of the cylinder. If it happens before or after, the engine will run rough, sputtering and coughing as it tries to run.

Temperature is also an important consideration. When the fuel is hot, either because the plane has just been flown or because it was parked in the sun, it expands. It can flow back to the fuel tank as it expands, leaving only small amounts of fuel in the lines or, possibly, only vapor. As a result, when the fuel is drawn into the cylinders, there isn't enough of it to make the proper fuel/air ratio that results in combustion. The engine will probably start up, then quickly die.

Air filters reduce the amount of dirt that gets into the engine compartment, and air filters need to be clean to be efficient. If your airplane is equipped with one of the replaceable element filters, do not wash and reuse it. These filters contain a special sticky substance whose job is to collect the dirt and dust and hold them, preventing them from entering the engine. By washing the element, the sticky substance is removed, allowing dirt and junk to be sucked into the engine. The foam material the element is made of will also start to disintegrate and be ingested into the engine. This does not help your engine live a long life. Filters are not that expensive.

FUEL SYSTEMS

Fuel systems rely on either gravity or pressure to deliver fuel from the tanks to the carburetor. On gravity systems, tanks must be located above the carburetor, and therefore this system is limited to planes with high-wing designs. It is a simple, inexpensive system that does not require a fuel pump.

On the other hand, pressure systems use a fuel pump to move the fuel from the tanks to the carburetor. This system permits for flexibility in design because the tanks can be located anywhere on the plane.

Water and contaminants can enter the fuel in your plane in a variety of ways. Refueling during rain or snowstorms can cause water to enter vents, seals, and caps. Water can also enter airport fuel systems just as easily. There might be leaks in underground tanks, or seals or hatches might have been open during rain or snowstorms or during transport of the fuel.

If you are fueling at an airport where you have reason to question the integrity of the fuel, you might want to check the storage tanks before fueling. To check underground tanks, lower a gauge or tape bob into the tank that has been treated with a water indicator paste. Allow at least 30 seconds for the paste to react.

For above-ground tanks, a fuel sample can be drawn into a container and checked for the presence of water. A few drops of vegetable dye added to the fuel will mix with any water that is present, but the dye is insoluble in fuel.

Refueling from drums or cans is discouraged since it increases the odds of water or contaminants being introduced into the fuel. If it is the only fuel available, check it carefully before fueling. Use a filter; even a chamois skin filter and filter funnel will help.

While refueling the airplane—especially if refueling from drums—make sure everything is grounded. This is what the line boy is doing when he attaches a large alligator clamp with a cable running back to the truck/pump to your airplane. This allows any difference in electrical charge between the airplane, the truck/pump, and the ground to equalize without arcing. If this is not done, the smallest arc produced by static electrical discharge can and will ignite fuel vapors. "Dry" fuel should appear clean and bright, not cloudy or hazy.

Condensation forms if the plane is stored with tanks that are not full. Adopt the habit of fueling at the end of each flight whenever possible to prevent the formation of condensation.

The fuel tanks in your plane have sumps designed to trap water. Since it isn't likely that all the water will drain from the tanks through the fuel lines, periodically drain the sumps to ensure that all water is removed from the system. Gently rocking the wings of some aircraft while draining the sumps will help get the last little bit out.

On some tailwheel planes, raising the tail to level flight attitude will get any water in the tank to flow to the main fuel strainer where it can be drained. With crossfeed systems, fuel should be pumped through the system and drained to ensure that the crossfeed lines are free of water.

If your plane has fuel tanks on each wing, position the fuel selector valve to each tank and drain the sump after each tank. Be sure to check fuel reservoirs beside the wing tanks if your plane is so equipped. The owner's manual will detail how to drain these reservoirs.

Use the grade of aviation gas recommended by the manufacturer. If that grade is not available, use the next highest grade. Only use automotive gasoline if that aircraft has been appropriately modified to permit the use of auto gas.

Warped, broken, or leaking fuel caps can be responsible for the introduction of water or other contaminants into the fuel system. Repair or replace the cap if there is any sign of deterioration.

Good fuel management begins with determining your plane's fuel consumption. By keeping careful records about flight time, power setting, and fuel purchases, you will have a good feel for how much fuel your plane uses in any given flight condition.

The *Pilot's Operating Handbook* will tell you how much usable fuel your plane has. The FAA recommends multiplying the usable fuel by 75 percent and dividing the result by your previously confirmed consumption rate. The resulting number will tell you how long you can fly and still have a comfortable fuel reserve.

More than one pilot has run afoul of the FARs by flying with inoperative fuel gauges. To be safe, it is wise to assume the gauges are not working correctly. Once you become familiar with your plane, you should know how long into a flight the gauge should read three-quarters or one-half full. Taking into account any variance in flight conditions such as headwinds or tailwinds, you should know if the gauges are reading accurately.

To lean or not to lean

Leaning the fuel mixture is a technique you learned during your training. From your basic grade-school science classes, you remember that three things are required for fire: fuel, air, and heat. Fuel and air can be mixed in varying percentages to make a rich or lean mixture. Changing the mixture during certain operations will maximize your plane's performance. Leaning improves engine efficiency and increases airspeed, as well as providing smoother engine performance. Leaning also improves fuel consumption, giving your plane a longer range. Spark plugs are also less likely to foul if the fuel mixture is properly leaned. If the engine begins to run rough, it could be telling you that the fuel and air mixture is not correct. Fix it immediately before the engine quits running.

On normally aspirated engines, lean any time the power setting is 75 percent or less. Use full rich for full-throttle operation at 5,000-feet density altitude or below. For high-altitude takeoffs and landings, adjust the fuel mixture setting by leaning to maximum rpm, and then enrichen slightly for carburetor engines. Lean to proper fuel flow and fuel pressure settings for injected engines. To ensure having maximum power in the event of a go-around, lean before entering the traffic pattern. Also, at high-altitude airports, lean for taxi, takeoff, and landing, and when entering the pattern. At cruising altitude, set the mixture to 65 to 75 percent for top performance, or reduce to 55 percent for better fuel consumption and greater range.

Enrich for descent only if the POH recommends it and then only enough to keep the engine running smoothly. Also, use full rich in the traffic pattern or if required by the POH for landing at high altitude.

There are a number of ways to accomplish leaning. There is the tachometer method (also called the engine "rough" method), fuel flowmeter method, and exhaust gas temperature (EGT) method.

If your plane is equipped with a fixed-pitched propeller, try the tachometer method. Check the POH and set the controls for the desired cruise power setting. Gradually lean the mixture from full rich until the tach reaches its peak rpm. At this stage, the engine is operating at maximum power. Enrichen the mixture to ensure that all cylinders of the engine are getting the proper fuel/air mixture because it is possible for one or more cylinders in the engine to be running leaner than the others.

Operating at maximum power does not provide the best fuel economy, however. In order to maximize your range, reduce the throttle to a cruise setting based on POH, then lean as previously mentioned. A plane with any type of propeller can also use the fuel flow gauges as a guide to leaning. Simply check your POH and set according to instructions.

You can also lean with an EGT system. There are two different systems in use: a single-probe system and a multiple-probe system. The typical EGT system consists of temperature-sensing probe(s), the instrument mounted on the instrument panel, and the appropriate wire bundle connecting everything together. The EGT system is self-sufficient since it utilizes different metals in the probe to generate a minute electrical current to move the needle or display on the indicator. By leaning the mixture, the exhaust gas temperature will rise until it gets to a point where the fuel/air mixture is at its theoretical perfect ratio. Any further leaning will cause the temperature of the exhaust gases to decrease. The point at which the temperature will decrease with further leaning is referred to as *peak EGT*.

As aircraft manufacturers change engine models, they might also change leaning procedures. Be sure you have the appropriate POH and updates for your airplane. Some engine models have the mixture set by leaning to peak EGT, then enrichening the mixture a certain number of degrees. Other engine models set the mixture by leaning to peak EGT, then leaning an additional amount. Use only the appropriate method for your engine. The engines that are run lean of peak are designed to run this way. Running an engine lean of peak that is not designed to be run this way will cause catastrophic engine damage.

A single-probe system is cheaper than the multiple-probe system, and is more common. A problem with the single-probe system is that it only measures the temperature of the exhaust gas of one cylinder. As we mentioned earlier, some cylinders can be running leaner or richer than the others. For a single-probe system to work properly, the probe must be mounted on the leanest running cylinder. The most common method for choosing which cylinder the probe is mounted on is the S.W.A.G. (scientific wild-ass guess) method. To properly mount the single probe on an engine exhaust system, it would be necessary to mount the probe on each exhaust stack, fly the aircraft, then move the probe to the next cylinder. You would then compare the exhaust gas temperature of each cylinder to each other, as well as engine roughness during each leaning.

Eliminate the problem of having to guess which cylinder is leanest by going to a multiple-probe system, which has an EGT probe for each cylinder. This now means you can lean the engine according to the leanest cylinder. Multiple EGT systems are also advantageous in troubleshooting problems and giving better notice of potential problems.

TURBOCHARGERS

A basic element of your flight training dealt with density altitude—the fact that air is "thinner" at higher altitudes and on warm days. You learned to adjust your flight procedures to accommodate this change in altitude.

A turbocharger helps overcome the problems of density altitude. Driven by the engine exhaust, this component essentially increases the amount of air entering the cylinders to prevent the loss of power at altitude. It tries to make the engine think it is running at sea level.

The turbocharger can be hard on an engine since it causes the engine to perform at higher power longer than a normally aspirated engine would. Higher performance can result in higher wear, so routine inspections become more critical. Also, the recommended hours between overhaul can be dramatically decreased due to increased stresses on all engine components.

Exhaust gases are channeled to make the turbine in the turbocharger spin, which makes the compressor spin. To control the amount of gas that is introduced, a wastegate is installed. The wastegate could be fixed (nonadjustable), manually controlled, or automatic.

An open wastegate prevents exhaust from entering the turbocharger at all, instead causing the exhaust to flow outside the plane through the exhaust pipe. As the wastegate is closed, more exhaust gases are funneled to the turbocharger, causing it to perform its function.

Manually controlled wastegates are open before takeoff, then as the plane climbs, the wastegates are closed to prevent reduction in power. Reopening the wastegates during descent "turns off" the turbocharger and allows the plane to fly with ambient air and standard fuel flow.

A fixed wastegate remains in one position all the time, taking some exhaust in and shedding some overboard. It can be adjusted on the ground, but not during flight. An automatic wastegate uses linkage to operate the wastegate as the pilot handles the throttle. This system might use manifold pressure or the density of the air discharged from the compressor to determine the placement of the wastegate.

A turbocharger greatly increases the amount of heat passing through the engine because forcing more air into the cylinders causes the air temperature to rise. This means it is critical for the pilot to watch the cylinder head temperature gauge (CHT) during operation. Attention to operating procedures as prescribed in the POH will help minimize damage due to heat.

Keep in mind that the turbocharger is part of the exhaust system and therefore gets extremely warm. Opening the cowl flaps is a simple method of getting more air through the engine compartment to compensate for the heat produced by the turbocharger. Increasing airspeed while executing a shallow climb will also help.

Rapid descents can cause thermal shock to a turbocharger since they run hotter at higher altitudes. (Though you might think it's colder up there, less dense air does not cool the engine as quickly.) Don't idle at high altitudes except in an emergency. Maintain power and increase vertical speed if necessary during descent. Allow a few minutes between speed reductions to allow the turbocharger to adjust to the new air density.

Turbochargers are fairly trouble-free. More often than not, any problem that seems to come from the turbocharger, is caused by the engine, so have it checked first. Turbochargers are most frequently damaged by loss of lubrication or dirty lubrication. Contaminants can also cause damage to the turbine blades.

If the turbocharger goes out during flight, fly the airplane as though it were normally aspirated, then land as soon as practical. Failure could be caused by malfunction of the exhaust stacks or failure of the wastegate. The oil system is an integral part of the turbocharger, providing lubrication for the turbine as well as controlling the wastegate in an automatic system. Failure of the oil system could result in dumping of the engine oil overboard, leading to engine failure from lack of lubrication.

ELECTRICAL SYSTEM

There are some basic differences between an aircraft electrical system and the one in an automobile. In your car, the battery is the source of power that ignites the fuel/air mixture and causes the explosion in a piston that makes the engine run. In your plane, that function is fulfilled by the magneto. The electrical system that uses the battery in a plane is used for lights, instruments, starters, and other accessories.

Aircraft built since the mid-1960s use an alternator rather than a generator to manufacture electricity, which is then stored in the battery. A voltage regulator ensures that a constant voltage is maintained regardless of engine rpm.

Lead-acid batteries are probably the most common in light aircraft because of their lower initial cost, but nickel-cadmium (nicad or NiCd) batteries are used in larger aircraft. The lead-acid variety tends to lose the electricity it stored if the plane isn't run occasionally. Nicad batteries do not suffer from this weakness. They also provide faster starts and better operation at wider temperature ranges, but they cost more initially. However, nicad batteries must have a deep discharge occasionally in order to maintain the ability to function. Additionally, they are sensitive to internal temperatures. Excessively high internal temperatures will result in the battery literally melting.

A battery master switch is installed to disconnect the electrical system in one move, rather than turning off each system individually in the event of an emergency. Manufacturers have developed a split master switch that controls the alternator and the battery separately. If the alternator fails during a flight, it is possible to turn off the alternator and still use the battery.

Batteries do not work at their optimum when cold. If the battery in your airplane is easily accessible, you might want to take it out and store it inside during cold weather. If you can't get to it or if you aren't inclined toward installing it before every flight with numb fingers, throw a blanket over it to reduce heat loss. (Better think of a system to remind you to take the blanket out, such as leaving a corner of the blanket hanging out to remind you it's there.)

THE PROP

Poor thing. It takes so much abuse. Dragging your plane through the air, deflecting stones and all manner of things. And it all looks so simple—just a couple of blades that spin around.

Sadly, many pilots are unaware of how sensitive an object the propeller is and how it is tied in with the internal workings of the plane. They run the plane off the runway, digging the prop into dirt, bending the blade. Then they whack it back into shape with a sledge hammer. They trim or file the nipped edges off, take it off to grease the hub, put it on backwards, and leave wooden props to dry and crack. Poor props.

If there is one thing you should know about working on the prop it is that you cannot work on the prop. Okay, so you can wash it, but that's it. You cannot whack it with a sledge hammer, file the edges down, or pop it off and put it back on.

Propellers can be of two types: tractor or pusher. The tractor prop is mounted on the front of the plane and is the most common type. The pusher, as you might imagine, is mounted on the back and pushes the plane through the air. (There is a plane design—the Cessna 337 Skymaster—that incorporates both types of props, which is compared to Dr. Doolittle's push-me-pull-you animal, but that's another story.)

The prop can have two or more blades, and it can be made of metal, fiberglass, or wood. A metal strip runs along the leading edge of a wooden blade to prevent damage. Specific props are designed to work with specific engine types and plane designs and cannot be interchanged.

The angle of the blade is an important consideration in prop design. The angle is greater at the point where the blade meets the hub than at the outer edge of the blade. (This change in angle is called *pitch distribution*.)

In older aircraft, the pitch of the prop can be changed before flight. These props are referred to as "ground-adjustable props." These props allow the pilot to fine-tune the aircraft's performance for the intended flight. If one flight requires a short-field takeoff the blade could be set at the necessary angle, but if the next flight is a long-distance one, another angle could be set appropriately. The settings can be changed easily without having to exchange propellers.

For a while, manufacturers made adjustable pitch props permitting pilots to set one pitch for takeoff and reset it for cruising. Then an automatic pitch prop was developed that would adjust itself. Usually, though, planes are equipped with a fixed-pitch prop.

The automatic-pitch prop or constant-speed prop uses a propeller governor to change the blade pitch. The pilot chooses an rpm, and the governor will sense small changes in the rpm, then change the blade angle to compensate.

The FAA takes a dim view of any work on the prop by anyone other than properly certificated people. Outside of inspecting and cleaning it, there is nothing a pilot might do to the prop. Forget replacing it or trying to relaminate it. An out-of-balance prop is another item best left to the experts. This is one thing you'll have to leave in the capable hands of your mechanic. And be sure the mechanic who does the work is certificated for prop work. Not everyone receives this training.

The prop is fastened to the end of the crankshaft, which runs, essentially, down the middle of the engine. Damage to the prop almost always results in damage to the crankshaft. A bent crankshaft throws everything else out of alignment and can cause untold damage. Bending the prop by running off the runway creates one set of problems, while hammering the dents out might bend everything further. The crankshaft probably looks like a pretzel by now. Best to call in Ace, your mechanic.

To further complicate the design and alignment of the prop, consider this. The FAA specifies minimum terrain clearance between the edge of the prop and the ground. This takes into account the landing gear, tire inflation, and size of floats on a seaplane. Underinflated or overinflated tires or a new tire size can change this dimension. This should deter you from wanting to take on any major projects with the prop.

Wooden props require even more special attention and considerations. Always position a wooden prop horizontally when you park the plane. If one blade is lower than the other for long periods of time, moisture in the higher blade will travel to the lower one and can cause the prop to be out of balance. (No, you can't rebalance it. Take it to an appropriately rated mechanic.) Regardless of what material the prop is made of, don't consider it a grab bar. To push or tow the plane, use sturdier parts made for the purpose.

Besides the propeller, consideration must be given to the governor. For most modern aircraft with constant-speed propeller systems, engine oil pressure is used to twist the blades from low to high pitch. An internal spring might help the process along.

The prop knob changes the spring tension, which matches rpms with blade pitch. When you manipulate the cockpit prop control, you are actually adjusting this spring. If you are used to having this control at a given position relative to rpm and you notice a change in that position at the same rpm, you might have a governor problem. If you discover the problem while you are on the ground, stay there. If you are flying, find the closest landing site, airport, or not. What happens to the prop is also affected by changes in airspeed.

Any changes in oil pressure will likely affect the ability of the prop to function properly. Dropping oil pressure in a single-engine plane will result in overspeed of the prop. Inside the prop governor is a positive-displacement oil pump that takes the engine oil pressure and increases it several times. Regardless of what your oil pressure gauge is showing, the actual oil pressure in the prop hub is substantially higher. A screen filters out the largest particles of foreign matter in the oil, but for all practical purposes, most things are not filtered, making it even more important to keep the oil changed.

You can keep the governor running properly by doing feather checks during runup. During the check, watch how the prop rpm responds. Anything abnormal should be checked before your next flight. If you have any question about what is normal, get to your local A&P and discuss it.

ENGINE BREAK-IN

One of the most crucial times in an engine's life is its first few hours. After you have had a new engine installed or had the old one overhauled, you must run it properly until it has a chance for all its parts to be adequately lubricated and to allow them to "settle." For example, the pistons and cylinders must work together for a period of time in order to become compatible, become properly lubricated, and run cooler than they will originally. Improper break-in procedures will result in cylinder glazing. This is but one example of how being overanxious about pushing the engine to maximum performance will substantially decrease the time till you need to have the job done all over again.

How you handle break-in should be guided by the manufacturer or the overhauler's recommendations. They have experience with their systems and with other pilots, and they know their equipment best. The few short hours between what you think you should be able to do and what they recommend, could spell the difference between early engine failure and long years of trouble-free flying. It could also make the difference in any warranty the manufacturer or overhauler offers.

Whether you have an opposed-piston engine or a radial engine, procedures and recommendations are essentially the same. First, the manufacturer or overhauler will put the engine through a run-in period before it is installed. It will be mounted on a platform, run, and tested in the shop. The break-in cycle, the first 50 hours, are your responsibility.

During run-in, the engine is placed in a test cell, where it is monitored under controlled conditions for such things as cylinder head temperatures, oil pressure, manifold pressure, and rpm. Operating at different speeds and for different times, technicians check all these things, adjusting anything that needs adjusting, but also using the information to establish criteria for that particular engine since no two run exactly the same. To avoid overheating, the engine is shut down periodically. During this time, the oil screens or filters are checked for any indications of metal particles. Oil consumption is also monitored during this test, which typically lasts two to two and one-half hours.

Cooling and lubrication are two items that are of particular concern to the person conducting the run-in. During shutdown, he or she might inspect such things as the pistons to ensure they are being properly lubricated to prevent cylinder glazing. The engine will likely run hotter during run-in until everything is properly lubricated and the rings are seated. To help keep the engine cooler during this stage, a shorter propeller is installed, which forces air around the engine.

Opinions vary considerably about what oil to use during run-in and break-in. Some technicians like to use mineral oil during run-in because of its tendency to keep the engine cooler. Other people prefer to use the same type of oil that will be running through the engine during its life. Single-viscosity mineral oil has been the traditional choice for break-in, though some are of the opinion that its heavy molecular base can contribute to cylinder glazing by forming lacquer and varnish deposits. Multiviscosity oil, whether mineral or ashless dispersant (AD), is designed to operate efficiently and provide cooling at a wide range of temperatures. Since the engine is heated and cooled several times during run-in, some prefer to use this oil. AD aviation mineral oil is designed to prevent deposits, and some feel it does a better job of holding any particles in suspension until they can be trapped in oil filters or screens. Regardless of your personal opinion of these oils, follow the manufacturer's or overhauler's recommendations carefully on this subject for best results at this crucial stage in your engine's life.

Despite the relative sensitivity to abuse the engine has when it is new or freshly overhauled, overhaulers do not recommend that it be babied. You need to run it at least 75 percent power in order to get the parts to adjust to each other and wear properly. Operating at low manifold pressures can cause cylinder glazing and other problems with the pistons and rings.

Once run-in is complete and the engine is installed, it's time for you to do your part of the break-in. Some estimate that approximately 75 percent of the wear of piston rings occurs during break-in. This is when the rings, pistons, and cylinders are making the most adjustment to each other. After break-in, they should be operating with minimum wear and maximum lubrication. Again, the manufacturer or overhauler will give you specific instructions, probably in writing, about what to do and not do during the first 50 hours or so of engine life. These are some of the things you will likely be told.

Keeping the engine as cool as possible is crucial, so fly during the coolest time of day during the summer. Do not run the engine for more than two or three minutes with the cowl flaps open, since this will inhibit proper airflow around the engine needed to keep it cool. Ground run-in should be done in as dust-free an area as you can find. You might want to run the engine a few minutes, shut it down, let it cool, then run it again when you first get your plane back. This gives you a chance to monitor gauges and listen for any noises that might indicate problems. Check the oil frequently and add any as needed. Oil consumption will vary considerably from one engine to another during this time, so don't go by anyone's advice. Check the oil yourself. Follow the manufacturer's or overhauler's recommendations to the letter about oil changes during this time. All manner of metal particles are likely to be circulating through the system after major work, and it's imperative you remove the particles as soon as possible.

So how long should you take to break in the engine? It will vary from one engine to another, even among engines of the same make and model. The manufacturers or overhaulers know their equipment best, so follow their recommendations, but several things will tell you when break-in is complete. First you will notice a decrease in oil consumption. Oil temperature and cylinder-head temperature will also drop when the engine is completely broken in.

GROUND RUN INSPECTIONS

Every few months, it's a good idea to do a ground run inspection in addition to your normal preflight. This is an additional check on systems which can help you find any problems early enough that they don't become major repairs.

First check to be sure all people and things are clear of the props. That includes tiedowns, chocks, tools, and your mother-in-law. And make sure no one is behind you. No sense in blasting another plane with full power and incurring the wrath of the pilot. Batten down any covers you might have removed from the plane so they aren't blown into the next county.

While you're walking around checking these things, also look for any indication of fluid leaks, both on the plane and on the ground. As airplanes age, they often develop leaks. Being familiar with your plane will help you determine if new leaks are developing or if a leak you already knew about has gotten worse. And while you are doing your walkaround, check control surfaces to make sure they are in good shape and move as expected.

Once inside the cockpit, before you touch anything, check the position of various controls. Curious fingers, cleaning, or just bumping could have caused some of the switches to end up in a position other than how you thought you left them. The radio master switch should be off to avoid power surge when you start up. Be sure the landing gear controls are in the "Down" position to avoid the embarrassment of having the nose gear retract when you fire up the engine. Weather radar should be off, and fuel selector valves should be set on the appropriate tank.

After turning on the battery master switch, check the landing-gear lights. If one or the other is not lit, push the test button. If you still don't have any lights, it's time to check the gear. And remember, the extinguished light might be telling you the landing gear is not locked, so don't move the plane until you have resolved the problem. Then check any fire warning or test mechanisms your plane might be equipped with to ensure they are all operating properly.

Prime according to instructions in your manual, set the mixture as the manufacturer recommends, then start the engine. If recommended by the manufacturer, adjust the mixture as the rpms increase.

Now verify that the alternators are on line and oil pressure is correct. Add a little load to the system by turning on landing lights and other high-amperage items. This will confirm that you are not running on just the battery.

Next turn on the radio master switch, dial the navigation and communication equipment, and turn up the volume. If you hear any clicking, you might have some problems in the ignition harness.

Check the magneto's grounding by pulling the throttles to idle. Quickly move the mag switch to the off position, then back to both. If the engine stops firing momentarily, you have confirmed that both the switch and the p-leads are operating normally. However, if the magneto is internally grounded, this test might not show up any problems with the p-lead. Now bring up the power while watching the rpm and manifold pressure to be sure they are coming up smoothly.

Turbocharged aircraft with automatic wastegates need a little extra attention. If the wastegate sticks, the rpm might continue to rise after you let go of the throttle, or the engine power might rise rapidly, stop, and rise again as the throttle is opened.

If throttle response is smooth, keep bringing up the power. If yours is a constant-speed prop, accelerate to 1500 rpm. Feather the prop levers and quickly bring them back out, listening for even deceleration of both engines. (If it's cold out when you are doing this, be sure engine and oil temps are up first.)

Using manufacturer's recommendations, bring the engines up to speed for doing mag checks. A properly operating mag system will show a 25- to 50-rpm drop during this check. A slightly greater drop than that could indicate problems with ignition timing or mag timing. A drop of more than 200 or severe roughness might mean a bad lead, faulty spark plug, or cracked distributor.

Now check fuel flow rates and fuel pressure gauges, if your plane is so equipped. Low pressure or jumping needles on the gauges need to be checked out before your next flight. The boost pump might help increase fuel pressure, but don't be lulled into a false sense of security. Get it checked.

Check the prop governor by setting the rpm at 2300 then pulling it back 50 rpm. Now start coming up on the throttle controls and watch the manifold pressure. It should steadily increase with no increase in engine rpm. If the rpm cannot be maintained at a steady rate, have it checked out by your mechanic.

On planes equipped with multicylinder EGTs, check to make sure they are reading normally, based on your experience with your plane. CHT temps should also be normal by now, so check that also. Watch the hydraulic pressure gauges for a minute to be sure pressure is holding steady. Check the circuit breaker or fuse panel to make sure everything is operational. Next check the idle mixture. With the throttle pulled all the way back, pull the mixture back slowly and watch for a slight rise in rpm. Check the magneto ground before shutting down by flipping the switch to off for a second. The engine should stop firing then continue firing as you flip the mags back on.

PITOT-STATIC SYSTEMS

Pitot or pitot-static tubes use static pressure ports or vents, heaters, and a system of tubing to give readings on instruments like the altimeter, airspeed, and vertical speed indicator. The system can also be connected to such units as air data transducers and automatic pilots.

The pitot tube is installed with its axis parallel to the longitudinal axis of the aircraft unless the manufacturer specifies something else. When lines are attached or disconnected, care must be taken that the opposite end is not loosened, twisted, or damaged during handling or fitting.

Whereas pitot tubes are usually easy to find since they are hanging out in the breeze, when it comes to static ports the manufacturer is playing hide-and-seek with you. Every manufacturer puts it in a different place. Some manufacturers put it somewhere on the fuselage. It could be forward of the cabin, sometimes aft of the cabin, sometimes on one side of the fuselage, sometimes on both sides. Other manufacturers can put it out on the wing, either combining it with the pitot tube or locating it in a tube alongside the pitot. Some airplanes don't even have a static system. They just vent the instruments to the cabin. This is primarily found in antique aircraft.

Always ensure that the pitot tube covers are in place when the airplane isn't being flown or use a flapper valve that screws on and remains in place permanently. As airspeed builds, the valve opens automatically. Both of these are deterrents to a pitot system's worst enemy, those pesky little bugs that build nests in tiny little openings.

If the pitot tube does become plugged, there are several ways to clear it. Some people will attempt to clear it by disconnecting the line off the back of the instrument, then trying to blow it out using compressed air. This is not a job to be taken lightly since there can be other connections directing this air to other instruments and equipment. If these instruments and equipment are not disconnected as well, applying compressed air to them will blow them apart. When using compressed air, the best thing to do is disconnect the pitot tube from the rest of the system at the first connection, then apply the air to the pitot tube only. Since this can entail some disassembly of systems, it would be best to leave this to the professionals. If the problem is a simple bug-plugged pitot tube, depending on the system, it could take the mechanic only a minute or two to clean the pitot out. If you're on real good terms with your mechanic, he or she might not even charge you for it. Besides, if the mechanic screws up, he or she gets to buy the instruments.

Static ports are usually tiny holes that get plugged up easily. When polishing your airplane, avoid using a lot of the wax or polish in the vicinity of the static ports, wherever they might be. If wax or polish plugs the static ports, the best thing to do is let everything dry, then clean the static port out with a small piece of safety wire. Do not disassemble anything. According to the regulations, if the aircraft is equipped with a transponder with encoder, and you disassemble a static line connection, the static system is now due the inspection required by the FAR Part 43, appendix E.

Some pitot-static tubes have replaceable heater elements. To check if the replaceable element is operating properly, check the ammeter current. Another check is to see if the tube or port gets too hot to touch.

If you suspect there is a leak in the pitot-static system, first check to see that all the tubing is securely connected to the instruments. Leaks anywhere else will have to be checked out by your A&P. Special equipment and standards must be met, depending on whether the equipment is flown in IFR or VFR conditions, so it's best left to the professionals.

4

Preflight

WE KNOW; WE KNOW. ALL YOU WANT TO DO IS GET IN YOUR PLANE and fly. Whether you're meeting someone for breakfast, taking a lesson, or just getting in some touch-and-goes, you're anxious to just get in the air. Of course, you understand all your instructor taught you about preflights and how important it is, but it is very tempting to cut corners. Especially if you fly frequently, you probably feel that you know your aircraft well enough to overlook a few things from time to time.

Your instructor's admonitions aside, there are two reasons why you need to conduct a thorough preflight. One is safety, which is obvious. To paraphrase a policeman, asking a pilot if he or she is a safe pilot is like asking someone if he or she is a good lover. Who is going to say no?

But if you are confident that you are conducting a thorough preflight inspection to ensure a safe flight, think of something else—your checkbook. A thorough preflight will turn up deteriorating conditions which can be attended to before they become expensive.

COOLING SYSTEM

Generally, you should be looking for anything that could obstruct the free flow of air around the engine. Birds and insects like air inlet ports and exhaust systems when they are overcome with the homing instinct. Use of covers over these areas is a good deterrent. Rags, cowl coverings, caps. etc., have all found their way into some pretty surprising places.

Periodically look inside the cowling with a bright flashlight and look at the baffling. These are the parts, usually metal and a heat-resistant fabric, that direct the airflow. Does the baffling extend all the way to the cowling? You want a relatively airtight seal since more air leaks result in less cooling air around the engine.

Look for broken or missing pieces and pieces that are out of position. Also check the fabric for flexibility. It needs to be flexible to ensure a seal since the cowling is fixed to the airframe and the engine shakes, rattles, and rolls on its rubber shock mounts. If the fabric has turned to stone, talk to your friendly A&P/IA about correcting any problems.

A visual inspection of the place where the baffles and the cowling meet will also tell you how tight a seal there is. If the plane is made of aluminum, it will be highly polished where the baffles rub the fuselage. If the plane is Fiberglas, there will be black marks if the baffles are making a good seal. If there are no signs of rubbing, the seals are not tight, which means air is flowing past them rather then being forced by the baffles into the area where it is needed for cooling.

MAGNETO SYSTEM

During preflight, you can conduct a simple test to determine if the magnetos are "hot." Set the throttle to idle and quickly switch the mag switch from "both" to "off," then back to "both." The engine should quit for a moment. If it doesn't, call Ace. One or both of the mags are hot and need work.

You have probably learned to do a differential magneto check during your training. This test measures the difference in rpm between both magnetos working and just one. Your plane's POH will indicate what the manufacturer considers to be a safe drop in rpms. Never exceed those recommendations. And remember, a drop in rpm during this check is normal. If there is no drop, call Ace. Moisture from the atmosphere can result in damage to the magneto, so inspect it for cracks or loose plates, which could let moisture in.

ELECTRICAL SYSTEM

While the magneto creates electricity for the engine to run, a separate electrical system is used to operate things like the starter, instruments, lights, and other accessories. It consists of a battery, alternator, or generator and regulator, much like an automobile.

If your plane's engine is configured so that you can see these parts, preflight should include an inspection of them. Ensure that battery cables are tight and free of corrosion. Mounting bolts on the alternator should be tight, and the alternator belt should be tight and free of cracks. (It is possible for the belt to be too tight, though. Ask your mechanic to show you what is correct on your plane.) Check the gauges to be sure the battery is charging and the alternator is working.

FUEL SYSTEM

The best preflight of the fuel system involves a complete understanding of how fuel gets from the tanks to the engine in your particular make and model aircraft. Study the POH and ask your mechanic, the manufacturer or both about anything you don't really understand.

Fuel vents should be open and free of obstruction. Look for cracked or missing fuel caps, as well. Check fuel lines for any indication of wear or abrasion. Hoses should be of sufficient length to allow for some flexing but not so long as to rub against engine components. If the lines have lost their flex, have them replaced. Where the lines pass near areas that generate heat, they can be wrapped with a high-temperature sleeving.

Fuel can be excessively hot because the airplane has been shut down too quickly or because fuel lines under the cowling have been subjected to high heat, such as being parked in the sun on a very warm day. If you are doing a hot start, follow the manufacturer's recommendations. Heat causes liquid fuel to become a vapor. When this happens, fuel flow is blocked and fuel starvation results. You'll find it preferable to have fuel flowing constantly to the engine. Proper hot-start techniques will minimize any problems.

Contaminants in the fuel will ruin your whole day. You learned during flight training to drain a fuel sample to check for clarity and color. If there is water in the fuel, it will sink to the bottom of the tanks and be drawn off in your test. Other contaminants will show up as floating "stuff" in the fuel. Be sure to use a clear container so you get a true picture of the fuel.

Here's a more involved test recommended by the FAA: Using an unchipped, spotlessly clean, white porcelain, enamel, or stainless-steel bucket, drain 4 or 5 inches of fuel from the sump. With a clean mixing paddle, stir the fuel into a swirling cone and remove the paddle. As the swirling stops, contaminants and water will gather under the vortex at the center of the bucket. Add several drops of red food dye. If there is water in the fuel, the dye will mix with it. If no water is present, the dye will settle in the bottom of the bucket. Water-sensitive papers are also available that will change colors if water is present. FBOs and fuel farms use a water-sensitive paste on the end of a dipstick to check for water.

During a ramp check, the FAA inspector might use a Hydro or Aqua-Glo II kit to check for water in jet fuel. The Hydro Kit is sensitive to water concentrations down to 30 parts per million (ppm), and the Aqua-Glo II kit can detect levels of water as low as 1 ppm.

Airplanes equipped with bladder-type fuel cells should be inspected to ensure the cells are secure and have not deteriorated. Wrinkles, wells, or depressions in the cells should be brought to the attention of a mechanic immediately.

If your plane is turbocharged, become familiar with the sound the turbocharger makes—a whistle or whine that is high pitched. If it sounds unusually high or shrill, see Ace. Check the turbocharger and exhaust pipes for loose fittings, oil leaks, blistered paint, or corrosion.

Be sure all fuel and oil tank covers are installed and secured. Fuel gauges must be operative before you leave the ground. There are a number of cases in the law books where a pilot left the ground, knowing there was enough fuel on board to complete the intended flight but with inoperative gauges. The NTSB took a dim view of this practice and suspended certificates. As a pilot, you are expected to use both the gauges and your watch to double-check the gauges when flying. Remember, running out of fuel is not only hazardous to your health, but also contrary to regulations.

For your information:

- FAR 91.151 requires that, when flying under VFR rules, enough fuel is available to reach the intended destination plus 30 minutes when flying during the day and plus 45 minutes when flying at night.

- FAR 91.155 requires that, when flying under IFR rules, there is enough fuel to reach the intended destination, then the alternate airport and then 45 minutes more.

THE PROPELLER

Before you even think about the preflight of your prop, make sure the mag switch is set at off. Even a little movement in the prop can start the engine if the mags are on.

Prop surfaces should be smooth and without blemish. Wearing a cotton work glove, run your hand over the edge of the prop to check for damage. On wooden props, check for any signs of separation in the plies of the wood. Nicks, scrapes, and bent edges in any type of prop should be repaired immediately.

Gripping the blade tip, wiggle it a little to check for tightness. Constant-speed props will move a little but others should not. Check the prop spinner for integrity and any sign of oil. (You shouldn't see any.) "Sight" down the prop blades from one end to the other to check for any bends. And unless you are fond of having the prop replaced, avoid runups on sand, loose pavement, and gravel. All that flying debris will damage your prop, windows, wings, and fuselage.

TIRES

Checking the tires on your airplane isn't vastly different from checking the tires on your car, and it is neglected just as much. Tires need to be properly inflated in order to give the best braking and the smoothest ride. Check for tread wear and replace bald tires. (There are few things worse than a blowout at 75 knots.) Any sign of the cord of the tire (that white fabric-looking stuff under the tread), whether it's from lack of tread or weather cracks in the sidewall, is cause for immediately replacing the tire.

HEATING AND
AIR-CONDITIONING SYSTEMS

During preflight, check for blockage to all ventilation and heater-exhaust outlets. Excessive soot buildup indicates too rich a fuel/air mixture that could be caused by a number of things. Check with your mechanic.

For planes with air-conditioning systems, a visual check of the compressor, hoses, and belts will reveal any signs of cracking or deterioration. And just like with your car, if you don't get cool air within a minute or two of start-up, the system should be checked out.

HYDRAULICS

Hydraulic systems rely on fluid to make them work. The best preflight inspection is to check under the fuselage, the ground under the plane, and the cowlings for any evidence of fluid escaping the hydraulic system. As the system is pressurized, the fluid will escape through any leaks faster than when the system is not pressurized. Therefore any leaks should be attended to before your next flight. As much as practical, check hydraulic lines for any signs of wear or abrasion.

Be sure you know what type of fluid is appropriate for your plane. Different fluids have different colors and the wrong one can do serious damage to your plane's system. Also determine where the reservoirs that hold the fluid are located, and check fluid levels.

When you start the engine, watch the oil pressure gauge. The needle should be in the green area within 60 seconds. If not, shut the engine down and investigate. Operate the engine at 1000 rpm until the oil pressure reading is steady and in the green area. Fluctuating oil pressure needs to be investigated.

PNEUMATICS

The pneumatic system relies on air passing through the system to create either a vacuum or pressure to make things like gyro instruments, de-icing boots, and other pressure-operated systems work.

More and more aircraft built in the Communist bloc are entering the general aviation fleet (Fig. 4-1). These aircraft can have some very interesting uses for a

Fig. 4-1. Aircraft manufactured in the former Communist bloc such as this Chujaio CJ6A (the Chinese version of the Russian Yak 18A), are becoming more common in the aviation fleet. They make some very interesting use of the pneumatic system. Pneumatics (air pressure) are used for such novel applications as starting the engine and operating the brakes, landing gear, and flaps. As a result, an interesting aspect of flying these aircraft is that there is no in-between with the flaps. They are either all the way down or all the way up.

pneumatic system, such as starting the engine, operating the landing gear and flaps, and applying brakes. Obviously, leaks in this system are not to be tolerated. Also there are special operation and maintenance items to be considered. The manuals will cover these.

The complexity and location of the system doesn't allow for much by way of a preflight inspection, but it is possible to check hoses and fittings for integrity and wear. In systems where the pump is visible, check for any indication of oil around the base of the pump, which could mean some problem with the system. Use your checklist and make sure that the pressure gauge reads the same at start-up as it did after your last flight. Familiarize yourself with the normal operating pressures and have any deviations checked out.

GYRO INSTRUMENTS

Before you can check these instruments (attitude, heading, and turn indicators) the gyros must attain the proper rpm. Allow a few minutes after start-up before checking them—three to five minutes, more in cold weather.

During taxi, the attitude indicator should not vary by more than five degrees except in very unusual circumstances. After level-off in flight, recalibrate the miniature airplane on the attitude indicator as a straight-and-level reference.

Prior to taxi, set the heading indicator using a reliable magnetic reference. Using the runway heading is not the most accurate reference. Use a magnetic compass after checking to be sure there are not watches, anything made of ferrous metals, or other magnetic articles around that alter the compass reading. Check the heading indicator during taxi to verify its accuracy.

PITOT-STATIC SYSTEMS

The pitot tube measures dynamic (ram) air pressure. It is generally located under the wing or on the nose. The tube is used for the airspeed indicator, altimeter, and vertical speed indicator. It needs to be clear of ice and obstruction in order to get proper readings on these instruments.

Insects love building nests in the pitot tube. If you cover the tube while the plane is on the ground, be sure to remove the cover before flight. The tube needs to be perpendicular to airflow for accurate readings, so be sure it is properly positioned. Turn on the pitot heat briefly and touch it to be sure it's operational. Don't leave it on.

Obtain the current barometric pressure and set it on the altimeter. Verify that the resulting altitude is the airport field elevation. Do not fly instrument flights if the altimeter is off by more than 75 feet.

The airspeed indicator and the vertical speed indicator should read zero. Wild gyrations of any of the instruments during taxi should be checked out. During takeoff the airspeed indicator should begin reading almost immediately. However, there is a slight lag in the vertical speed indicator. Some pilots like to tap it lightly, though it's anyone guess if that really helps.

AVIONICS

Of all the components of an airplane, few are more baffling to the operator than avionics. Technological advances make instruments and radios more efficient—and even more baffling—but we rely on them to give us vital information about the flight.

Moisture in the instruments is one of the biggest threats to the equipment. Loose seals around the face of instruments is one way moisture can get in. If you notice instrument faces fogged up, moisture is likely the cause. An avionics specialist can clear up the problem. Moisture can get in through cracks or poor seals in the windows. It's most important to find the source of the leaks and stop them as soon as possible.

Background noise in the headset could be caused by the engine, bad electrical grounds, or even the strobe. If it is the engine, the noise will change as the rpms change. Filters are available that will eliminate this noise.

The microphone can also be a source of trouble, so check it to be sure the button doesn't stick and the cord is in good shape. Check the attachment point between the cord and the mike to be sure it is sound.

Though a valuable piece of equipment in the event of a crash, the emergency locator transmitter (ELT) is a major source of headaches for the Civil Air Patrol. They have been called out more than once to track down the signal from an ELT that turned out to be sitting on a bench in the repair station.

When you put a new battery in the ELT, note the expiration date of the battery and write it on the outside. During the preflight, it will be easy to check the expiration date and get the battery changed in time.

There are only a few things you are permitted to do if you are having trouble with the instruments. Check to make sure they are pushed all the way in and have a good electrical contact. You can also check the fuses, if they are easily accessible. Otherwise, you have to go to a repair station. This is another area that requires a special rating. Not every A&P is so rated, so be sure the station you go to has the appropriate rating.

Under the FARs, you are permitted to fly the plane with inoperable gauges, provided it is not a required gauge. But you must place a placard over the gauge that states it is inoperable.

Keeping avionics cool is one of the best things you can do to ensure their longevity. Temperatures inside the cockpit can reach 170 degrees or more on a warm, sunny day. Use of sun shields on the windows can greatly reduce that figure.

LIFE PRESERVERS AND LIFE RAFTS

The rubberized fabric used for inflatable life preservers and life rafts can be damaged or just deteriorate over time. Periodic inspections will ensure that the equipment you have aboard will be operational if you ever need it. Chafing can occur from vibration of the aircraft, and leaks can develop in the folds of the material.

Check for cuts or tears and inspect the mouth valves and tubes for leakage, corrosion, or deterioration. Remove the carbon dioxide cylinder and operate the discharge mechanism several times to be sure it operates properly. Inspect the cylinder for any signs of degradation or damage.

If you haven't found any damage, perform a pressure check by inflating the raft or preserver to two pounds of pressure and letting it stand for 12 hours. You should notice no appreciable loss of pressure at the end of that time. A quicker method of locating leaks involves immersing the preserver in soapy water. Any leaks will make bubbles in the water. Mark the preservers or raft with the date of inspection. Now that you are sure your plane is in top shape, let's go flying.

5

Preventive maintenance

OKAY, GO AHEAD AND SAY WE SOUND LIKE YOUR MOTHER. WE KEEP saying the same thing over and over, but we are doing this for your own good. You cannot do whatever work you want to on your airplane, no matter how talented you are. You might be a lifelong auto mechanic known far and wide for your ability to repair anything. You might be an aeronautical engineer who has dedicated decades to designing aircraft systems. None of these skills permits you to work on your plane. (In fact, if you are an engineer, you are probably better off not even owning tools.)

Even though the things you are allowed to do are mostly simple, they can be done incorrectly and can result in serious damage (meaning repair bills with three or four numbers to the left of the decimal). Following some basic instructions and complying with industry standards can keep your preventive maintenance from becoming a repair bill.

If you are indeed mechanically inclined and have developed a good relationship with your mechanic, you might be able to do work beyond the scope of Part 43 under the A&P's supervision. Not all mechanics are inclined toward working this way, though, because their ticket is at stake so don't be too surprised if you are turned down when you bring up the subject.

This section of the book is organized in the same order as appendix A of FAR 43 to make it easier for you to locate the item or items you are interested in. Besides, we thought it would make you think we were well organized. There are some things listed in appendix A that you are permitted to do which we have only lightly touched on here. This is because in order for you to do them properly, you will need instructions specific to your airplane. If you do not find all the information here you need to accomplish a given job, check with your mechanic or read the maintenance manual before beginning the work. Other areas in appendix A we have combined since they are related.

We have also added a few tips at the end of this section, which we thought would be advantageous to you. There are some things you can legally do which are not directly addressed in Part 43 but that will help you keep your plane in top condition. Those things primarily involve inspections of various systems and what to look for. Optional equipment such as oxygen can be cleaned and inspected by the owner/operator and should be. We offer some tips on what to check.

We hope it goes without saying that, before beginning any work, you must read the maintenance manual to ensure performing the job properly. Read the appropriate section all the way through before picking up the first tool. That way, you will know the procedure and any special instructions before you get into too much trouble. You know how some authors are. (Naturally, not us.) They give you a list of 16 things to do then throw in—on the next page, of course—something like, "But before you do that," or, "Notice!" So read it all first so you can avoid such unpleasant surprises.

TIRES, WHEELS, AND
LANDING-GEAR SERVICING

Wheel bearings should be serviced every six months or 100 hours, whichever comes first. Tires should be checked during each preflight and changed when cracks appear in the sidewalls or when the tread is thin.

Jacking the airplane up in order to accomplish these tasks requires some careful considerations. The safest procedure is to do just one wheel at a time. Read the POH to learn how the manufacturer suggests the jacking be done. As with a car, there are places that can safely handle the jack, while others will cause considerable damage. If possible, work inside a hangar. If not, don't work on a windy day. Wind can pick up the plane and tip it off the jacks.

Improper jacking can also cause the plane to tip on its side or nose or tail. Manufacturer's recommendations for jacking take into account the plane's center of gravity to prevent this from happening, so do it their way. It might be necessary to use sandbags at the nose or tail to maintain balance.

Jack pads might be permanently installed, or they might have to be bolted into place. Don't shortcut this step. The pads help distribute the load in a wider area, thereby protecting the body of the plane from being punctured by the jack.

No one should be inside the plane unless the manufacturer requires that someone monitor how level the plane is. Chock all of the wheels that are not being raised, both fore and aft. On taildraggers, lock the tailwheel if it is so equipped.

Place the jack so its legs do not interfere with the work you are going to perform. Tripping over it might bring the plane crashing down—possibly even on you. Review the POH or maintenance manuals for any special instructions applicable to your plane.

Before proceeding to work on the wheel and tire, take out the valve stem core to be sure the tire is completely flat. Disassembly of the wheel with an inflated tire can cause serious injury. A safety tip here is to remove the valve stem core before removing the wheel nut from the axle. That way, if one or more of the wheel half bolts are broken, the wheel will not be blown apart.

Most wheels are made in two halves bolted together (Fig. 5-1). Before removing the bolts, the tire will need to be separated from the wheel rim. This is referred to as "breaking the tire bead." You might see people doing this by running a long screwdriver between the tire and rim, but this can damage the wheel halves. There are tools available called bead breakers that support the wheel halves and apply pressure to the tire next to the rim, pushing the tire away from the rim. You might be able to break the bead on some of the lighter weight tires by simply applying your weight next to the rim.

Remove the bearings and clean with an appropriate solvent. Make sure the bearing is dry before packing with grease. Do not dry the bearing by blowing com-

Fig. 5-1. Shown here is a typical wheel assembly disassembled and showing the inside and the outside of the wheel. Also shown is the hardware used to hold the wheel together, a bearing, and a dust cover. At the top of the picture is the two wheel halves, then in the center of the photo, left to right, are a wheel bearing cone, inner dust cover plate, felt dust cover, outer dust cover, and snap ring that holds these parts in the wheel. The bottom of the photo shows three bolts with washers and nuts that hold it all together. This is a nosewheel assembly. A main wheel assembly would have a brake disc bolted on.

pressed air across it and allowing it to spin. The bearing can fly apart with deadly force. Before repacking the bearings, inspect all components. The bearing is composed of two components: the cone and the cup. The cone is the assembly with the rollers. The cup is usually pressed into the wheel half. They are a set. If one piece needs to be replaced, replace the set. If any rollers fall out of the roller cage or they are pitted or scored, the bearing must be replaced.

If there are black marks on the bearing cup or on the rollers, here's a quick check to determine whether or not they need to be replaced. Lightly run your fingernail across it at about a 90° angle. If you can feel any roughness, replace it.

Use an approved bearing grease, working it into the bearing cone assembly with your hands. There are bearing packers available commercially in which you place the bearing and use a grease gun to fill the bearing . Either way, make sure that the bearing is completely filled with grease. Don't be stingy. Too much grease just makes a mess, whereas not enough grease results in bearing failure. Reinstall the bearings and wipe away any excess grease from the outside of the wheel.

While the wheel is disassembled, inspect it for any signs of corrosion, cracks, and other defects. Small amounts of corrosion can be cleaned off, and then the surface can be repainted or lacquered to prevent return of the corrosion. If you discover severe corrosion, cracks, and other defects, the wheel must be replaced. Give the bolts a good inspection, too. Any corrosion, cracks, or stretching are cause to replace the bolt.

If you use tube-type tires, and most of you will, sprinkle a fair amount of tire talc powder inside the tire. This provides some lubrication between the tire and the tube. Inflate the tube inside the tire before remounting it to check for proper fit. Then deflate it, leaving just enough air in so it stays in place and won't get pinched between the two wheel halves during reassembly (Fig. 5-2).

Airplane tires and some tubes have balancing marks (Figs. 5-3 and 5-4). If the tube does not have a balance mark, align the stem with the balance mark on the tire. If the tube does have a balance mark, align it with the mark on the tire. Aligning these balance marks will not guarantee a balanced tire, although it is the first step. Most tires and tubes will require little if no external balance weight to roll smoothly. If there is some vibration or shimmy, take the airplane into the shop and have the wheel and tire balanced together. Some aircraft are very susceptible to nosewheel shimmy if the nosewheel and tire are out of balance.

Insert the wheel halves into the tire, beginning with the half that has the valve hole. Some wheels are marked to assure the halves are properly lined up. If yours are this type, look for the marks and line up accordingly. Watch that you don't pinch the inner tube between the two halves.

Bolt the two halves together, making sure you use washers under the nut and the head of the bolt if that was how you found them. If inserts on self-locking nuts are sufficiently worn that you can fasten them with your fingers, replace the nuts. If the bolts are not tightened properly, this can result in elongated holes, cracks, or other failures of the rim. This will result in the need to replace the wheel half. Assemble the wheel in accordance with the maintenance manual. Some wheels might have a certain order in tightening the bolts, and by all means, use the proper

Fig. 5-2. A wheel and tire reassembled.

Fig. 5-3. The tire and inner tube are ready to be installed. Balance marks are obvious in this photograph—the dot on the tire and the stripe on the inner tube.

Fig. 5-4. The inner tube is inserted into the tire. Be sure to use tire talc to help lubricate inside the tire and help make the tube last longer. Notice how the balance marks are lined up. If no balance marks are on the tube, align the valve stem with the balance mark on the tire.

torque values on the bolts. Reinstall the valve core and inflate the tires to recommended pressure. Safety-wise, it is best to inflate the tire inside a cagelike structure, which will contain the pieces if a wheel comes apart. If this is not available, don't inflate the tire until after the wheel is on the axle and the axle nut is installed.

Replace the wheel on the axle, tightening the nut enough to prevent any side play in the wheel. Use a new cotter key, positioning it so that the sharp edge doesn't damage any bearing seals. Inspect the wheel pants for any cracks before reinstalling them. Here's a good time to clean out the insides of the wheel pants. When you are taxiing in the rain, mud will get thrown into the pant. This buildup will add unnecessary weight, and in a severe case, too much mud will pack in and cause the pant to blow apart. If practical, let the plane sit overnight after performing these repairs. If there is a problem or a leak develops in the tire, it will show up before your next flight.

Lubricating grease tends to attract dust and dirt. Use an approved cleaning solution that is noncorrosive to remove the old, dirty gunk from the exterior. Corrosive cleaners might work faster, but any cleaner that gets trapped in the parts will cause problems. Relube any wear points such as jack screws, door hinges, pulleys, and cables. Wipe away any excess grease. Make sure actuating mechanisms are properly safetyed and that required placards and accessories are in place.

SHOCK STRUTS AND ELASTIC CORDS

Older airplanes used a shock strut with only fluid in it to absorb shock when you touch down and taxi around the airport. Most modern planes, however, use the oleo strut consisting of two telescoping tubes, the cylinder and the piston, which use a combination of compressed air and hydraulic fluid to absorb shock during landing and taxiing. An opening between the two tubes permits fluid to flow from the lower chamber to the upper one, then back again during compression of the strut. A metering rod in the lower chamber looks like a stretched-out cone with its base at the bottom of the lower strut and is used to control the flow of fluid between the two chambers. As the strut compresses, the metering rod slides into the upper chamber through the opening between the two chambers, reducing the diameter of the opening. This has the effect of reducing the amount of fluid that can move through the orifice, which increases resistance as the strut compresses. The more the strut is compressed, the smaller the orifice becomes. Hydraulic fluid is forced through the orifice, compressing the air in the upper chamber and increasing the air pressure. This is what gives you that nice cushioned ride.

Some struts reverse this design, putting the hydraulic fluid on the top and the air or nitrogen on the bottom. The innards of this design are different also. They use a free-floating piston to separate the air and the fluid, and a metering pin on top of the piston performs the function of the metering rod. The workings are the same as the other design, and so is the shock absorption.

Oleos have developed a good reputation for being easy to maintain, rugged, and providing excellent shock absorption. They are very reliable and require amazingly little maintenance, given the amount of stress they are under. You do need to inspect them from time to time to make sure they are still in good shape, particularly after a hard landing. And you need to maintain the levels of fluid and air. (Many mechanics replace the air with nitrogen. More on that later.)

A filler valve and air valve assembly are located near the upper end of the strut to permit adding air and fluid. Instructions for adding air and hydraulic fluid are written on the outside of most struts, but they might fade or disappear over time, so refer to the manufacturer's manual for directions.

The strut must be fully deflated in order to add oil. Jack the airplane up to permit the strut to be fully extended before adding oil. Deflating the strut while it is compressed will cause oil to gush out of the valve. The air inside the strut is under extreme pressure, so keep your face away while deflating. Release the air slowly.

With the strut fully extended and deflated, attach a narrow tube to the valve and immerse the other end in the can of hydraulic fluid. By compressing and extending the strut by hand you can pump fluid out of the can and into the strut. If the fluid doesn't pump, it means the seals need replacing.

Most mechanics prefer using nitrogen rather than air in the struts. Air contains moisture and can lead to corrosion. You might get lucky and discover the corrosion when a seal fails and the strut is overhauled. Or you might not notice the problem until the strut fails, resulting in a dent in your checking account. Equipment for adding nitrogen is too costly for a single plane owner to bother with, but your mechanic might allow you to drive up to the shop and use shop equipment to add nitrogen when you need it.

While the airplane is still on jacks, check all the bolts for tightness. Loose struts can result in a lot of vibration as you taxi, abnormal tire wear, premature wear on parts, and hidden damage. Particularly on steerable nose struts, any looseness results in the shimmy dampener working even harder to prevent shimmy from occurring.

O-rings are used to seal the area around the orifice between the chambers to force the fluid to flow through the opening, not around it. Other O-rings are located in the filler port, the air valve, and the plate that holds the air valve at the top of the strut. These O-rings are all fixed in place and usually don't need any attention but should be periodically inspected for indications of nicks or deterioration, particularly if you live in a hot, dry climate. Other O-rings in the struts are dynamic, meaning either the O-rings move around as the strut is compressed and decompressed or parts of the strut move past a stationary O-ring. They might also have a Teflon backup or spacer O-ring to try to limit the amount of twisting the O-ring can do. These O-rings are more prone toward cutting and damage from the movement around them and should be periodically inspected.

The inspection you can do on shock struts is strictly a visual one. Don't start taking things apart. Notify your A&P if you think they need repairing.

While it is legal for you to replace rubber shock cord rings, you might prefer to leave this job to your A&P since special tools are required. Basically, a shock cord is nothing but a rubber band with a thyroid problem. They can be anywhere from ½-inch to 1-inch thick, and when you try to stretch them with your hands, they seem to have the same stretch as a piece of iron. However, they will stretch and that's why you need the special tools. They can be used either for shock absorbers or in assisting retractable landing gear in retracting or extending. All shock absorbers have a woven fabric covering that is usually white, but you will also find various colored threads. While these might look to be just cosmetic, they are in fact a code as to when the shock cord was manufactured. If the paperwork that comes with the shock cord (which will have the date of manufacture on it) becomes lost, by contacting the shock cord manufacturer, you can find out when they were manufactured.

Shock cords need to be replaced periodically due to loss of elasticity. When you replace the shock cords, use brand new ones, since old ones will deteriorate from age. Shock cords also deteriorate from exposure to fluids and Mother Nature. Your maintenance manual will have the replacement schedule and procedures in it. Please exercise extreme caution when replacing shock cords if you have the special tools, since an accident here can result in severe bodily injury. You do not want to get your hands, fingers, or other body parts caught between the tool, the bungee, and anything it's attached to.

THE NUTS AND BOLTS OF IT

You are about to learn more about aircraft hardware than you ever thought you needed to know. We are doing this because, in our experience, substituting hardware is one of the most common misunderstandings aircraft owners have. Perhaps if you have a better understanding of why a particular type of hardware was chosen by the manufacturer, you will be a little more careful about just grabbing any screw or bolt or nut to use as a fastener.

Aircraft hardware must adhere to stringent standards, generally established by the military. The strength and dimensional details for hardware are specified by the Army/Navy Aeronautical Standard Drawings. Hardware that meets these specs is referred to as AN hardware. It will bear some markings that tell the mechanic much about the hardware (Fig. 5-5). The markings indicate the manufacturer, whether it is a standard AN or special-purpose bolt, and the material used to

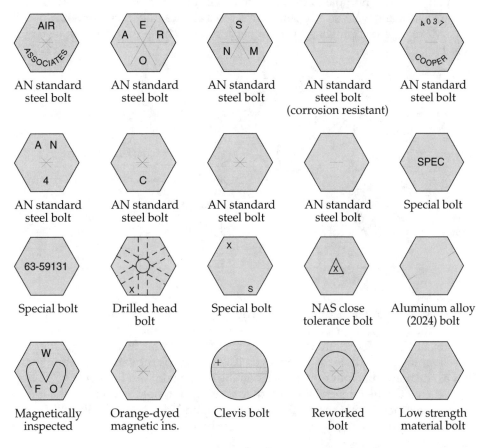

Fig. 5-5. Hardware that is approved for use in aircraft must meet stringent standards, which are usually established by the military. Above are examples of the markings used on bolts to inform the user of what type the bolt is and what applications it can be used for.

make the bolt. Typical markings include such things as a raised or recessed triangle indicating close-tolerance, a manufacturer's part number, and type of inspection conducted on the bolt. Screws also meet these standards, though markings are not on the heads of screws. For this reason, it is important that you purchase hardware from a reliable aircraft supply house so that you are sure you are using approved parts that meet strength requirements set forth by the manufacturer.

Most bolts and screws used in aircraft applications are steel. Aluminum just doesn't have the same inherent strength. Fasteners have a given degree of strength in both shear (perpendicular to the shank) and tension (parallel to the shank). The greatest strength of a bolt is between the head and the threads (Fig. 5-6). When selecting a bolt to fasten two items that will require greatest sheer strength, it is necessary to choose one that permits the two items to be fastened to meet at the unthreaded part of the shank. Threads should extend completely beyond these items. The end of AN bolts often have a hole drilled to accommodate cotter pins or safety wires. If no hole is drilled, use a self-locking nut or a lock washer between the nut and washer. AN bolts and screws are designed to work with specific nuts. Make sure you purchase a complete set so you have the strongest fastening possible.

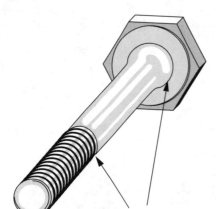

Fig. 5-6. A bolt is strongest in the portion of the shank that has no threads. The right bolt for any application will provide gripping in the area between the head and the threads. If the bolt you have selected is not long enough for the threads to extend out the other side, you are using the improper hardware.

Those of you who like to get out your taps and dies and alter bolts or retap holes should think twice before doing so on your airplane. Running a die up the shaft of a bolt to make more threads weaken the bolt. Take the time to get the right size. Tapping a new hole for a bolt, even if your tap has the same pitch and diameter as the bolt, could alter the threads on the bolt, again, weakening it.

When a torque wrench is required, torque the nut, not the bolt. Set the torque wrench to exactly what the manufacturer recommends. A loose bolt will fatigue more easily; an overtightened bolt actually bends and becomes weaker in the sheer.

Before fastening any nut and bolt, whether torqued or not, follow a few precautions, and you'll get the proper fastening. Make sure that all threads are clean and dry unless the manufacturer calls for lubrication on the particular application.

When using a wrench, torque or otherwise, apply a smooth, even pressure rather than applying a sudden pull. If there are any special adaptors on the end of the torque wrench, you'll need to take the additional length into account, especially if you are using inch-pounds. Read the directions that came with the wrench, or ask the salesperson that sold it to you.

Cotter pins and safety wire should never be reused, nor should self-locking nuts that can be finger tightened. Considering their cost and the important role they play in keeping items secure, throw out the old ones and use new. As for the proper way to install cotter pins and safety wire, see (Figs. 5-7 through 5-11).

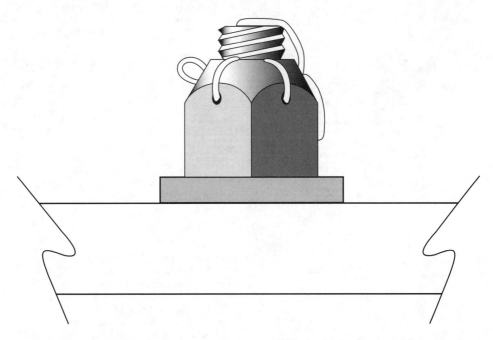

Fig. 5-7. Two methods of installing cotter pins in nuts and bolts can be employed. In cases where a single cotter pin is required, such as on the axle nut, the method in diagram number four is preferred. The pin is pushed through the hole in the nut or bolt, then one half of it is bent down, and the other half is bent over the top.

As a safety precaution, after making your final twist safetying, cut the final twisted section to a length of approximately an inch, then double it over. This puts the sharp edges of the safety wire up against the fastener being safetyed. You will invent a whole new vocabulary when you reach into a closely confined area and find safety wires with straight pigtails sticking out. This will result in getting red fluid all over your airplane, and it won't be hydraulic fluic.

The most common safety wire in use is 032 stainless. It comes in 1-pound rolls and can be purchased contained inside a can or on a spool. Save yourself a lot of grief and buy the one in the can. The spool will come unwound inside your tool-box and create a nest any sparrow would be roud to call home. When using the can, don't forget to leave a losse end hanging out so you can find it.

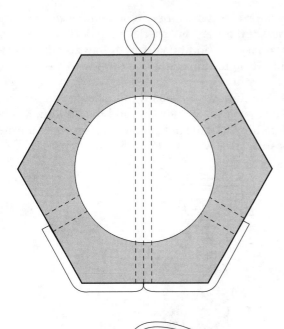

Fig. 5-8. If the cotter pin in Fig. 5-7 is likely to catch on something, bend the cotter pin around the side, as shown here.

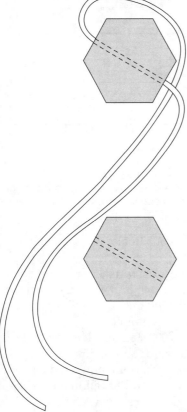

Fig. 5-9. These drawings show the correct way to safety wire two or more standard bolts together. If the bolts you are safetying are left-hand threads, reverse the procedure. Insert the safety wire through the hole, in this case, in the bolt head. Pull the wire approximately halfway through and loop one half of the wire around the bolt. The wire needs to be wrapped in such a way that, when you pull on it, it is tightening the bolt. The safety wire is then wrapped around the side of the head of the bolt and under the wire that came out of the bolt head.

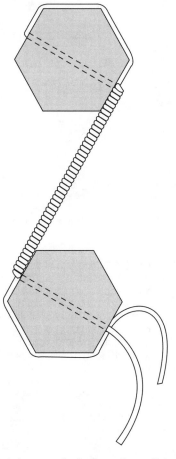

Fig. 5-10. Approximate the distance between the first and second bolt heads, grab the wire at this point with a pair of pliers, and twist clockwise. Make 10 to 12 tight, uniform twists per inch. The twists should be made almost all the way to the hole in the head of the second bolt.

The FAA has a whole list of conditions under which self-locking nuts can be reused (wouldn't you know?). In short, they can be reused only where the manufacturer approves, where they won't do any damage if they loosen and fall off, and where there is at least one full thread protruding beyond the nut. There are also places in the engine that get hot enough to exceed temperature limits on the nylon self-locking nuts, so avoid using them in those places. There are self-locking nuts that are designed for high temperature applications. Replace any hardware with the type that is approved by the manufacturer. Here is where the parts manuals can come in handy. Not only do they list the parts, they usually list all of the attaching hardware.

Rivets are used throughout the fuselage to hold two sheets of metal together. They are used instead of nuts and bolts in part because they fasten in a different way. Whereas nuts and bolts simply clamp the pieces of metal together, a rivet expands to fit the hole, making a tighter bond. You might be familiar with pop rivets, which have a wide variety of uses in the real world (as opposed to the aviation world). However, they don't really give a secure joint, so their use in aircraft is limited to nonstructural areas.

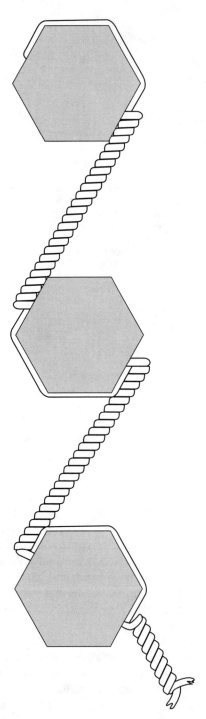

Fig. 5-11. Take one of the two pigtails and wrap it around the top of the second bolt just under the head. Draw the second pigtail through the hole in the bolt. Wrap the pigtails in a counterclockwise direction, again 10 to 12 twists per inch. If there is a third bolt to be safetyed, use the same process, going back to a clockwise wrap. Cut the wire about 1 inch beyond the last twist and fold the cut ends against the bolt.

Conventional rivets are used in most structural locations in aircraft except those where you cannot get a bucking bar behind the item being riveted. In those instances, blind rivets are the ones to use. If you replace any rivets you remove with those specified by the manufacturer, you won't have any problems (Fig. 5-12).

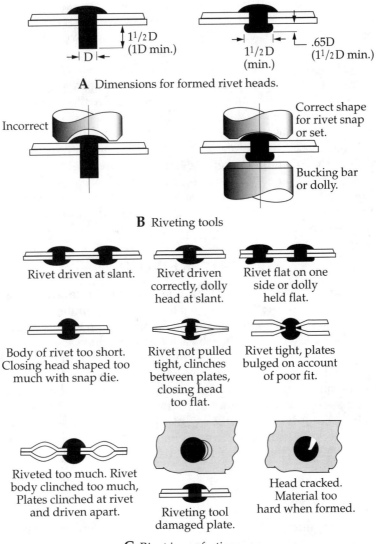

A Dimensions for formed rivet heads.

B Riveting tools

C Rivet imperfections

Fig. 5-12. These are some examples of seating of rivets, one proper and the rest improper. The rivet should be snug and entirely fill in the hole. These diagrams show before and after ratios of the rivet to the hole they are installed in. If any of these improper conditions exist on rivets you have installed, drill them out and try it again.

It isn't necessarily a good idea to replace them with whatever you take out unless you are sure it is original equipment.

You might hear the expression "icebox" rivets from your mechanic. This refers to a specific type of rivet made of an alloy that age-hardens pretty quickly unless it is kept refrigerated. At one time, they were shipped packed in ice, but now mechanics just apply heat to soften them before use. Use of these stronger rivets is primarily in areas such as the skin and control surfaces, which you are not permitted to work on. In all likelihood, about all you will be riveting is something like engine baffles or simple patches.

Use of a rivet gun requires a little technique to make sure the rivet is straight and properly installed. Make a few practice installations before going to work on your airplane until you feel comfortable with the gun. See the section on metal repairs for more information.

Once you have removed any broken hardware, don't just throw it out. Try to determine what caused the failure so that you can make any necessary repairs rather than simply continuing to replace hardware. The rivet or bolt might have pulled through the material it is fastening, or it could have broken either in shear or tension. A careful inspection of the area should reveal the source of the problem, which could be as simple as the wrong fastener being used. If you can't identify the problem, have a mechanic take a look.

FABRIC REPAIRS

Cotton, linen, and several synthetic fabrics are used in the covering of airplanes. Substituting fabrics can result in problems like adhesion failures, variances of decay, etc. It's best to use what's already on the airplane, even for the smallest repair.

A few basic tools will make the job easier, all obtainable at a fabric store. You will need a pair of pinking shears—they're the ones that cut in that cute little zig zag pattern—and a set of tapestry needles, including a curved one.

Part 43 permits you to perform small fabric repairs that do not include rib stitching or the removal of structural or control surfaces. "Small" isn't defined in the regulations, but Advisory Circular 43.13-1A indicates that holes larger than 16 inches involve techniques best left to a mechanic. The manufacturer of your plane might have set limits on the size patch you are permitted to do, so check the maintenance manual first.

Small repairs

If the tear is straight or L-shaped, use the curved needle and waxed thread to "whip stitch" or baseball stitch the sides together. Clean 1½ inches in all directions from the stitching with a dope thinner or acetone, then apply a patch of the same size using fabric dope approved for the type of fabric on your plane.

If the edges cannot be sewn back together, you have two methods to choose from. The first is the sewed patch repair, which you can use if the damage is not longer than 16 inches in any one direction. First, cut out the damaged section, making the opening round or oval shaped. Clean the area of the old fabric the same as if you were repairing a tear. Cut a piece of fabric approximately 1 inch larger than the hole. Turn the edges of the patch ½ inch all around and insert into the hole, sewing the edges together using the baseball stitch (Fig. 5-13). To help hold the patch in place while you stitch, temporary stitches at several points will help. Now dope the fabric and apply surface tapes.

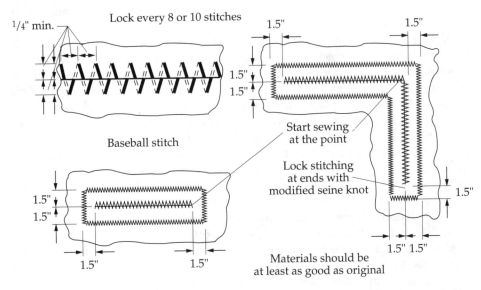

Fig. 5-13. Fabric covering of an airplane can be sewn in a number of ways. Zigzag stitching, which might be called a baseball or whip stitch, is the approved stitch and creates the strongest bond. Any thread or material you use to make the patch should be the same as the fabric being patched, since interchange of materials will likely create uneven stresses.

The other choice for repairing small holes is the unsewed or doped-on repair. You may do this type of repair only if the airplane has a never-exceed speed of 150 mph. Like the sewed patch repair, a doped patch repair can be used if the damage does not exceed 16 inches in any one direction. Cut out the damaged section in a round or oval shape, then clean the edges of the opening, which will be covered by the patch with a solvent.

Remove the dope from the area around the patch with thinner, or lightly sand it off. If you sand the old dope off, make sure to support the fabric from underneath. For holes up to 8 inches, the patch must provide an overlap of at least 2 inches all the way around. If the hole is 8 inches or larger, make the patch at least one-quarter of the hole diameter larger, with a maximum lap of 4 inches. All doped patches should have pinked edges (that's one cut with those fancy pinking shears), although you can use smooth edges. However, if you use a smooth edge, you should use a pinked surface tape to finish it. Raw edges that are not pinked will fray quickly, even with the dope on.

If the damage exceeds 16 inches in any one direction, or is close enough to a rib to result in the patch going over the rib, the repair must be done by a mechanic. Of course, all fabric repairs must be performed in accordance with the appropriate maintenance manual and Advisory Circular 43.13-1A.

Tensile tests are required on fabric coverings to ensure that they have not degraded from exposure to the elements. The tests vary for different types of fabric and are probably spelled out in your manual. They are also spelled out in Advisory Circular 43.13-1A. When the fabric reaches a certain level of degradation, it must be replaced.

Not all repair stations have the expertise for major fabric replacement, so this might be one area in which you can persuade your A&P to let you do the job. However, major fabric replacement is a major repair that requires paperwork signed by both an appropriately rated mechanic and an authorized inspector. And a word to the wise: don't tackle this job unless you have considerable sewing experience and a large shop to work in. Angles, curves, and fittings all present unique problems for sizing the fabric exactly right. You might think you can just use the old cover as a pattern, but the minute you remove it from the plane it will change size and shape. Allowing for this change is necessary in order to minimize waste and end up with a good finished project. Unless you have expertise in compensating for all these changes, leave it to the pros.

You will need a large workshop for a long time to accomplish recovering your plane. Working full time, it can take as long as one week to recover just one wing panel. Completely recovering the plane can take in excess of three months. And weather can affect how quickly you can finish. High humidity, blowing dust, and extreme changes in temperature can all lengthen the job.

HYDRAULIC SYSTEMS

Inspect lines for any indication of nicks or abrasion. Lines should be free of twists and kinks (Fig. 5-14) and have sufficient slack that they are not under tension. Those lines running near moving parts should be especially watched for signs of wear. If necessary, tie them up out of the way, taking care that there is still the required slack in them. Do not use nylon ties on flexible lines, as they might cut into the material used to make the lines. Check the areas around the lines for signs of leakage. Anchor points should be secure and free of scratches. Make a note of any damage or defects you see and refer them to your mechanic.

Check the hydraulic reservoir for proper fluid level and replenish using only approved hydraulic fluid. Except for inspection of the system, this is the only maintenance you are permitted to perform.

Each hydraulic system has its own reservoir, which might not be located in the most convenient of spots, but you should learn where the system is so you can periodically check fluid levels. Consult the maintenance manual for any special instructions, such as whether the system is pressurized or not. If you find the fluid low in the brake reservoir, check the thickness of the brake pads before adding fluid. Thin pads result in the pistons in the brake calipers being extended slightly

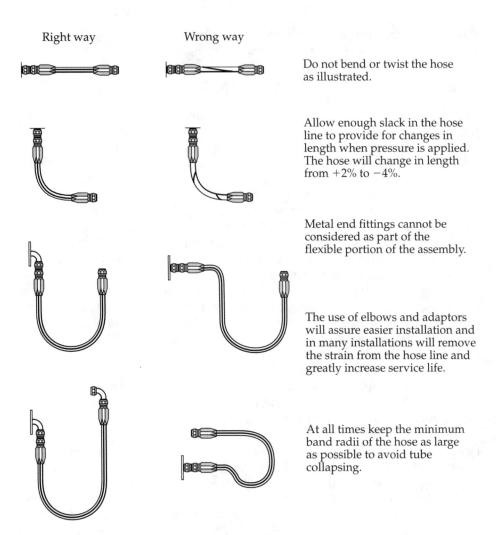

Right way   Wrong way

Do not bend or twist the hose as illustrated.

Allow enough slack in the hose line to provide for changes in length when pressure is applied. The hose will change in length from +2% to −4%.

Metal end fittings cannot be considered as part of the flexible portion of the assembly.

The use of elbows and adaptors will assure easier installation and in many installations will remove the strain from the hose line and greatly increase service life.

At all times keep the minimum band radii of the hose as large as possible to avoid tube collapsing.

Fig. 5-14. When hoses are replaced, care should be taken that the hoses do not become twisted during installation. Colored lines along the covering of the hose will help you keep the hoses straight. If the lines appear to be wrapped around the hose rather than running along the sides, disconnect and start over.

more than normal, which means you will add more fliud. When you replace the pads, the piston will be forced back into the caliper and fluid will be forced into the reservoir, which will overflow and create a mess. Replace thin brake pads before adding fluid.

The maintenance manual will specify which type of hydraulic fluid is appropriate for use in your plane. The most common type is a petroleum-based one referred to as 5606. But some systems, such as those in antique airplanes, might use automotive brake fluid or a synthetic fluid. Fluids are color-coded so you can tell them apart. Since different fluids require different O-rings and seals, using the wrong fluid can create serious problems.

PAINTING

Even if you hangar your plane, time and the elements will eventually take their toll on the finish. Painting or having your plane painted is no small task, which means it will likely put a major dent in your operating budget. Before you undertake this expense, try a few things to see if you can restore the finish without more paint. This won't work if paint is actually chipped or worn off, but if the problem is a dull, chalky finish you might be surprised at the result.

First you will need to determine what type of paint is on the plane. With any luck, the information will be found in the maintenance manual if it is still the original paint. If the plane has been repainted since manufacture, the maintenance records should give you the information you need. If all else fails, ask a repair station that specializes in painting aircraft.

A number of products are available that can restore oxidized paint. Some are made for automobiles, some for aircraft, and some for boats. If you are of the scientific bent, you might want to pick up several different types and try them to see what gives the best results. Test an inconspicuous part of the plane so you don't wind up with uneven color.

As with any other product, read the instructions carefully. Some products need to be hand applied, others will work well with an electric buffer. And products interact with each other in a variety of ways. If you have any questions about the product you have chosen, call the manufacturer or ask your mechanic.

But in some cases, nothing but a new paint job will do, partial or complete. Here are some tips that might make the job less nerve-wracking. Safety precaution: People with respiratory problems might exhibit flulike symptoms after using urethane paints, particularly if the paint has been sprayed on. If you have such problems, either select another product or have someone else do the job for you. Regardless of your health, use a face mask and rubber gloves while doing this work. Be sure you use them in a well-ventilated area. Some have a relatively low flash point, which means they will spontaneously combust at low temperatures, so familiarize yourself with the properties of the chemicals you are going to use.

Paint jobs fall into two categories: a complete repaint (major) or a touch-up (minor). You probably won't be painting the whole plane, since this would require disassembly of the type only a mechanic can do. You are also not permitted to paint balanced flight controls. So before you begin, determine how big a job you are going to take on.

There are several ways to approach painting. You can either strip the area down to bare metal and start from scratch. Or, if the old paint job is still in good condition, you can use it as a base and paint over the top. Each has its advantages and disadvantages.

Stripping the paint is ideally the best method, since each layer of paint on the airplane equals weight subtracted from your useful load. Stripping might mean taking off a multitude of previous paint jobs. Unfortunately, this is a very messy job. Most stripping is done with chemical strippers, which are not environmentally friendly. The glop you end up with after the stripping is technically hazardous waste and must be disposed of properly. Another disadvantage of chemical stripping is that if you do not properly clean and neutralize after the stripping, corrosion begins. Any stripper left in seams and cracks will just cause the paint you spray over it to blister, creating more corrosion.

Another method of stripping is the "dry media" method, which involves removing the paint by directing a blast of air with particles in it, similar to sandblasting. This takes special equipment (read expensive equipment) and skill in the use of this technique, but it is a wonderful method. Museums and restoration shops can use this process and remove the paint one layer at a time, finding previous paint jobs and in the case of former military aircraft, unit markings and other identification signs. The greatest disadvantage of the process is that, improperly used, it can severely warp thin aluminum skin. This would require replacement of all damaged panels. Another disadvantage is that, no matter how careful you are in the spraying and masking, the dry media gets everywhere.

If you elect to paint over the top of the old paint, you are adding more weight to the airplane, but this is a viable option if you are just touching up small areas or changing the color of the stripes. You'll just sand the areas, roughening the surface to provide better adhesion for the new paint.

Proper preparation of the surface is imperative for a good end product. The paint job will be only as good as the base it is put on. Properly applied, paint will be a very thin layer, usually measured in mils. If the base has scratches, chips, runs, sanding swirls, and other flaws, paint will not only not cover them, it might even magnify them.

Masking anything not to be painted is another important step in preparation. Don't try to skimp and save by using newspapers to cover these areas. Newspapers are wonderful for lining canary cages, but they leave a lot to be desired for masking purposes. Some paints and solvents will bleed through, holes in the papers won't show up until the paint runs through, and the ink comes off on everything. A roll of good quality masking paper can actually pay for itself in retouch jobs you won't have to do. Even if you are going to be touching-up a very tiny spot, be on the safe side and cover everything. Overspray can carry a long distance. You can be touching up the trim on the vertical stabilizer and when you're done, discover your wing tips are now speckled with the same color. And be sure all masking materials are securely taped—every little edge. Be especially attentive to any identification tags or plates which must remain visible. These include serial number plates as well as the aircraft data plate.

Plastic-sheet drop cloths can be used for covering large areas, but keep them well away from areas that are being painted. Static electricity buildup on the plastic will cause it to attach to anything you don't want it to.

Make sure there is nothing else in the vicinity that will attract paint, i.e., your spouse's new car or a transient Learjet. If you're painting outside, be aware of weather, since temperature and humidity greatly affect the paint. Wind can destroy an otherwise wonderful paint job by covering it all with a coat of dust, which then must be sanded off before you repaint.

When choosing tape for the masking process, don't buy the cheapest you can find. Go to a paint supply store and get tape with good adhesion properties. Also buy the thin, plastic tapes used for defining the paint lines. Regular masking tape is wonderful for holding the masking in place, but paint has a tendency to bleed under the edges, resulting in an irregular line. With the plastic tapes and careful application of the tape and the paint, you will have a nice, crisp color line—something you can point to with pride and say, "I did that."

Probably the best time to paint is early morning—very early. Breezes haven't come up, the temperature will be rising rather than falling, and the bugs are still asleep. Unfortunately, that means you have to get up at O-Dark:30 and begin the preparation. But think of all the money you're saving.

A good end product also means choosing the right primers and paints. Epoxy primers tend to provide better adhesion, particularly to aluminum surfaces. Urethane finish coats are the best protection against corrosion and solvents. Whichever one you choose, use the entire system—primer, solvent, and paint—which are designed to work together.

Before beginning, remove any acrylic or plastic parts such as windows that can be removed. These parts are easily damaged by solvents and paints. Trying to scrape overspray off them with a razor blade will only damage them further.

Aluminum surfaces

Corrosion and rust must be removed using appropriate solvents. Before applying any solvents, mask off any areas that will be damaged by use of the product you have selected or that you simply don't need to treat.

Now is not the time to play Mr. Wizard, however. If you are not familiar with the types of materials we discuss here, read the labels of the product you are thinking of using. You will likely find these solvents listed as ingredients. Using the wrong product can do more harm than good, so ask for assistance on anything you aren't sure of.

Chromic acid inhibitor, sodium dichromate, dry-cleaning solvent, and kerosene are some of the chemicals that can be used for cleaning away corrosion and rust. Some chemicals attack rubber or acrylic parts and will likely state so on the label. It might be best to avoid those products altogether since they could inadvertently get on some of those materials and eat away at them.

Also before selecting the product you will use, make sure you know what material you are working on. Aluminum, stainless steel, and magnesium all react differently to various chemicals. If you are not sure what the material is, ask a mechanic or call the manufacturer.

If you need to scrub some areas, use fine aluminum wool or a plastic scrubber. Never use steel wool or emery cloth on an aluminum surface. Particles from these materials will become embedded in the aluminum and cause more corrosion. An alkaline cleaner can be used on areas that are heavily caked with mud, oil, or dirt. Clad aluminum can be polished by hand with household abrasives or with metal polish, but not so with anodized aluminum. The anodized film can be removed with these products. A 50/50 solution of mineral spirits can be used on areas of heavy corrosion, but for superficial corrosion, a 10 percent solution of sodium dichromate with 1 percent of chromium trioxide will do the trick.

A phosphoric acid bath after cleaning will etch the surface, permitting the paint to adhere better. Rinse thoroughly after using phosphoric acid, but don't use hot water. Within eight hours of this bath, treat the surface with chromic acid. If more than eight hours elapse, repeat the phosphoric acid bath first. Depending on the paint process used, some of the new primers do not require use of the acid baths. These are advertised as "self-etching." Again, use the complete paint/prime process and when all else fails, read the directions.

Use two coats of an epoxy primer on the prepared surface. If more than three days go by before you apply the final coat, lightly sand the epoxy to provide better adhesion. An intermediate primer can be applied before the finish coat and is recommended in areas of high humidity, where there is lots of rain, or on seaplanes.

Use a good-quality tack cloth to remove any dust and loose particles before each coat, whether it's primer or color. These can be picked up at a painting supply store. When using the tack rag, do not press hard or continually rub in one area. All this succeeds in doing is transferring the wax from the rag to the surface to be painted. The paint has not yet been invented that will flow properly over wax.

Aluminum surfaces that are not to be painted can be restored by using an alkaline treatment on any dirt, corrosion, or rust. Then mask off any areas that are not to be treated, and working small areas at a time, apply a phosphoric cream or solution.

Thoroughly rinse with clean water or wipe with wet cloths. If you want a bright aluminum finish as the end product, buff the surface now. Be sure to remove all buffing compound before proceeding. Treat the surface with chromic acid within eight hours of the phosphoric treatment. This step is recommended whether the surface is to be left bare, painted with a clear finish, or waxed.

Steel surfaces

Using a product recommended for steel surfaces, first remove all rust, grease, oil, mud, or other contaminants. Steel wool, wire brushes, and abrasive papers can be used on particularly dirty areas. Apply phosphoric acid to etch the surface for better paint adhesion. While applying the acid, use a wire brush to remove any rust or corrosion that remains.

Use two coats of an epoxy primer under the finish coat. An intermediate primer is recommended if you live in an area of high humidity or a lot of rain. To avoid painting over dirt or oil that might accumulate, do not let more than a few hours elapse before applying the finish coat.

Magnesium

Magnesium is the most chemically active of all the metals used in aircraft and is the most difficult to protect. Prompt removal and treatment of corrosion found on these parts is imperative if the part is to be protected. Magnesium is most commonly found as an alloy in castings such as wheels and various engine components. Other common areas to find magnesium are skins of control surfaces. Treat the corroded area with a 10 percent chromic acid solution to which has been added approximately 20 drops of battery electrolyte per gallon.

Fiberglass

Remove old paint and primer using a product specifically made for fiberglass. Sand with a fine-grit sandpaper to provide better paint adhesion, then use an epoxy primer and three coats of enamel finish.

Depending on the extent of the paint job you did, you might need to repaint the N numbers. Unfortunately, you may not use your calligraphic style here. One whole part of the FARs is dedicated to identification and registration marks.

According to the regulations, you may not do anything to the registration number that obscures or modifies the nationality and registration marks. No fancy typefaces, no shading or outlining that would make the numbers difficult to read at a distance. In fact, the FARs require that you use the Roman style capital letters. The registration number must also be of a color that contrasts with the background of the fuselage. And except for a rare occasion, the numbers must be permanent.

All characters must be of equal height and at least 12 inches high with, naturally, some exceptions. For a couple of years, the FAA permitted aircraft to carry 3-inch-high numbers, but it became a problem for drug enforcement officials, so the rule was rescinded. Aircraft that already had the 3-inch-high numbers, however, could keep them unless the planes were repainted, the numbers needed repainting, or the aircraft was restored or changed in some way. Aircraft used for exhibition, amateur-built aircraft that do not exceed 180 knots, gliders, and balloons are permitted to carry the 3-inch numbers. Numbers must be two-thirds as wide as they are high except the number one that must be one-sixth as wide as it is high, and the letters "M" and "W," which may be as wide as they are high. You didn't think Washington would leave anything to chance, did you?

On fixed-wing aircraft, the N-number must be displayed on either the vertical tail surfaces or the sides of the fuselage. Those planes that must have 12-inch numbers must have them displayed horizontally. Three-inch-high numbers may be displayed vertically on the vertical tail surfaces. If the numbers are placed on the fuselage, they must be placed horizontally between the trailing edge of the wing and the leading edge of the horizontal stabilizer.

Any aircraft flying internationally must have 12-inch numbers. That means if you have an airplane with the 3-inch numbers, before you can take your vacation trip to Mexico or Canada you must either repaint the numbers or apply temporary markings. These temporary markings can be as crude as duct tape, or they can be as exotic as pressure-sensitive vinyl decals. Either way, dimensions of these temporary numbers must meet the same requirements mentioned previously.

There are some exceptions, of course. If the aircraft does not have enough side area to put the regulation numbers on it, the numbers can be a smaller size with the appropriate height/width/spacing ratios. Some aircraft are eligible for N-numbers as small as 2 inches high. These aircraft are antiques, ex-military aircraft sporting the appropriate military paint job, and some home-built aircraft. Aircraft that are operated exclusively for exhibition, such as in a movie or television show or airshow, do not have to meet the previously discussed requirements. Airplanes that qualify for this exemption will have operations limited to test or practice flights, flying between exhibition points and between an exhibition point and the home base of the aircraft. You must get prior approval from your local flight standards district office (FSDO) before operating without the N-number on display.

Anytime these aircraft leave the United States, however, they will have to have the 12-inch numbers for U.S. Customs. Before doing anything with the N-numbers, check with your favorite IA, who can look up this regulation and get the pertinent requirements for your application.

CORROSION

Almost all the metals used in aircraft will corrode to some degree or another. Corrosion might be just on the surface, or it could penetrate into deeper layers. It can be aggravated by external loads and stresses, improper care, and contact with materials that absorb water such as wood, rubber, felt, and dirt. Salt water, salt air, and even exhaust from the engine will also accelerate corrosion. Metals must be protected against this natural phenomenon.

Metals also interact with each other to cause corrosion. In most cases, special protection is necessary to prevent dissimilar metals from interacting and causing corrosion. One exception is that tin can be used with aluminum alloys without added protection.

Pitting can occur in any metal and is usually a result of the breakdown of whatever protection the metal had been given. Unlike corrosion, which might follow the grain line of the metals, pitting can occur at random, not following any grainline. Pitting is generally a deeper attack on the metal than surface corrosion.

Stress corrosion is the result of static tensile stresses applied to a surface over a period of time under corrosive conditions. As stress increases, the material becomes more susceptible to cracking. Then as temperature, exposure, and concentration of corrosive ingredients increase, cracking becomes even more likely. Aluminum alloys used in shock struts, taper pins, and clevis joints are examples of areas of your plane that are subject to this type of stress corrosion cracking.

Corrosion fatigue occurs when stresses cycle through a part that is flexed. Continued flexing makes it difficult to repair the protective coating on the part that is being damaged by corrosion. Parts that rub together can also corrode as the rubbing wears away the protective film that might have been applied to the metal. Small particles of the metal can also be worked loose, which act as an abrasive on anything they touch.

Metals are given corrosion protection during manufacture through such means as phosphate rust-proofing, special heat treatments, anodizing, or plating. However, as an airplane owner, you will be using such methods as oiling, greasing, and painting to protect metallic surfaces. Because corrosion is so insidious and can cause extensive damage and astronomical repair bills, it is necessary for you to constantly inspect your airplane for any signs of degradation in the metals.

Now that you have a basic idea of what corrosion is, what do you look for? Common places to look are on the belly of the airplane, along seams, anywhere water can collect, near drain holes, and near rivets. If your plane has an aluminum skin, look very carefully at the paint. It will blister when corrosion exists underneath. If you wonder whether you are looking at corrosion or an imperfection in the paint job, scratch the suspect area with your fingernail. If the paint flakes off with a lot of white powder underneath, congratulations; you've just found corrosion.

Some aircraft have magnesium skins. Usual corrosion here is a discoloration of the metal after the paint flakes off. Anytime the paint starts flaking off a magnesium surface, it would be best to have that area stripped to bare metal and repainted.

Two pieces of metal rubbing can create corrosion, so it is necessary to determine if this is occurring. This is particularly important if the pieces are not supposed to be rubbing, such as two pieces forming the skin of an airplane. The telltale sign of this type of corrosion is black powder streaking from rivets and joints with the slipstream. As the individual pieces of skin loosen and rub against each other, the aluminum actually turns to powder and washes out at the rivets (giving them the name of "smoking rivets"). You might notice this streaking particularly after flying through rain or giving your airplane a good bath. A common misconception is to attribute the black streaking to oil, particularly if it is around the engine compartment, but this streaking should be brought to your mechanic's attention, as continued corrosion can get very expensive.

You can also reduce the onset of corrosion by avoiding putting two metals together that will interact to produce corrosion. Do not use small aluminum clips on large stainless-steel webs. Use stainless-steel fasteners in stainless-steel assemblies. Insulate dissimilar metals, but avoid using materials that absorb moisture. Paint cut edges and seal edges on butt joints. And never cover over drain holes.

Special corrosion consideration must be given to landplanes that have been converted to seaplanes since landplanes do not typically receive the type of corrosion-proofing that seaplanes do. Seaplanes should be washed with clear, fresh water immediately following extended water operation, particularly if the water is salty or brackish.

The FAA considers the following procedures to be the minimum precautions necessary for landplanes converted to seaplanes:

- Unless already protected, treat exposed fittings or fittings that can be reached through inspection openings with two coats of zinc chromate primer, paralketone, nonwater-soluble heavy grease, or comparable materials. This applies to items such as wing-root fittings, wing-strut fittings, control surface hinges, horns, mating edges of fittings, and attach bolts, etc.

- Coat nonstainless control cables with grease or paralketone or other comparable protective coating if not replaced with corrosion-resistant cables.

- Inspect all accessible sections of aircraft structure. Clean structural parts showing corrosion and refinish if corrosion attack is superficial. If a part is severely corroded, replace with an adequately corrosion-proofed part.

The FAA also recommends the following additional precautions for converted airplanes:

- Provide additional inspection openings to assist in detecting corrosion. Experience has shown openings to allow inspection of the lower and rearward portion of the fuselage to be particularly desirable.
- Incorporate additional provisions for free drainage and ventilation of all interiors to prevent collection of moisture (scoop-type drain grommets).
- Protect the interior of structural steel tubing. This can be done by air and watertight sealing or by flushing with hot linseed oil and plugging the openings. Inspect tubing for missing sealing screws, presence of entrapped water, local corrosion around sealing screws, welded clusters, and bolted fittings, which might be indicative of entrapped moisture.
- Slit the fabric of fabric-covered aircraft longitudinally on the bottom of the fuselage and tail structure for access to these sections. Coat the lower structural members with zinc chromate primer (two coats). Follow by a coat of dope-proof paint, or wrap with cellophane tape and rejoin the fabric. This precaution is advisable within a few months after start of operation as a seaplane.
- Spray the interior of metal-covered wings and fuselages with an adherent corrosion inhibitor.
- Place bags of potassium or sodium dichromate in the bottom of floats and boat hulls to inhibit corrosion.
- Prevent the entry of water by sealing as completely as possible all openings in wings, fuselage, control surface members, openings for control cables, tailwheel wells, etc.

In view of the inordinate number of natural disasters such as hurricanes and floods in recent years, you might want to know how to care for your airplane if it has been subjected to partial or total immersion in water. Some of these things, you can do. Others must be done by an appropriately rated person.

Water immersion increases the likelihood of corrosion, the removal of lubrication, the deterioration of aircraft materials, and the degradation of electrical and avionic equipment. Salt water enhances this likelihood even further. Simple air drying followed by a cursory inspection of the craft isn't enough to ensure safe flying. Some of this work must be done by an appropriately rated mechanic, but there is much you can do.

Prompt action is mandatory after a plane has been immersed in water. Considerable disassembly might be necessary in order to get to all the affected parts and properly clean and protect them. As soon as possible, wash the plane's interior and exterior with a liquid detergent and isopropyl alcohol in a ratio of eight parts detergent to 20 parts alcohol. Add this mixture to 72 parts of tap water and mix thoroughly. This is a concentrate and should be mixed again with nine parts tap water for use. Alternatively, you can use a water emulsion cleaning compound mixed one part compound to nine parts water.

If the plane is supported by its landing gear, install a spreader bar, jury strut, or some other additional supports to ensure the gear doesn't collapse. Electrically ground the aircraft by attaching a ground lead to the aircraft at a point that is outside the area that could contain explosive vapors. Disconnect and remove any wet- and/or dry-cell batteries and isolate the aircraft from all sources of electricity or other spark-producing devices. Static electricity sparks can be produced by air hose outlets, so don't use them for ventilating or purging fuel vapors. Electrical wiring that has been exposed to corrosive water should be replaced. If it was just splashed or sprayed, it can probably be rinsed and dried with compressed air.

Remove all fuel, oil, and hydraulic fluid and flush the fuel and oil cells with clean, fresh water. Flush the oil system with a water-displacing preservative and clean fuel cells with fresh water. Spray the interior of the cells with oil. Flush fuel lines with hot water, then dry using clean, dry, compressed air. Replenish the fluids using all new ones. Deflate the tires, especially on magnesium wheels, and depressurize landing gear struts, pneumatic systems, and hydraulic accumulators.

Both the propeller and the engine should be removed and washed with steam or fresh water. Major components of the engine and accessories should be removed and flushed with water, preferably hot. If you have the facilities, you should immerse the parts in hot oil also for a short period of time. Change the water and oil frequently. Wipe the parts with a dry cloth and air dry as completely as possible before reassembly. Constant-speed propellers should be disassembled, cleaned with steam or water and dried thoroughly before reassembly.

All fabric on fabric-covered planes should be replaced, as well as upholstery, leather, insulation, and plastic or rubber foam that cannot be cleaned. The airframe should be cleaned with steam under pressure. Pay particular attention to seams and crevices in which corrosion can start. You might need to drill temporary drain holes to be sure all water has been removed. Do not steam clean electrical equipment. Following the steam bath, rinse immediately with either hot or cold fresh water. Touch up any scratches on painted surfaces with an appropriate primer or preservative. Wood, metalite, acrylic, and other nonmetallic materials can be cleaned if they had been sealed, but porous and nonsealed items should be replaced.

UPHOLSTERY AND INTERIORS

The most important thing you can remember when tackling upholstery and interiors is that the material you use must meet FAA standards for fire protection. If you wish to plow through the FARs, you can look up Part 121.312 if you operate under 121, 123, or 135. Otherwise, contact the manufacturer or your local flight district standards office giving them the make, model, serial number, and operating rules you fly under (probably Part 91). They will tell you what you need to know.

It's easiest to buy from a reputable parts supply house or an aircraft upholstery shop who has done all the homework for you. These outfits will supply certification that the fabrics and materials used are in accordance with the appropriate FARs.

As with fabric skin repairs, if you are not an experienced upholsterer, hire this job done. We have seen too many pilots pay for this job twice—once when they did it wrong and once when they hired someone to do it right. An experienced upholsterer will know how to handle this job, but for those of you who wish to make this your first adventure with a sewing machine, here are some tips.

Depending on the material you use, you might need an industrial sewing machine. Most newer home sewing machines can handle a lot of fabrics with just two layers, but with the seat, you are going to find corners where you might have four or six layers of fabric to get through. A home sewing machine will work on loosely woven fabrics, but for heavier fabrics or leather, you'll need the power of an industrial machine.

If you have never sewn before, take some scraps of fabric and practice sewing until you feel comfortable with the machine. This is also true if you are going to use an industrial machine and have never used one before. They go extremely fast and take a little practice to make sure you sew straight and don't catch your thumb in the needle.

Remove the old seat coverings and iron them flat to use as patterns. The longer they have been on the seats, the more distorted they will be, but with some adjustments, you should be able to come up with a decent pattern. The biggest thing to look for is to get the pattern straight because, in all likelihood, there are bows and sags in the material. To make it straight, you will need to identify the grain of the fabric. The grain can be either the warp or woof (the crosswise or the lengthwise threads). It will probably be easier to work crosswise with the fabric, from side to side on the seat, since there are shorter distances between the edges and you are less likely to get lost following the grain.

Lay the new fabric on a flat surface, if possible one that is large enough to hold the entire seat cover without hanging over the edges. Most fabrics that are used for upholstery are pretty heavy, so save your fingers and lay the fabric out in only one layer and cut each seat cover separately. This will also give you the most accurately sized piece.

Starting at one side near one horizontal edge, identify one thread that runs clear across the seat covering. Pin that thread in place on the new fabric you will be cutting. Follow the thread across the pattern piece to the other side of the fabric and pin it on the new fabric on the same thread as the other side is pinned on. Repeat this process every few inches until you have pulled the pattern piece back into shape. If the fabric isn't too much out of shape, you might only have to do this every 6 or 8 inches. If it's badly distorted, you might need to do it every 4 inches or so to get a good straight pattern. This isn't as painful as it sounds, though. You'll only have to do it for one seat back and one seat front. The more pinning you do, the more professional your finished project will look. After you have finished pinning the pattern piece, cut the new seat cover, adding ¼ inch to the outside edge all the way around.

For you brave souls who are doing this without having ever sewn before, keep this in mind. If you are using striped or plaid fabric, the job will look much better if you line up the plaid or stripes so that it appears to be one continuous piece of fabric where the back meets the front. This will require purchasing a little extra fabric. The person who cuts the fabric can help you figure out how much extra you will need. In fact, it isn't a bad idea to take one of the old seat covers with you so you make sure you get the right amount of fabric.

Piping, that cording around the edges of the seat, gives the seat a more finished look but can make you crazy if you haven't worked with it. You need to decide how much you want to tackle. Piping needs to be covered with the fabric you are using so it will match the seat when sewn into the seams.

No matter which kind of sewing machine you are going to use, you need to set the stitch length appropriately. For upholstery, a fairly long stitch is best—say, 8 to 10 stitches per inch. Tighter stitches might seem like they would be better, but in fact, you are only perforating the fabric, and it will tear the first time it is under stress.

Seat covers can also be stapled on the seat or velcroed into place. If you decide to velcro it, do not buy adhesive-back velcro. It will gum up your sewing machine after only a few minutes. Turn the edge of the seat cover under and sew the velcro on. The other side of the velcro, which goes on the seat, can be either glued (use a glue gun) or stapled in place.

METAL REPAIRS

All repairs must be done so as to return the aircraft to its original strength and condition, taking into account stresses, function, and aerodynamics. You are not permitted to repair anything that is structural or is part of any control surface. That caveat aside, there are some things you need to know before attempting any repairs.

The use of annealed 2017 or 2024 aluminum is not considered satisfactory for use in aircraft because it does not resist corrosion very well. Use only the type of materials used in original construction or an approved replacement.

If you need to replace bolts, rivets, or other fasteners, use the size used during manufacture. Too small a fastener will not adequately hold the parts. Too large a fastener will require drilling a larger hole, which will weaken the tensile strength of the part and could result in catastrophic failures.

If you are going to replace some rivets, first weaken the one in place by drilling out the head. Use a drill of a slightly smaller diameter than the rivet, and drill in the exact center to avoid damaging any surrounding areas. Break off the head with a pin punch and carefully drive out the shaft of the rivet with the punch and gentle tapping with a hammer. Use of a chisel and hammer to break the head of the rivet, while effective, can also cause damage to surrounding areas.

When removing screws, take care not to apply excessive loads to the screw, which can cause damage to surrounding structures. Excessive loads often result from trying to remove a screw that has seized from corrosion. If you discover a screw that has seized from corrosion, overtightening, or lack of use, here's a little trick to try before the screw head gets wallowed out. Try tightening the screw.

Sometimes you can tighten it just enough to break the screw free. Penetrating oils can also be used, but they work best when they are allowed to set for a period of time. Easy-outs or stud removers can also be used but extreme care must be taken in choosing the correct size and drilling the hole.

Common mistakes here are using too large a remover or drilling the hole off center. Either way, you end up with damaged threads in the receptacle. Another way of removing a frozen screw is similar to drilling out a rivet. Very carefully drill the head off the screw, which will enable you to remove the fairing, panel or whatever you are trying to remove. You might be able to reach inside with a pair of vise grips and screw the threaded shank out of the nut plate. The worst that can happen is having to replace the nut plate.

After removing rivets or screws, inspect surrounding areas for any indication of stress cracks or any other damage. Elongated holes can occur when the screw or rivet has been loose for some time or if you drill it out off center. If you encounter this problem, talk to your A&P about the best method for repair.

According to appendix A, you are allowed to make small, simple repairs to fairings, nonstructural cover plates, cowlings, and small patches and reinforcements not changing the contour of the airframe so as to interfere with the proper airflow. For most aircraft today, this means sheet-metal repairs. As we have commented before, everything we use on an aircraft must be aircraft quality. "Pop" rivets found at your local hardware store do not fall into this category. If you own or have access to riveting tools such as a pneumatic hammer and bucking bars, use of these can result in probably the most aesthetically pleasing patches.

There are blind rivets similar to the hardware store pop rivets that can be used, but these are usually more expensive. Your maintenance manual will have a section on structural repairs, which you can use as a reference since it will give such information as patterns and spacing for the rivets. AC 43.13-1A will have a section on identifying rivets, another section on proper riveting, and another on patterns and spacings. We have included a diagram from this publication on the proper method of riveting for your information (see Fig. 5-15).

Using the smallest rivets necessary will help your repair to remain inconspicuous. Nothing looks worse than a 2-inch patch held on with rivets big enough to hold the Golden Gate Bridge together. If the metal in the patch or the item to be patched is thick enough to allow flush riveting, this will help make the repair virtually invisible.

A word to the wise: riveting is an art. Done properly, you can't see it. Done improperly, it will result in even more damage to the part you are trying to repair. If you do decide to attempt this form of repair, take the time and spend the money to get lots of practice material. Then practice, practice, practice. When you think you're ready to do the repair, practice some more. By all means, consult with your favorite mechanic and have him or her critique your practice work before you do the actual repair.

FIBERGLAS AND PLASTIC REPAIRS

Many aircraft manufacturers today are using some forms of plastics and Fiberglas in making cowlings, fairings, and other nonstructural parts. Forming these various parts from these materials can result in a part that is as strong as metal but a lot cheaper. Refer to the maintenance manual on what materials to use. With Fiberglas there are several different types of resin used, and they are not all compatible with each other. The key to a good Fiberglas repair is getting the patch to stick to the part that needs repairing. While this sounds fairly obvious and stupid, this is probably the most violated rule in repairs. Be sure to properly prepare the surface to be patched. Fiberglas repairs will not stick to paint or any glossy surface. Even if you remove the paint down to the base Fiberglas, you will find that the original Fiberglas has a smooth texture. This will need to be roughened up to provide some teeth for the patch to properly adhere. Lightly sand the surface enough to eliminate the shininess but not enough to get into the Fiberglas cloth itself.

When making the patch, use Fiberglas cloth, not Fiberglas mat unless, of course, specifically called for in the maintenance manuals. Mix the resin and hardener in the appropriate ratio as called for in the instructions and work in small batches. Exercise caution since relative humidity and the air temperature can adversely affect the resin/hardener combination. If it is real cold out, the resin will set up slower, but don't be tempted to add more hardener to speed up this process. This will result in a weaker substance. Likewise, a warmer temperature will help the chemical process along in less time.

Working in small batches will be an advantage since the chemical reaction between the resin and the hardener will generate heat. If it is already a warm day and you mix a large batch, the ambient air will cause the batch to set up faster, probably before you have time to apply it. In a severe case, the temperature generated will melt the typical mixing cups used and cause burns to unprotected skin. For best results, make the patches small and mix up only enough resin mixture to thoroughly soak the fabric patch. After this patch has set up, lightly sand and apply a mixture of resin and filler. The most common fillers are microballoons, made up of microscopic glass spheres. Sand most of this layer off, which will give you a nice, smooth base to paint over.

Repairing plastic can be difficult since the typical plastic used today can be an absolute bear to repair. Typically, most adhesives do not bond well to the plastic, and Fiberglas will not adhere well either. The maintenance manual should be a big help here since it will list what materials work well with the particular plastic the manufacturer decided to use. In some cases, the easiest repair for plastic parts is replacement with new parts made by either the manufacturer or after-market parts manufacturers. Some of the after-market parts can actually be made of a plastic, that is easier to repair or, in some cases, the plastic is replaced with Fiberglas. If you decide to go the route of buying the parts, make sure the parts have FAA approval to be used on your make and model of airplane. Some extra paperwork might be required, such as a Form 337. Consult with your favorite mechanic before buying the part so things will go much easier.

WINDOW REPLACEMENT

According to appendix A of Part 43, you are permitted to replace side windows, but not the front windshield. The difference is that side windows are relatively flat and don't require the special consideration for dimensional change due to temperature fluctuations as the curved front windows require.

If the window isn't badly scratched, you might be able to buff the scratches out rather than replacing the window. Use an automotive rubbing compound or a mixture of turpentine and chalk. Be sure to use cloths that are soft so you don't make more scratches.

Replacing the window can be done either by ordering a precut one from the manufacturer or purchasing a sheet of acrylic and cutting the window yourself. There are a number of things that should be taken into consideration about which way to go.

Price is no small consideration, of course. It will cost more if you order a precut window from the manufacturer, but it should fit fairly well with some minor adjustments. You might—emphasize might—be able to buy a sheet of acrylic for less money than a precut window, but you then have to cut and shape the window and make it fit. We say it might be less expensive because suppliers might require that you buy a minimum size sheet, which could be more than you want. If you are replacing more than one window, that might not be a problem. Alternatively, you might have a friend who also needs a new window.

Acrylic comes in different types. You need to make sure you get the right material for use as a window if you don't want to have it all turn to an opaque blob in a short time. Cell cast is the highest grade acrylic you can buy. It is manufactured by being cast between two sheets of glass, then it is cured to give it superior optical qualities and strength. The most common acrylic found in stores is extruded. It is less expensive because it does not go through the sophisticated curing process. A third type, continuously manufactured, is a combination of the two processes. The acrylic is extruded and goes through the more extensive curing process.

Your choice of acrylics depends on the intended use. Most precut windows available on the market are cell cast. Since we are talking about side window replacement here, you might be able to get away with extruded acrylic if you can find a piece relatively free of blemishes. But because you are starting out with a product that doesn't have the best optical qualities, it becomes even more important that you properly care for the window once installed by not using any cleaning solutions that will damage it.

There is another acrylic available sold under the brand name of Lexan. This is great stuff for the bulletproof bubble you want to put on the family car, but it might not be so good in airplanes. If you were to need a quick escape from the plane, you probably won't be able to kick one of these things out.

If the acrylic or window comes with a masking material already in place, leave it on until you have finished installation. If there is no masking material, cover the surface with something like plastic wrap. The masking material will prevent any scratches or nicks from appearing while you are handling it.

Having made an executive decision about whether to buy or cut your window, you can begin assembling the tools you need. While acrylic is relatively soft, drilling and cutting can lead to nicks and cracks that will weaken it. Use of proper tools will minimize the chances of doing any damage. Special drill bits and saws are available that are made specifically for acrylic and will make the job easier. Whatever you will use to cut the material should have a fine-tooth blade used for cutting laminate or plywood. Be careful when using power tools such as a circular or table saw on acrylic, since the heat generated by the blade cutting is enough to melt the acrylic. The acrylic will then weld itself back together behind the tool and just when you think you have finished making the cut, you'll discover you still have one sheet of acrylic. Cutting fast enough so as not to concentrate heat in one spot might crack or chip the acrylic. Experiment on scrap pieces to determine how fast the blade gets hot enough to produce problems before you start cutting on the full sheet. Try an abrasive blade used for cutting masonry and see if this works better for you.

Some people have better luck scoring the acrylic with a tool designed specially for this, then cracking it, much as you would glass. This, too, takes a special touch and should be practiced before you attempt to cut the final product.

Your success in drilling holes for the fasteners will also depend on your technique and equipment. Special drill bits are made for plastic and are worth the expense, even if you only use them once. Drill bits used on metal might work, but they tend to chew their way through plastic, leaving a lot of chips behind. If possible, and if you know how, you might prefer using a drill press, which gives you better control over the process. Whatever you use, place a piece of scrap wood under the spot where you will be drilling. This permits the drill bit to ease out the other side rather than bursting through, which can cause chipping.

Use the same type of fasteners the manufacturer used in the original window. If you have reason to suspect the window you are replacing is not original equipment, verify with your A&P what hardware should be used. You are permitted to substitute bolts or screws for rivets and might decide to do so if you have never worked with rivets before. In this case, be sure the bolts are at least as strong as the rivets, and use spacers or washers so the bolt head and nut are not biting straight into the plastic. You will need a good caulking compound to seal the window and again, use what the manufacturer recommends.

Now to the job. You can mark cutting lines directly on the masking material. When marking these lines, remember to add $\frac{1}{16}$ inch in all directions as "fudge factor." You can always sand down any extra, but you won't be able to add that $\frac{1}{16}$ inch later.

Before you cut the window, lay the sheet of acrylic out in the sun or somewhere where it will get nice and warm. Cold acrylic is brittle and will crack or shatter easily. By warming it up, you will find it easier to work with. For this reason and a number of other obvious ones, replacing windows is a nice summertime job. Warm temperatures will also permit the caulk to cure better.

Once you get it cut and fitted, make sure you keep the acrylic good and warm during the installation. This is especially important if there is a slight curvature to your side windows. Never force the plastic into place. By making sure you have a nice, relatively easy slide-in fit, you will eliminate stress points that will result in cracks.

Some windows are actually assemblies in which a retaining strip is used to hold the acrylic in place. You should have fewer headaches if your plane is made this way, since you won't be drilling or riveting straight into the acrylic. Remove the old window and use it as a pattern. Clean any caulk that remains in the window frame using an appropriate solvent. Be careful not to damage any of the surrounding skin or paint job while doing this.

Check the fit of the new window before proceeding. Sand down any areas where necessary, either by hand or with an electric sander using very fine sandpaper. If you apply the foam tape used to mount the window before you check the fit, you'll go nuts trying to get it off to trim the acrylic. When you're sure the fit is accurate, run a bead of caulk around the window frame and fit the window into place.

A little tip here: if you are not skilled with a caulk gun and your caulk bead looks more like a diagram of the Great Wall of China, you might want to use some masking material around the window frame to protect the paint and save you hours of cleanup time. Let the caulk set a few days, then trim any excess off.

Cracks in side windows can be arrested by a method called stop-drilling, drilling a small hole at the end of the crack to prevent it from spreading. It won't give you a perfect window, but it will extend its life. Care needs to be exercised here in drilling the hole, since improper drilling can cause more cracks to appear. Special Plexiglas drill bits used at the appropriate drill speed will give you a nice, clean hole that won't develop more cracks. The recommended drill size for stop-drilling cracks is ⅛ inch or a number-30 size drill bit.

When possible, have someone hold up a piece of wood on the other side of the window from where you are drilling. The wood will stabilize the Plexiglas and prevent it from flexing, which could make even more cracks. Allow the drill bit to feed slowly through the plastic, especially towards the end, since you want the bit to exit the plastic without grabbing or bursting out the other side. After drilling the hole, fill it with a dab of clear RTV silicone to keep the water and air out.

Clean plastic windows with water and a mild soap, using a clean, soft sponge or cloth. Do not use gasoline, alcohol, benzene, acetone, or window cleaning sprays because they will soften the plastic and cause crazing. Don't rub plastics with a dry cloth, either, since this can scratch them as well as causing static electricity. Static electricity will cause every piece of dust in your county to glom onto your windshield. You'll wind up flying IFR on a perfectly sunny day. When the window is clean, apply a thin, even coat of commercial wax and buff it with a soft cloth. Rubbing too long in one place on such thermoplastics as acrylic and cellulose acetate can cause just enough friction buildup that the heat created can soften the plastic.

SAFETY BELTS AND SHOULDER HARNESSES

You are, according to the regulations, allowed to replace safety belts, more commonly referred to as seat belts and shoulder harnesses. Aircraft seat belts might look like automotive seat belts, but they are manufactured to more stringent specifications. The specifications are referred to as Technical Standard Order (TSO) TSO-C22f.

Shoulder harnesses are designed to prevent debilitating or fatal injuries to pilots and passengers involved in a survivable crash. Following much testing, aircraft designers have developed systems that provide those onboard the plane some sort of structural protection that might help them survive a crash landing.

Military experiments have shown that the human body can inherently withstand decelerations of 20gs for up to 200 milliseconds (.2 second) without injury. These tests, as well as ones with agricultural aircraft, have shown a relatively high rate of survival when a restraint is designed taking this data into account. An effective system requires that both the belts and the anchor points be selected with this information in mind.

Two types of shoulder harnesses are currently in use: the single diagonal type harness and the double over-the-shoulder type. The over-the-shoulder type might use two separate anchor points or a "Y" configuration and one attachment point. The shoulder harness is not a substitute for the lap or seat belt. The best system makes use of both shoulder and seat belts for maximum protection.

Each system has its own advantages. The single diagonal chest strap—like those installed in automobiles—is the simplest system and works best at longitudinal decelerations. However, during side decelerations, a pilot or passenger in this type of restraint might slip out and away from the chest strap, even when it fits properly. The double over-the-shoulder type harness works well for both longitudinal and side decelerations.

Several attachment points are available that will adequately support either type of shoulder harness and provide maximum protection for pilot and passengers. The harnesses can be mounted to either the seat or to one of several points on the airframe. They include the side, ceiling, floor, or a point directly to the rear of the seat.

Oddly enough, the FAA has never addressed the issue of what are acceptable materials for the installation of shoulder harnesses. Manufacturers offer the best guidance here, and their instructions should be followed carefully.

Webbing used for shoulder harnesses and seat belts is typically made from nylon or dacron. These materials provide maximum strength with minimum deterioration over time. Both shoulder harnesses and seat belts should be made from the same webbing to prevent the pilot's or passenger's body from moving at different rates of speed, which could cause additional injury. In addition, use of the same materials will make it easier to clean and will eliminate the need to stagger replacement of each belt or harness.

An inertia reel is used to lock and restrain the occupant in a crash while at the same time providing the ability for normal movement without restrictions.

Your car seat belt uses one of these inertia reels. If you move forward quickly, the belt locks, preventing further forward movement. Moving slowly, however, prevents the inertia reel from locking and you can move about as necessary. The inertia reel also uses a rewind mechanism to take up the slack of the belt as you move.

Seat belts can be mounted in a variety of ways. Some can be attached with a quick-disconnect fitting, or they could be bolted to the airframe. Others could even be wrapped around a structural member or tubing and then weaved through a buckle. When replacing the seat belt, install the new belt in the same manner as the old.

When you are inspecting your belts, look for any fraying, broken stitches, and loose attach fittings. While you are giving your belts a good close inspection, look for a tag identifying the belt as being manufactured as per the TSO. If there are any defects in the webbing or latches or if the TSO tag is missing, the belt needs to be replaced or repaired. There are companies that specialize in the remanufacturing of seat belts. They will replace the webbing and fix the latches and fittings, making the belt as good as new. If you want, they can even change the color so it will be color-coordinated with your new interior.

Periodic inspection of these components will reveal any deterioration or defect that prevents them from working properly and therefore, causing injury to pilot and passengers. Sit in the seat and fasten the belt and/or harness. Check for freedom of movement and inadvertent lockup. The webbing should be long enough to permit the person being restrained to reach all necessary switches and controls. The inertia reel should be able to take up any excess webbing so straps remain lying against the body while fastened. The belt opening should be aligned in such a manner that it is aligned in the direction of loading.

Check all attachment points to make sure they are securely fastened. Fasteners should be free of corrosion or damage. Buckles should fasten and unfasten easily. Belts should lie flat with no twists or kinks and should have no frays, slices, or other damage. Check inertia reels to make sure they are securely mounted and operate as designed. They should take up and release the webbing as the occupant of the seat moves around. The manufacturer of the belt might offer a structural repair kit that will handle most common repairs. Follow instructions provided in the kit.

SEATS

The FAA permits the owner/operator to not only remove the seats, but also to repair or replace them as long as no disassembling of any primary structure or operating system is necessary to accomplish the repair. If you replace the seat, it must be with a seat assembly that has been certified on that particular make and model of airplane. Repairing a seat is limited to replacing the seat parts with approved replacement parts. As we have said before and will say again, perform the work in accordance with the appropriate maintenance manual. Sometimes the parts manual will show an exploded view of the seat as well as other assemblies, thus allowing you to see how everything fits together.

It doesn't hurt to occasionally remove the seats and inspect the tracks on which the seat rides for any sign of deterioration or cracks. In fact, if you fly certain models of Cessna, this inspection is required by an airworthiness directive. Cleaning the tracks will help them work easier, too. Vacuum around the tracks to remove all dirt, sand, gum wrappers, or anything else you find there. (Just like cleaning the couch, though, you get to keep all the money you find.) Some seats can be lubricated. Others cannot. Check your maintenance manual.

Familiarize yourself with how the tracks on your seats are manufactured. Something that you might think is a crack might actually be nothing more than a seam made during construction. Run your hand lightly along the rail to check for any burrs, nicks, or dents that might have developed in the tracks. Using your maintenance manual as a guide, lubricate the runners using an approved oil or grease. The seat tracks are a structural item and require the attention of an A&P, so if you think they are in bad enough condition to need replacing, make an appointment at your local repair facility.

ELECTRICAL SYSTEM

You should inspect the electrical system periodically in those areas you can see without any disassembly other than inspection panels. Check for damage, general condition, and proper functioning. Although there is little an owner/operator is permitted to do with the electrical system, when you do attempt a repair, be sure to use recommended parts and procedures.

When you inspect the system, you should be looking for any indication of overheating of connections or wiring, indicated by bubbled or blackened insulation. Most problems are caused by loose connections. Make sure all connections are tight, especially ground connections. All it takes is a little bit of corrosion at this connection, and you no longer have an electrical circuit.

Most aircraft use the airframe as a part of the electrical circuit, to create a "negative ground." This means the negative terminal of the battery and all electrical equipment are directly attached to the airframe. By using the metal airframe, the need to run additional wires to the electrical equipment to complete the circuit is eliminated, saving the weight of the second set of wires. Unfortunately, if your airplane is wood or composite, you have to run the second wire.

According to the regs, the only thing you can do that is preventive maintenance in this area is troubleshooting and repairing broken circuits in landing light circuits and replacing bulbs, reflectors, and lenses of position and landing lights. A cursory inspection of light bulbs and fuses might indicate that everything is fine but the break could be where you can't see it. Here's where you use the multimeter to check for electrical continuity.

Another common problem in light circuits is installing the wrong bulbs. This might seem rather obvious, but it's amazing to see how often it's done. Putting a 12-volt bulb in a 24-volt system can get very expensive, considering that the typical price of a landing light bulb can be $25 to $40. Installing a 12-volt bulb in a 24-volt system will produce a very bright light—but not for long. Maybe two seconds. Then it gets very dark and you can't see where you're going. However, if you put a 24-volt bulb in a 12-volt system, the bulb will last a very, very, very long time, and you still can't see where you're going.

One thing that might not be too obvious but can cause problems is installing the wrong wattage in the system. You might want to have a brighter landing light, so you try to replace a 100-watt bulb with a 250-watt bulb. This is not good. The electrical circuit was designed for the 100-watt bulb and has a circuit protection device (fuses or circuit breakers) with an appropriate rating. You will recall from your elementary science classes that volts times amps equals watts. With a little simple math, you'll find a 100-watt, 24-volt bulb will require a little over four amps. And a 250-watt, 24-volt bulb will require a little over 10 amps. By installing the larger watt bulb, you will overtax the electrical system. If the circuit protection device fails to open in this instance, the electrical wiring could overheat and cause a fire.

If your light doesn't work, check whether you are getting voltage at the various components of the electrical system. With luck, the electrical bus circuit breakers and switches will be easy to reach on your airplane. By using your multimeter, you can measure voltage at the bus, before the circuit breaker, after the circuit breaker, before the switch, and after the switch. As your airplane ages, keep in mind that the electrical components are getting old, too. Switches and circuit breakers fail internally. When they are overloaded, circuit breakers also fail to open when you need them overloaded. They might get so old and tired that they open during an underloaded situation. Or they might just internally open and not allow electricity to pass, even though it still appears to be in the engaged position and hasn't "popped." The switch might click and act like it's working, but it has failed internally, too.

If the items underneath the instrument panel and out at the light fixture test satisfactorily, its time for the frustrating part—trying to find where, in between, the wire is broken. The lights are usually placed somewhere out on the extremities of the airplane. This means that somewhere inside there probably is some kind of a quick-disconnect plug, so the appropriate extremity can be removed and replaced. Sometimes trying to find this plug can be best compared to playing hide-and-go-seek. This portion of the troubleshooting usually entails opening lots of inspection panels. While you are looking for this plug, keep your eyes open for various varmints. For some unknown reason, God has made rats, rabbits and mice think wire insulation is edible. Once you find the plugs and determine that no varmints have been using your airplane as a deli, disconnect the plugs and start checking for voltage. You can also check each segment of wire for continuity. If the insulation is still intact and the wire is broken internally, a continuity check will reveal the problems.

Another thing to look for is misalignment of electrically driven equipment. Even the smallest misalignment can result in a poor connection. Misalignment can be caused by dirt or corrosion or improper support of wiring that has pulled things askew and by poorly soldered or loosely swaged bundles, broken clamps, and insufficient clearance between exposed current-carrying parts and ground.

Also check for loose or missing safety wires or cotter pins. Dust and light corrosion can be removed from terminals and connections with emery cloth or very fine sandpaper, but do not use emery cloth on commutators since particles from the cloth could cause shorting and burning.

And, of course, your problem might be something as simple as a burned out bulb in your airplane, but changing it isn't as simple as changing the one over the kitchen sink. Here are a few tips to make you and the bulb last longer. First, make sure power is off. Few things are more exciting than hooking up a bulb with the power on and having the bulb come to life in your hands. The bulb will heat up quite rapidly and get hot enough to cause burns. There is also the possibility of the terminals on the back of the bulb coming into contact with the structure of the airplane. If the power is on, you can have your own version of the Fourth of July because the sparks will fly. There is also the possibility, depending on which bulbs you are working on, of getting electrocuted. So definitely disconnect the power. The best way to do this is to disconnect the negative terminal at the battery and secure it far away from the battery.

Avoid handling the bulb with your bare fingers. The oil from your fingers left on the exterior of the bulb will cause uneven heating and can cause some bulbs to crack or shatter. Bulbs in flashing beacons are particularly vulnerable to this. Whenever handling the bulbs, wear gloves, or handle the bulbs with either tissue or the packing the bulb came in.

Some installations have a clear plastic fairing over the bulbs, which must be removed first. Either way, you need to get to the bulb so if you have the fairing, go ahead and remove it. Most landing light bulbs are held in place by some kind of a clamp arrangement. Take a close look at any screws and make sure that any you start to undo are part of the clamp assembly and not the screws used to aim the bulbs. Remove the screws and the clamp, and the bulb will come free in your hand. There will be enough slack in the electrical wiring to the bulb to allow you to pull the bulb away, then rotate it so you can get to the back of it. There you will find two terminals in the back of the bulb with screws attached to the electrical wiring. Unscrew the screws, remove the bulb, and throw it away.

While you are removing the bulb, you might notice a rubber ring approximately the same diameter as the bulb. This is a cushion that goes between the bulb and the clamps. Not all installations have them. Sometimes these rings are attached to the clamp parts; sometimes they are loose.

Installing the new bulb is the reverse of removing the old one. There are some things to look for, though. There might be a notch in the clamp assembly that will correspond to a raised bump on the back of the bulb. These notches and bumps, when aligned, help prevent the bulb from rotating, as well as ensuring that the bulb is returned to the same position as the old bulb so you don't have to re-aim the lights. If you do try to put the bulb in without these notches properly aligned, the bulb will not lay flat in the clamp, and you might have a hard time getting the screws back in.

Once you do have all of the parts in the correct alignment, tighten the screws so they are just snug. If you tighten it too hard, this can lead to a decreased bulb life or, in an extreme case, will result in a broken bulb. Before you finish your installation, take a look behind the bulb and make sure the terminals won't come in contact with anything. Before you put the fairings back on, perform a quick function test and make sure the light comes on.

As for replacing other bulbs such as navigation lights and beacons, most use a bayonet mount. This mount requires that you push in on the bulb slightly, then twist. The bulb should pull straight out. Exercise extreme caution when removing these bulbs, since corrosion can build up between the brass bottom of the bulb and the steel fixture. This can cause the bulb to seize and become very difficult to remove. The corrosion can be severe enough so that when you push in and twist, you will break the bulb. And you don't want to go to the emergency room for stitches. When you install the new bulb, make sure it locks into place. You should feel a slight click when it's properly seated. Before you get it all covered up, make sure you check it to make sure it works.

One bulb you should probably stay away from is the bulb for strobe lights. Whereas these bulbs can be fairly simple to replace in some installations or fairly complex in others, they all have some kind of a powerpack that supplies the voltage. These powerpacks will supply a very high voltage to the bulb and can retain this voltage for a period of time after the unit is turned off. To be on the safe side, if you are going to be replacing these bulbs, disconnect the power from the powerpack, then go have lunch. This should allow the powerpack to discharge, but still exercise caution.

WHEELS AND SKIS

You may replace wheels and skis provided no changes to weight and balance are required. You may not, however, make the original conversion to skis. See your mechanic if you wish to have this work done.

As with any other component of the aircraft, when replacing wheels or skis, you must use approved parts that maintain the aircraft in at least its originally manufactured or properly altered condition. Changing the size of the wheels or skis is considered an alteration, which must be performed by an A&P.

SPARK PLUGS

Various manufacturers have different recommendations for how often the spark plugs should be changed. For best performance, follow these recommendations. Spark plugs can be easily damaged by mishandling or dropping, so extreme care must be taken during installation. One IA we know says, "Drop it once, drop it twice." The second drop is into the waste bin. Do not attempt to use a spark plug that has been dropped. Dropped plugs could have cracked the insulation inside, with such results as internal shorts or arcing causing the plug to misfire. In addition, ceramic, which might have broken off from around the center electrode of the plug, could drop into the engine and cause all sorts of headaches.

To remove the old plugs, disconnect the ignition harness by removing the coupling nut (Fig. 5-15), ensuring that you do not allow the ignition lead to twist while you loosen the nut. Some ignition leads have a metal elbow that you can hold onto with your fingers (Fig. 5-16). Others have a small nut that must be held with the appropriate-size wrench (Fig. 5-17). Pull the lead straight out to avoid damaging the barrel insulator and lead terminal (Fig. 5-18). The neoprene collar sometimes sticks to the shielding barrel but can be broken loose by carefully twisting it like a nut. Use the proper size deep socket to remove the spark plug, pulling it straight out to prevent damage to the barrel or to the threads on the ends (Figs. 5-19 and 5-20). As you remove each spark plug, make sure you maintain some kind of order so you know where each spark plug was removed. By looking at each spark plug, you'll be able to tell a lot about what's going on inside the engine. You'll be able to tell if any cylinders are running too lean or too rich, if a spark plug is misfiring, or

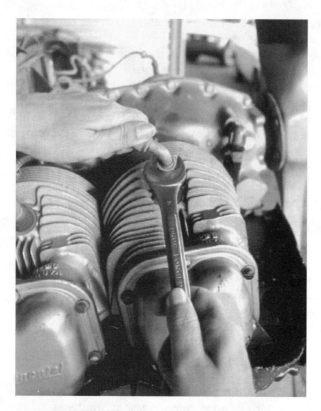

Fig. 5-15. To remove the spark plug, begin by loosening the harness nut. Make sure the ignition lead is not allowed to turn with the nut.

Fig. 5-16. Ignition harnesses use one of two styles of nuts to hold the harness to the spark plug. This style can be grasped by hand while the nut is tightened.

Fig. 5-17. This style ignition harness requires a small wrench to hold the harness while the nut is tightened.

where the oil is going if your oil consumption has increased. Each spark plug has a story to tell and it would be a good idea to know where the story is taking place. There are spark plug trays available that will hold 12 spark plugs. These trays are usually numbered 1 through 6 for the cylinders and a corresponding hole for the top spark plug and the bottom spark plug.

If you don't want to buy one, you can always make one, and it doesn't need to be exotic. A piece of wood, cardboard, or foam with the appropriate number of holes will work just as well. Of course, if you are one of the lucky ones with something exotic with a radial engine, you're definitely going to need to make up your own. If all else fails, simply tag the plugs with a piece of tape and a notation on the tape of where the plug came from. However, keep in mind that you're going to be cleaning the plugs, and the solvent has a tendency to take tape off.

Occasionally the bushings or Heli-Coil inserts on the cylinders might need to be cleaned. The FAA suggests cleaning the bushings using a clean-out tap. Fill the channels between the threads on the tap with clean grease before inserting it in the

Fig. 5-18. When the nut is loose, remove the spark plug lead from the spark plug and pull the lead straight out. You might have to twist the lead just slightly to get it to separate.

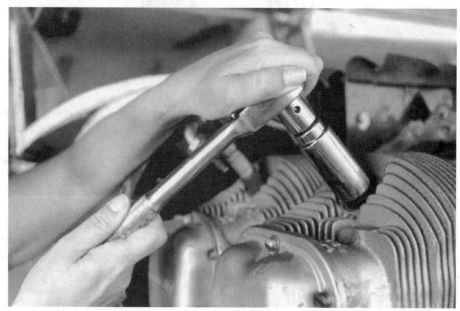

Fig. 5-19. Remove the spark plug using the proper socket. Make sure the socket is square on the plug. Do not allow the socket to contact the threads on the end where the harness is attached.

Fig. 5-20. Remove the spark plug from the cylinder; inspect and clean gap, and test the spark plug.

hole. The grease will pick up any deposits that are inside. Start the tap by hand to avoid any cross-threading. Exercise caution here since you run the risk of backing out any Heli-coils. If the bushing is loose or cross-threaded, the cylinder will have to be replaced. A substitute method is to clean the threads with a bristle brush.

Heli-coil inserts can be cleaned with a round wire brush on a power tool. Be sure the brush is in good shape and won't crumble in the cylinder, leaving bristles behind. The brush should be just slightly larger in diameter than the spark plug hole. Be careful not to remove any of the seating gasket surface during this proce-dure. If the Heli-coil becomes damaged, it will have to be replaced. Wipe the seat-ing gasket with a clean rag and solvent.

Now that you have the plugs out, it's time to clean them with solvent. Use a good, stiff-bristle brush to get down inside the firing cavity of the plug. This will clean out loose lead and deposits of fuel and oil. Dry off the plugs as much as pos-sible. The next step is to clean out the deposits still down in the firing cavity. Ide-ally, the best tool for this is a vibrating tong cleaner. However, these can be a bit expensive. The next-best alternative is some kind of a sharp, pointed tool with a very small tip. Dental picks can work very nicely here. While digging around knocking loose all of those lead deposits, be careful you don't crack or break insu-lation around the center electrode. If you do break the insulation, drop the spark plug and drop it a second time—into the trash can.

Once you have removed all the deposits you can, if you have access to one, lightly blast the plugs using an abrasive medium. Whether you use a portable sandblaster, a bead blast cabinet, or the blast cleaning side of a spark plug tester machine, don't blast the spark plugs for very long. Once you get the combustion residue off, blasting them longer just succeeds in eroding the electrodes, thus shortening the spark plug's life. After blast cleaning, wash the plugs again in solvent to make sure none of the blasting agent gets into the cylinders of your engine. Set the gap according to instructions, using a round wire feeler gauge (Fig. 5-21). At this point, exercise caution while setting the gap. If the spark plug is the massive electrode style and the gap is set too small, you cannot spread the electrodes like you can a car's spark plugs. Unfortunately, this requires the spark plug to be replaced. If the spark plug is a fine wire style and the gap is set too small, you can spread the gap. Inspect the spark plugs before installation to make sure there are no cracks in the insulator or nicks in the threads. If you are replacing the spark plugs, make sure you replace them with plugs that are identical to the ones you removed (Fig. 5-22).

Correct

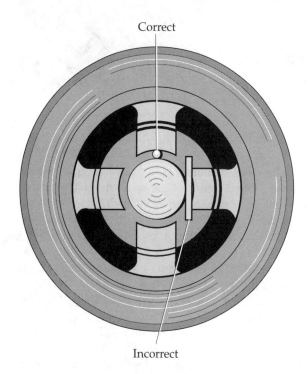

Fig. 5-21. The gap on the spark plug needs to be precise. Use of a round feeler gauge rather than a flat one will give the best setting.

Incorrect

Before you reinstall your spark plugs, something needs to be done to the gaskets. In theory, replace the old gasket with a new one. However, in the real world, this might be a little impractical since you might not have new gaskets. Therefore, the next best thing is to anneal the old ones before you reuse them. To do this, you will need access to a torch and some kind of table to do this on—a steel one, not the dining room kind. Fire up the torch and use it to heat the old gaskets until they are

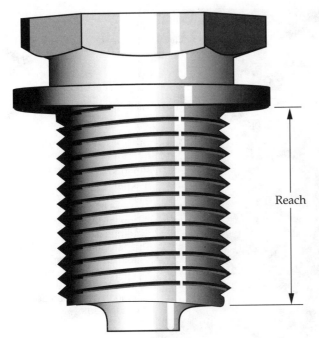

Fig. 5-22. The spark plug reach is a crucial consideration when you change spark plugs. The reach is that portion of the plug that is threaded. If you use the spark plug called for by the manufacturer, you should have no trouble. Substituting spark plugs could lead to unseen problems. A spark plug might fit into the hole, but if the reach is too long, it will fill a portion of the combustion chamber, preventing the piston from traveling its full range or causing the piston to ram the spark plug.

Reach

cherry hot, then slide the gaskets into a can of water. Since the gaskets are made of copper, the water quench gives the copper extra softness as compared to just air cooling. Failure to anneal the old gaskets can lead to exhaust leaks or the spark plugs loosening and even falling out.

You're almost ready to install the spark plugs. The next step is to inspect the threads on both ends of the spark plug. This is assuming your engine is equipped with a shielded ignition. If not, you will have only half as much inspection since the plugs are only threaded on one end. The threads that screw into the cylinder can have deposits in the threads, either from the combustion process or from cleaning. These deposits will make the spark plug more difficult to install and could prevent the spark plug from being properly torqued. Use a wire brush and clean all deposits from the threads. Inspect the threads at the terminal end for thread damage resulting from cross threading, overtorqueing, or allowing the spark plug socket to cant sideways. Very minor damage here might be corrected with the use of a thread file.

It's necessary to apply an antiseize compound on the threads before installing any plug. Put a dab on the threads that go into the cylinder. Be careful not to get any on the rest of the plug. If antiseize compound is allowed to get on the electrodes, this will short out the plug, preventing it from sparking. Start the plug by hand to make sure it isn't cross-threaded, then tighten down with the spark plug wrench. In most cases, you should be able to screw the spark plug all the way down by hand. At this point, use your torque wrench set to the appropriate value (Fig. 5-23). Don't overtighten, or you'll damage the plug.

Fig. 5-23. After the spark plug is clean, gapped, and tested, hand thread it into the cylinder. Use the torque wrench and torque it to the appropriate value. When reinstalling the spark plug, make sure the socket is square on the plug to avoid damage to the threads.

Before reattaching the lead, clean it with acetone or some other approved solvent and inspect it for cracks or other damage. Slip the lead into the shielding barrel of the plug and tighten, making sure the ignition lead does not rotate (Fig. 5-24). When tightening the terminal nut, do not overtorque. A rule of thumb is to tighten finger tight, then turn a maximum of one flat (60°) more. As a minimum, overtorqueing these nuts makes them difficult to remove the next time. An overtorqued terminal nut might mean that, when you try to remove it next time, you will succeed in loosening the spark plug in the cylinder. Depending on which spark plug this is, it can be an absolute bear trying to get a wrench on the base nut of the spark plug to hold it still while you break the terminal nut. These terminal nuts are rather thin, and overtorqueing them can also cause them to split.

Plugs can become fouled with lead or graphite deposits, affecting their ability to function. Lead fouling is the result of using the incorrect fuel or of improper leaning technique. If the deposit isn't too heavy, it can be burned off by carefully causing thermal shock of the plugs. A sharp rise or sharp drop in combustion tem-

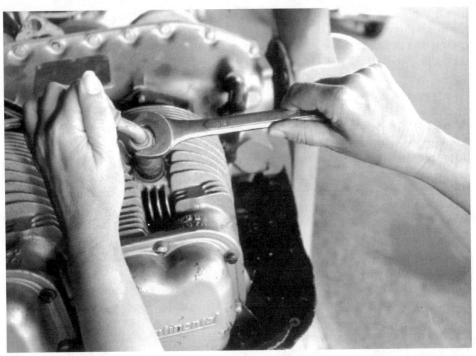

Fig. 5-24. Install the ignition lead and the nut in the correct manner. Support the lead to prevent twisting it as the nut is tightened.

perature causes the cylinders to expand or contract. The lead deposit and the spark plugs expand at different rates, so the lead chips off or breaks loose and is burned.

Depending on the equipment on your airplane, there are various methods of producing this thermal shock. Simply running at full takeoff power for one minute is enough to raise the combustion temperature enough to get the desired effect. The propeller must be in low pitch and the throttle advanced slowly to produce takeoff rpm and manifold pressure.

Using a rich fuel/air mixture will also produce thermal shock by suddenly cooling the combustion chamber. Two-position mixtures are not rich enough, so you'll need to use the primer system to add fuel. Use it continuously for about two minutes. If deposits cannot be easily burned off, pull the plugs and clean them.

If this doesn't resolve the problem, you might have a problem with graphite fouling. Graphite fouling is caused by getting the lubricant used during installation of the plugs on the electrodes. This cannot be burned off. Remove the plugs and wipe them clean.

The gap between the electrodes on the spark plug must be precise in order to produce the spark necessary. As the plugs are used, the electrodes will erode and the gaps widen. The magneto must produce higher voltage to bridge the gap, and problems can arise. You might notice misfiring, hard starting, or excessive rpm drop during your mag check. This can be occurring due to too wide a gap of the spark plug or any defects in the components of the ignition system. If the gap is too wide and the magneto cannot produce enough voltage to spark the plug, the plug won't work. If there is a defect in any of the components, a wide spark plug gap will just cause the voltage to find the defect, since voltage looks for the path of least resistance.

HOSE CONNECTIONS

Item 21 under preventive maintenance in Part 43 allows you to replace any hose connection, with the exception of hydraulic hoses and connections. Hydraulic hoses are different because they are generally continuously filled with fluid, and any air entering the system will create problems. As for replacing the connections, fittings, and what have you, refer to the maintenance manuals for details and procedures and the parts manuals for the correct part. Afterwards, perform a function test of the system to ensure that no leaks are present. Use safety wires as required.

FUEL LINES AND FILTERS

You are permitted to replace fuel lines as a part of preventive maintenance as long as they are prefabricated assemblies and no major disassembly is required. Fuel lines come in two styles: the hard line, which is made of metal, and the flexible line, which is made up of a fabric and sometimes metal-braid-reinforced rubber. These assemblies can be obtained from either the aircraft manufacturer or from FAA-approved after-market sources. Inspection criteria for fuel lines is the same as discussed for hydraulic lines. Ensure that the lines are properly mounted after replacement and are not twisted (Fig. 5-14). Make sure the fuel lines are routed in the same way that the manufacturer did.

Replacing hard lines can be difficult due to the length of metal tubing and the bends in them. You also have to run them through bulkheads and around other items. It might be easier to let the mechanic handle this since he or she can fabricate the lines in place.

Fuel filters generally come in one style—a metallic mesh screen and are found in various places in the airplane. The most common filter that needs to be cleaned periodically is the screen in the gascolator bowl, which is usually located at the low point of the fuel system. These gascolators come in different shapes and sizes, so it's time to listen to the broken record: follow the instructions in the appropriate maintenance manual. Some things are common to all systems. Before performing any work, make sure the fuel is turned off. It is no fun to take a bath in high-octane fuel, and avgas does not work well as a cologne or after shave. Look for corrosion and other indicators of the fuel system having had water in it. Dirt and other contaminants usually collect here, so watch for them. You might also find indications that parts in your fuel tank are starting to disintegrate. Clean the bowl and screen in solvent, reassemble and safety in the appropriate manner. Before doing anything else, turn the fuel on, and check for leaks.

There can also be fuel screens located in the carburetor, various fuel pumps, and fuel tanks. Check with Ace, to find out where they are located in your airplane and whether you can get to them to clean them. Inspection of some of the filters will require major disassembly and draining of the fuel system, which is a bit beyond the scope of the work you are allowed to do.

Another job you are permitted to do but which you or the manufacturer likely have already done is replace the fuel filler port to prevent misfueling accidents. Approximately 10 years ago, general aviation experienced a rash of misfueling accidents. Much of the problem stemmed from misunderstanding by the line people of what "turbo" meant. An airplane like a Turbo Centurion would taxi up, the person refueling saw the word turbo and assumed jet fuel was required. Manufacturers and aircraft owners alike began installing restrictor plates, while FBOs changed their fuel nozzles to prevent such misfueling problems. The situation is much the same as the difference in fueling nozzles at the local gas station. You can inadvertently put unleaded gas in a vehicle that burns regular gas, but you cannot put regular gas in a vehicle that requires unleaded because of the size of the nozzles and the filler port.

Many planes that have been flying in recent years already have these restrictor plates in place, but if you have purchased a used airplane which has been a hangar queen, you might want to consider installing the device or having it installed. Retrofit kits are available from the aircraft manufacturer.

Back in the 1950s and 1960s, some aircraft engineers decided that fuel caps that were not flush with the body of the aircraft created too much drag. They reinvented the cap so that it is flush with the surface. The problem with this design is that water collects around the recessed cap and can get in the fuel tank. A new raised fuel cap will help keep out water. These new caps have a smaller diameter, which will prevent the large jet fuel nozzles from being inserted. Unfortunately for you, this is a job for your mechanic, since opening of the fuel tanks is required. In our humble opinion, you are better off not worrying about the tiny difference in drag made by the raised cap. Water in the fuel is a far greater hazard.

CHANGING OIL

Changing your oil regularly is one of the most important things you can do to extend the life of your airplane's engine. It isn't complicated, takes very little time, and with a few tips, doesn't even have to be particularly messy. In between oil changes, it is just as important to keep the oil level up to recommended levels as indicated in the POH. Many pilots check the oil level before every flight.

How often should the oil be changed? You need to develop some standard that combines how much you fly and how long since the last oil change. Many pilots change oil every 25 to 50 hours, but if you don't fly that much in one year, you need to change oil according to the calendar. Two or three changes a year will extend the life of your engine.

Gather all your tools before you start. You'll need a clean bucket to drain the old oil in. A clean bucket is especially important if you are going to send an oil sample in for analysis. You don't want to get a phone call from the lab saying, "I found the strangest thing in your oil. Plant fertilizer. How would that get there?"

Place the bucket in a large pan like one of those throwaway aluminum foil baking pans available at the grocery store. It will catch any drips that wander down the side of the bucket.

Equipment for removing and reinstalling safety wires is needed. Wire cutters, pliers, and .032 safety wire should be all you need. Have your sockets handy for removing the drain plug, as well as a new filter, if necessary, and the amount and type of oil you need. If you are averse to getting this stuff on your hands, you can wear a pair of work gloves.

The oil should be drained when it is warm to hot. First, the hot oil will be thinner and will drain easier, but most important, it will pick up as much foreign matter and sludge as possible, which will be drained off. So run the engine a few minutes before starting your oil change and get it up to normal operating temperatures. Better yet, take it around the patch once. Shut the engine down and take off the cowling. (Be careful. The engine is hot.)

Refer to your POH or maintenance manual for the location of the drain plug. You might have to access it through the bottom of the cowl, the nosegear doors, or from the side of the engine. The manual should tell you what you are looking for. You will remember to put the bucket under the drain hole before you pull the plug, won't you? The plug should be safetyed, so cut the wire and use the appropriate socket to loosen the plug. Let the oil drain a bit before you take a sample for oil analysis.

Remove the oil filter while the oil is draining. If you aren't sure where it is, check the manuals again. Depending on the type of filter you have, you might need to use a special filter wrench, which the filter manufacturer can provide. Of course, over time, these filters can get firmly implanted in place. Try using a solvent if elbow grease doesn't work. You can also get a better grip on the filter by placing some scraps of sandpaper between the filter and the wrench with the grit facing towards you. Depending on the type of engine you have, you might need to get the new filter on right away to avoid losing prime. The maintenance manual will tell you if this is the case for your plane.

Oil can also be sent to a laboratory for analysis (Figs. 5-25 and 5-26). While the engine is running, minute particles of metal are discharged from various components and get into the oil. The larger particles are trapped in filters or screens, but particles smaller than about 10 microns will pass through filters and screens. Since different metals are used for different components, an analysis of the oil can tell you which parts are showing wear.

Laboratories that perform this type of analysis offer kits that have everything you will need to draw off a sample of the oil and ship it to the lab. They will then conduct tests, often within 24 hours, and let you know the results. If they find something that requires immediate attention, they will call you with the results.

The oil sample should be a "midstream" sample, meaning you don't want the first oil that comes out of the sump, nor do you want the stuff you scoop out of the drain bucket. Run a little oil out before taking a sample. The oil should also be hot rather than cold so that the dissolved metallic salts will be detectable.

You need to provide the lab with some information about your plane so they can provide you with some meaningful data. How long since the last oil change?

AVIATION LABORATORIES

918 MARIA STREET
KENNER, LOUISIANA 70062
(504) 469-6751

ANALYSIS RESULTS

DATE: 7/05/94

INDEPENDENT AVIATION INC.
ATTN:DIRECTOR OF MAINTENANCE
12 GEORGE STREET
HANGAR # 4
HOUSTON   TX 77011

ENGINE S/N:99999
ENGINE MODEL:
AIRCRAFT:
S/N:
TAIL NO.:

**** CURRENT   RECOMMENDATION ** CONTACT A SERVICE REPRESENTATIVE DUE TO SAMPLE RESULTS!

SAMPLE DATE:10/21/93
ANALYSIS DATE:10/23/93
SAMPLE NUMBER: 1
TSN HRS: 800
TSO HRS: 25
OIL HRS: 25
FILTER HRS: 25
OIL ADDED: 3.0
FILTER MGS:
FLASHPOINT:

*** FILTER ANALYSIS RESULTS ***										
MATL:	ST ST	CB ST	AL ST	M50	COPPER	SILVER	MAGNS	ALUM	GRIT	MISC
AMOUNT:	-----	-----	-----	-----	-----	-----	-----	-----	-----	-----
TYPE:										
FORM:										

*** OIL ANALYSIS RESULTS ***										
Iron	Copper	Nickel	Chromium	Silver	Magnesium	Aluminum	Lead	Silicon	Titanium	Tin
48.5	35.3	1.0	7.0	0.1	0.2	7.0	4100	3.0	1.0	

LAB FINDINGS: COPPER VALUE IS STILL HIGH.
LAB COMMENTS: POSSIBLE WEAR SOURCE ARE VALVE GUIDES, FAX'D REPORT 10/23.

**** PREVIOUS 1   RECOMMENDATION ** RESAMPLE THIS ENGINE AFTER 25 FLIGHT HOURS.

SAMPLE DATE: 8/21/93
ANALYSIS DATE: 8/23/93
SAMPLE NUMBER: 73
TSN HRS: 750
TSO HRS:
OIL HRS: 50
FILTER HRS: 50
OIL ADDED: 3.0
FILTER MGS:
FLASHPOINT:

*** FILTER ANALYSIS RESULTS ***										
MATL:	ST ST	CB ST	AL ST	M50	COPPER	SILVER	MAGNS	ALUM	GRIT	MISC
AMOUNT:	-----	-----	-----	-----	-----	-----	-----	-----	-----	-----
TYPE:										
FORM:										

*** OIL ANALYSIS RESULTS ***										
Iron	Copper	Nickel	Chromium	Silver	Magnesium	Aluminum	Lead	Silicon	Titanium	Tin
60.2	30.5	1.0	11.0	0.1	0.3	9.0	4620	6.0	1.0	

LAB FINDINGS: COPPER VALUE APPEARS HIGH.
LAB COMMENTS: FAX'D REPORT 8/23.

**** PREVIOUS 2   RECOMMENDATION ** NORMAL SAMPLE RESULTS, SEND SAMPLES AT NORMAL INTERVALS.

SAMPLE DATE: 6/21/93
ANALYSIS DATE: 6/23/93
SAMPLE NUMBER: 33
TSN HRS: 700
TSO HRS:
OIL HRS: 50
FILTER HRS: 50
OIL ADDED: 2.0
FILTER MGS:
FLASHPOINT:

*** FILTER ANALYSIS RESULTS ***										
MATL:	ST ST	CB ST	AL ST	M50	COPPER	SILVER	MAGNS	ALUM	GRIT	MISC
AMOUNT:	-----	-----	-----	-----	-----	-----	-----	-----	-----	-----
TYPE:										
FORM:										

*** OIL ANALYSIS RESULTS ***										
Iron	Copper	Nickel	Chromium	Silver	Magnesium	Aluminum	Lead	Silicon	Titanium	Tin
50.2	10.3	1.0	8.0	0.1	0.3	8.0	4530	4.0	1.0	

LAB FINDINGS:
LAB COMMENTS:

HOUSTON • NEW ORLEANS • LOS ANGELES

Fig. 5-25. Laboratories that conduct oil analysis on aircraft oil provide a report such as the one above from Aviation Laboratories. The report tracks a variety of characteristics about the oil, including any metallic particles that might be found in the oil. The laboratories track these reports over time, which provides the best indication of the internal condition of your airplane. Regular oil analysis together with frequent oil changes can prevent unexpected repair bills.

Changing oil 121

MATL:
Filter Material Codes

ST	ST	Stainless Steel
CB	ST	Carbon Steel
AL	ST	Alloy Steel
M50		Bearing Alloy
MAGNS		Magnesium
ALUM		Aluminum

ELEMENTS:
Reported Parts
Per Million

AMOUNT:
Filter Amount Codes
Percent of Total

TRACE	0 - 10%
MINOR	10 - 40%
MAJOR	40 - 100%

T.A.N.   Total Acid Number

TYPE:
Filter Material
Type Codes

BR	Black Rubber / Elastic
CM	Carbon Seal Material
CS	Plain Carbon Steel
CU	Copper
DL	Moly Drylube
FE	Iron
FI	Fibers
FP	Fel - Pro C5A
GB	Glass Beads
HR	Hylomar Sealant
MG	Magnesium
MO	Moly (Metal Spray)
MS	400 Stainless Steel
NI	Nickel
OX	Iron Oxide
PH	17 - 4 PH Iron
PC	Paint Chips
SG	Silicon Grease
SI.	Silicon
SS	300 Stainless Steel

FORM:
Filter Material
Form Codes

BF	Brass Fines
BZ	Bronze Fines
CK	Chunks
CP	Corrosion Products
FL	Flakes
FN	Fines
MC	Machining Chips
OP	Oxidized Platelets
PL	Plating
PT	Platelets
SL	Slivers
ST	Stringers

TS	BRNG Alloy (M50)
VO	Voishan Seal Material

:matlform

Fig. 5-25. Continued.

Filter material codes

ST ST	Stainless Steel
CB ST	Carbon Steel
AL ST	Alloy Steel
M50	Bearing Alloy
Magns	Magnesium
ALUM	Aluminum

Amount:
Filter amount codes
Percent of total

Trace	0–10%
Minor	10–40%
Major	40–100%

T.A.N. Total Acid Number

Form:
Filter material form codes

BF	Brass Fines
BZ	Bronze fines
CK	Chunks
CP	Corrosion products
FL	Flakes
FN	Fines
MC	Machining chips
OP	Oxidized platelets
PL	Plating
PT	Platelets
SL	Slivers
ST	Stringers

Elements: Reported parts per million

FE	Iron
CU	Copper
NI	Nickel
CR	Chromium
AG	Silver
MG	Magnesium
AL	Aluminum
PB	Lead
SI	Silicon
TI	Titanium
BE	Berylium
SN	TIN

Type:
Filter material type codes

BR	Black rubber/elastic
CM	Carbon seal material
CS	Plain carbon steel
CU	Copper
DL	Moly drylube
FE	Iron
FI	Fibers
FP	Fel-Pro C5A
GB	Glass beads
HR	Hylomar sealant
MG	Magnesium
MO	Moly (metal spray)
MS	500 stainless steel
NI	Nickel
OX	Iron oxide
PH	17-4 PH iron
PC	Paint chips
SG	Silicon grease
SI	Silicon
SS	300 stainless steel
TS	BRNG alloy (M50)
VO	Voishan seal material

Fig. 5-26. A key to the codes in the oil analysis report.

What is your engine time in service? How much oil is the engine consuming? The data they need will be on the form you send in.

Figure 5-25 is an example of the type of information that will be garnered during the oil analysis. This particular company stores all its analyses on computer for each customer so they can determine trends in wear of your engine. They might recommend having the analysis done more frequently if they think something is awry.

OIL FILTERS

An important step in changing the filter is an autopsy of the old filter. It can reveal a great deal of information about the condition of your plane's innards. Pour the oil out of the filter into a separate container until you have a chance to look at the filter.

Special filter cutting tools are available that will make the job easier and are worth the expense (Figs. 5-27 and 5-28). Some knives or blades might leave traces of metal behind which will cause you all sorts of grief when you have the oil analyzed and can't figure out where traces came from.

Two diagnostic procedures are recommended and are common practice with airplane owners and repair stations, and these procedures are vital to the longevity of your engine. One is an examination of the oil filter and the other is oil analysis.

Pull the filter out and stretch it out so you can see into the pleats (Figs. 5-29 through 5-30). Examine the filter for any foreign matter such as metal chips. It might be difficult to detect the metal particles because of all the oil, so you

Fig. 5-27. After removing the oil filter, allow as much oil to drain out as possible, then cut the filter open using the appropriate tool and begin the autopsy of your oil.

Fig. 5-28. This shows the oil filter with its base cut off. Exercise extreme caution since the metal edges of the oil filter canister can be sharp with burrs.

might want to use a magnet and run it down the filter to see what you pick up. Metal flakes in the filter can be an early indication of some deterioration in the engine, which you can catch before it becomes a disaster. Metal particles in the filter can also indicate normal wear and tear inside the engine. After you have done a few oil changes, you will know what is normal for your engine. After cutting the filter open, it's a good idea to get a second opinion, so go show it to your mechanic.

The purpose of this exercise is to find any minute particles of metal that might indicate deterioration of some engine parts. The earlier you catch them, the earlier you can resolve the problem, which means you are looking for very tiny shavings. They might not be visible, so run a magnet down each pleat of the filter and see what you find.

You can also take the filter and rinse it in a pan of solvent, then run the solvent through a cloth. If there are any particles in the solvent, they will remain on the cloth. Then do the same thing with the oil you poured out of the filter.

Fig. 5-29. Remove the filter by grasping the element and pulling it out of the canister.

Fig. 5-30. Collect the oil from the filter and inspect it for metal shavings. This is a messy job. Do it in an area that is easy to clean. Do not wear your Sunday go-to-church clothes.

Before installing the new filter, examine it for any signs of dirt or damage, and to be sure the gasket is secure. It doesn't hurt to turn the filter over and tap it on the workbench a time or two to make sure no foreign objects found their way into during manufacture or shipping.

Now check the filter adaptor on the engine to be sure it's in good condition and nothing is clinging to it that doesn't belong there. Lubricate the gasket on the new filter according to manufacturer's instructions. And don't be stingy with the lubricant. Some filters allow you to fill them with oil before you install them. If yours does, do it. It's just easier.

It isn't necessary to tighten the filter down so tight that you create an inertia weld. The manufacturer might recommend a certain torque—18- to 20-foot pounds—or provide special instructions for tightening properly. Don't reinvent the wheel here. Follow the recommendations.

Don't forget to safety the filter in place. Some pilots like to do a runup and leak check before this step, which is fine as long as you don't forget to go back and do it. (Try holding the safety wire in your hand while you go through this process. It'll remind you to install it.)

Different filters are safetyed in different manners. Some have safety wire holes on the top, while others are at the base. Using .032 wire, insert it in the appropriate place and anchor it according to manufacturer's instructions. The anchor point should pull the filter in a tightening direction. Twist the wire 10 or 12 times per inch and clip off any excess wire.

And take the time to do a runup and leak check before you go for a flight. Oil leaks at 6000 feet aren't a good time.

MAGNETIC CHIP DETECTORS

For those of you who haven't heard of these, a magnetic chip detector is a little gadget located in a fluid system that has a magnet that collects metal particles suspended in the fluid. When enough of these particles have collected on the magnet, an electrical circuit is completed and turns on a warning light. This warns the pilot of a possible pending failure of something. Chip detectors can be found in areas such as the transmissions and gearboxes in helicopters. The removal, cleaning, and reinstallation of these chip detectors can vary from installation to installation, so do the work in accordance with the manual.

STORAGE BATTERIES

Operating storage batteries beyond their ambient temperature or charging voltage limits will result in all sorts of disgusting things happening: electrolyte boiling, deterioration of the cell, and battery failure. For lead-acid batteries, the voltage per cell should not exceed 2.35 volts. For nickel-cadmium (nicad) batteries, the limit varies with design from 1.4 to 1.5 volts per cell. For best results, follow manufacturer's instructions.

Lead-acid batteries exposed to cold temperatures are subject to plate damage due to freezing of the electrolyte. Nicad batteries are not as susceptible to freezing because no appreciable chemical change takes place between the charged and discharged state. However, the electrolyte will freeze at approximately –75°F.

Temperature ratings are based on specific gravity—the difference between the weight of the electrolyte compared to the weight of pure water. Specific gravity can be measured by using a hydrometer. Figure 5-31 indicates temperature limits for lead-acid batteries at various specific gravity readings. Lead batteries manufactured in this country are considered fully charged when the specific gravity reading is between 1.275 and 1.300. A battery that is ⅓ discharged reads approximately 1.240, and a ⅔ discharged battery reads about 1.200.

Lead-acid battery electrolyte freezing points

Specific gravity	Freezing point C.	F.
1,300	–70	–95
1,275	–62	–80
1,250	–52	–62
1,225	–37	–35
1,200	–26	–16
1,175	–20	–4
1,150	–15	+5
1,125	–10	+13
1,100	–8	+19

Fig. 5-31. As a lead-acid battery becomes discharged, it will freeze at higher temperatures. Care should be taken during cold weather to protect the battery as it ages.

Nicad batteries cannot be checked in this manner, however. The only accurate way to determine the state of charge of this type of battery is by a measured discharge. After the battery has been fully charged and left to stand for at least two hours, distilled or demineralized water can be added if necessary.

Before adding fluid to the battery, particularly nicad types, it is best to remove it from the plane. Contact with the fluid and even its fumes can cause serious damage to eyes and other body parts, so use rubber gloves, a rubber apron, and protective goggles while performing this task.

Have available sodium bicarbonate for acid electrolyte or boric acid, vinegar, or a 3 percent solution of acetic acid for potassium hydroxide electrolyte. If you inadvertently spill any of the electrolyte, you can immediately wash the area to prevent corrosion.

If you decide to replace your lead acid battery with a nicad type, neutralize the battery box with baking soda or borax, 20 percent by weight, dissolved in water, and flush it with clear water and dry it. You might want to paint the area with an acid-proof paint to prevent future corrosion.

Insulate the terminal posts to prevent accidental discharge and serious damage to the plane.

Check the condition of parts that hold the battery in place to be sure they are tight. If a quick disconnect type of battery connect that prohibits crossing the battery lead is not employed, check that the aircraft wiring is connected to the proper battery.

EMERGENCY LOCATOR TRANSMITTER

There are two kinds of aircraft owners in the world: those who have had trouble with their ELTs and those who are going to have trouble. Actually, it isn't quite that bad, but anyone who has been in aviation any length of time has heard of problems with these required pieces of equipment. They seem to send their best signals out when sitting on a workbench in the avionics shop. Many a Civil Air Patrol pilot has spent an afternoon looking for just such a signal. But at least, they often don't work when they are needed.

Because of so many problems with them, the FAA and NASA jointly undertook a study in 1990 to try to determine what the real problems are and what, if anything, can be done to reduce or eliminate the problems. They found, pretty much to no one's surprise, that in at least 15 percent of the cases where the ELT failed by either giving off a false signal or giving off no signal, the problem could be tied directly to maintenance—more precisely, to the lack thereof. Consequently, a change to the FARs was made requiring an inspection of the ELT every 12 months. (One would have thought this item would be included in annual inspection, but it rarely was.) Not only must the ELT be inspected, but also certain functional tests must be done to ensure the ELT is operational. We go into that in more detail in the troubleshooting section in chapter 7.

Several models of ELTs are available. Some use a foldout antenna, making them somewhat portable. Switches to arm and disarm the ELT will be located directly on the instrument, and a second switch can be in the cockpit, depending on the model.

ELTs are generally mounted in the aft section of the plane, but if you don't know where yours is, follow the outside antenna. It's usually within a foot or two of its antenna. The ELT should have a label on the exterior showing the installation date and expiration date of the battery. Under the FARs, you must replace the battery when over half its shelf life has expired. The manufacturer calculates the shelf life and labels the ELT with the date of manufacture and the date for replacement of the battery. You must also replace the battery when cumulative time in operation is one hour.

Inspection of the ELT and replacing the battery in most cases is a relatively simple procedure. Disarm the ELT by turning the switch to the off position. Disconnect the antenna by twisting the coax connection. The ELT can be mounted by either screws or an overcenter latch, which ought to be safetyed in place. Cut the safety wire and throw it out. If in the process you realize it was the wire, not the latch, holding the ELT in place, have the latch or mount replaced.

Remove the ELT and set it somewhere where you can work on it comfortably. Remove the screws holding the ELT together and open the ELT. Slide out the battery pack. Inspect the interior for any signs of broken wires, corrosion, moisture, and foreign objects. You can clean anything out you find in there, but repairs to wiring must be referred to an avionics technician or to the ELT manufacturer. If the battery has not expired, return it and fasten the cover back in place. Remount the ELT in your plane and safety the latch.

The ELT must be tested for proper operation. In the old days this was accomplished by turning the aircraft radio to 121.5 and turning on the ELT, listening for the sweeps on the radio. This is no longer the correct method since the aircraft antennae are too close together and the aircraft com radio will receive an ELT signal too weak to be received by the satellites. These days, the ELT must be tested for sufficient signal strength as well as proper operation of the "G" switch. The FAA states that this must be performed by an "appropriately rated technician," so check with your mechanic. Since the FARs might have changed since you last looked this subject up, we are reprinting the pertinent parts of the FARs relating to ELTs here.

§ 91.207 Emergency locator transmitters.

(a) Except as provided in paragraphs (e) and (f) of this section, no person may operate a U.S.-registered civil airplane unless—

(1) There is attached to the airplane an approved automatic type emergency locator transmitter that is in operable condition for the following operations, except that after June 21, 1995, an emergency locator transmitter that meets the requirements of TSO-C91 may not be used for new installations:

(i) Those operations governed by the supplemental air carrier and commercial operator rules of Parts 121 and 125;

(ii) Charter flights governed by the domestic and flag air carrier rules of Part 121 of this chapter; and

(iii) Operations governed by Part 135 of this chapter; or

(2) For operations other than those specified in paragraph (a)(1) of this section, there must be attached to the airplane an approved personal type or an approved automatic type emergency locator transmitter that is in operable condition, except that after June 21, 1995, an emergency locator transmitter that meets the requirements of TSO-C91 may not be used for new installations.

(b) Each emergency locator transmitter required by paragraph (a) of this section must be attached to the airplane in such a manner that the probability of damage to the transmitter in the event of crash impact is minimized. Fixed and deployable automatic type transmitters must be attached to the airplane as far aft as practicable.

(c) Batteries used in the emergency locator transmitters required by paragraphs (a) and (b) of this section must be replaced (or recharged, if the batteries are rechargeable)—

(1) When the transmitter has been in use for more than 1 cumulative hour; or

(2) When 50 percent of their useful life (or, for rechargeable batteries, 50 percent of their useful life of charge) has expired, as established by the transmitter manufacturer under its approval.

The new expiration date for replacing (or recharging) the battery must be legibly marked on the outside of the transmitter and entered in the aircraft maintenance record. Paragraph (c)(2) of this section does not apply to batteries (such as water-activated batteries) that are essentially unaffected during probable storage intervals.

(d) Each emergency locator transmitter required by paragraph (a) of this section must be inspected within 12 calendar months after the last inspection for—

(1) Proper installation;

(2) Battery corrosion;

(3) Operation of the controls and crash sensor; and

(4) The presence of a sufficient signal radiated from its antenna.

(e) Notwithstanding paragraph (a) of this section, a person may—

(1) Ferry a newly acquired airplane from the place where possession of it was taken to a place where the emergency locator transmitter is to be installed; and

(2) Ferry an airplane with an inoperative emergency locator transmitter from a place where repairs or replacements cannot be made to a place where they can be made.

No person other than required crewmembers may be carried aboard an airplane being ferried under paragraph (e) of this section.

(f) Paragraph (a) of this section does not apply to—

(1) Turbojet-powered aircraft;

(2) Aircraft while engaged in scheduled flights by scheduled air carriers;

(3) Aircraft while engaged in training operations conducted entirely within a 50-nautical-mile radius of the airport from which such local flight operations began;

(4) Aircraft while engaged in flight operations incident to design and testing;

(5) New aircraft while engaged in flight operations incident to their manufacture, preparation, and delivery;

(6) Aircraft while engaged in flight operations incident to the aerial application of chemicals and other substances for agricultural purposes;

(7) Aircraft certificated by the Administrator for research and development purposes;

(8) Aircraft while used for showing compliance with regulations, crew training, exhibition, air racing, or market surveys;

(9) Aircraft equipped to carry not more than one person; and

(10) An aircraft during any period for which the transmitter has been temporarily removed for inspection, repair, modification, or replacement, subject to the following:

(i) No person may operate the aircraft unless the aircraft records contain an entry which includes the date of initial removal, the make, model, serial number, and reason for removing the transmitter, and a placard located in view of the pilot to show "ELT not installed."

(ii) No person may operate the aircraft more than 90 days after the ELT is initially removed from the aircraft.

THE PROPELLER

Pilots are always trying to do things to their propellers. As we discussed earlier, about the only thing you can do legally and safely is wash it. You might not bang it with a hammer, file it down, relaminate it, or any of the other things that look so simple but which so adversely affect your safety and the ability of the airplane to function.

Every little nick or scratch in the prop creates a stress point. Filing it down alters airflow, and though it might not seem like much, also alters the balance of the prop. When the prop is out of balance, the loads are shifted throughout the entire aircraft. The crankshaft gets twisted, and everything that is attached to it is altered. We have seen some very frightening cases in which a failure of the propeller resulted in a blade being thrown off. Because the prop was then completely out of balance, the engine was ripped from its mounts. The consequences to the pilot and passengers are obvious. The best advice we can give you about maintenance on the prop is don't do it.

Having said that, let's go back to what you can do. When you clean your airplane, you can polish the prop, get all the bugs off it, and remove any fluid you find there. Don't forget the back of the prop. Air flows over and around the blades. Any obstructions, nicks, or other damage on the back of the blades will have a detrimental effect on the operational characteristics of the prop.

DOORS AND EMERGENCY EXITS

Not all aircraft have emergency exits, but all aircraft have some sort of entry door. All moving parts of doors and emergency exits can be lubricated with a light film of lubricant. Be sure to use lubricant that is compatible with the material used on the seals. Apply a light film of graphite stick or latch lubricant.

The maintenance manual should have any specific instructions necessary for replacing seals. Be sure to use only lubricants, and solvents, and adhesives that will not destroy the particular seal material you are working with. Wipe away any excess adhesives or cements that could cause doors, windows, or mechanisms to bind.

Failure of emergency exits to open easily could be caused by paint or primers that have bonded surfaces together, inadequate lubrication of moving parts, corrosion, or improper installation. After you have performed any of these procedures on your airplane, check the emergency exit to ensure that it functions properly. During routine maintenance is the time to discover that the emergency exit is stuck closed. This is one item that should be covered during the annual inspection. Unfortunately, on more than one occasion the emergency exit was jammed when it was needed most.

AVIONICS

Avionics have become so sophisticated these days that the manufacturers have become more stringent about who works on their equipment than the FAA is. While the FAA requires that a mechanic have an avionics rating to work on navcoms, autopilots, distance-measuring equipment, and such, some manufacturers require that only factory-authorized repair stations work on their equipment. Others will not permit any work to be done in the field. They want it back at the factory. Violating this kind of instruction not only might invalidate a warranty, it definitely makes the unit illegal.

As an owner/operator you are permitted by the FAA to check to see that the units are getting electrical power—period. No other work on avionics can be accomplished by a pilot. But you can do some things to prevent problems from starting in the first place.

Installing new radios can be done in certain circumstances. Many radios that are designed to be easily installed are available in the aftermarket. You simply slide out the old radio and slide in the new one. If you decide to do this, however, make a commitment to do it right. It does little good to pull out a 50-year-old radio and replace it with a brand new one, then expect the new one to work on 50-year-old wiring. The same is true of the coax running to the antenna. As a minimum, have the wiring checked out before reinstalling the new equipment.

RADIO AND ELECTRONIC SYSTEMS

You've heard the expression, "If they can put men on the moon why can't they . . .?" If it's any consolation, even NASA hasn't developed radios and instruments that work all the time. Pilots are used to relying on radios and instruments to provide vital flight data, and the equipment seems to always malfunction when you need it most.

Except for inspection of the system, there isn't anything you as an owner/operator are permitted to do on these systems. Even many mechanics cannot perform repairs or maintenance on avionics, since a special rating is required. Forget about popping off the instrument panel and trying to find out why something isn't operating. Even if you have a good deal of electronics training, aircraft instruments are different, and the FAA requires you be specifically trained to handle them.

There are a few things you can check during an inspection that might help isolate the problem you are experiencing, thereby reducing the size of your repair bill. These things are covered in our section on troubleshooting in chapter 7.

CONTROL CABLES AND TERMINALS

As a rule, carbon steel or corrosion-resistant steel wire is used to make aircraft control cables. The cables could be either flexible or nonflexible. Several terms are used to describe the various types of cables and their construction characteristics.

Wire refers to the individual steel thread, and a strand is a group of wires twisted together. The core strand is the one around which other strands are twisted. The cable is the core strand plus all the other ones twisted around it.

In the old days, control cables were attached to fittings and spliced by weaving the strands together in the FAA-approved way. This is still legal, but it is very time-consuming, and not many mechanics know how to do it. Cable attachments today consist of nicropress sleeves and thimbles which are swaged to form the attachment.

The cable is laced through the sleeve then looped and laced back through. A thimble is placed inside the loop to prevent wear then the sleeve is crimped in placed—a process known as swaging. The process must be done precisely in accordance with instructions to assure a snug assembly so the cable doesn't pull loose. Go/no-go gauges are used to make sure the process was done correctly.

Whether the cable assemblies are swaged or woven, the inspection is basically the same. Inspect cables, swaging, and nicropress sleeves and thimbles for signs of wear and degradation. Any frayed wires, rust, or corrosion should be noted so the cable can be repaired or replaced immediately. Pay particular attention to locations where the cables pass through fairleads or around pulleys. Wearing a cotton work glove, carefully run your hand along the cable, checking for any irregularities. Look for signs of wear indicated by several wires appearing to blend together as one. Internal wear occurs from the wires chafing against each other and is usually not possible to detect by visual inspection. Your mechanic will know what to look for. Also carefully check cables that are located near any source of moisture, such as wheel wells and battery compartments. They can corrode much quicker. Light rust can be removed using a steel brush, taking care you do not damage the wires of the cable.

Where cables pass through pulleys, they can be protected with a light coating of graphite grease or general-purpose lubricant. Inspect the pulleys, checking for ease of operation and general integrity. Look for any sharp edges or any foreign material embedded in the grooves, which could prevent smooth operation. Signs of wear on the pulleys could be an indication of some irregularity with the cables and should be referred to your IA (Fig. 5-32). Check all brackets and guards for corrosion, looseness, or damage. Check pressure seals, guides, and antiabrasion strips for security, signs of wear, damage, and corrosion.

Cables might look similar, but their construction and material could be very different. An owner/operator is not permitted to repair or replace any control cables. During an inspection, if you detect any corrosion or damage to the cables, refer the matter to your mechanic.

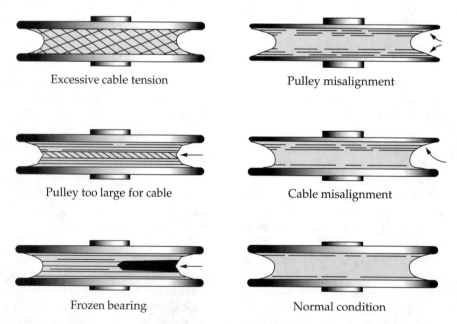

Excessive cable tension   Pulley misalignment

Pulley too large for cable   Cable misalignment

Frozen bearing   Normal condition

Fig. 5-32. Scoring or other damage to the pulleys could be an indication of damage to the cables that pass over the pulleys. The pulley should be free of any markings except for the normal dulling of the surface caused by use.

EXHAUST SYSTEM

Before cleaning any part of the exhaust system, you'll need to remove any cowlings to expose the complete system. Examine the cowling and nacelle areas adjacent to the exhaust system components for any indication of soot. This could lead you to the location of any leakage points. Look for any signs of the cowling chafing or abrasion on the engine control cable.

Extreme temperatures generated by the exhaust system can damage leads, hoses, fuel lines, and air ducts. These components need to be protected from radiation and convection heating by heat shields or adequate clearance. Any exhaust shields or shrouds should be removed for a thorough inspection.

While cleaning the system, check for cracks, dents, and missing parts. Pay particular attention to welds, clamps, supports, and support attachment lugs. Products of combustion can cause thinning, pitting, and an accumulation of moisture. Examine the heel of each bend in any components for any signs of deterioration, as well as any dented areas, low spots, or bulges.

LIFE PRESERVERS AND LIFE RAFTS

The rubberized material used in life preservers and life rafts should be repaired according to manufacturer's instructions. Replace corroded or damaged metal parts and any weakened or mildewed lanyards.

Life preservers and life rafts can be checked for leaks by inflating them to two pounds of pressure and letting them stand for at least 12 hours. If they do not hold this pressure, they should be replaced.

OXYGEN SYSTEMS

The four basic types of oxygen systems, classified according to the type of regulator used are demand, diluter-demand, pressure-demand, and continuous flow. Systems used to deliver oxygen to aircraft pilots and passengers must meet specific FAA and ICC requirements. Medical oxygen is not approved for use in aircraft since it might not have been tested and approved for high altitudes. Oxygen cylinders must indicate they conform with Interstate Commerce Commission requirements, which carry the ICC 3A, 3AA, or 3HT designation. Flexible connections, tubing, and other components specifically designed for oxygen must be used.

A slow-opening valve should be installed as a cylinder shutoff valve rather than a rapid opening one. Sudden and fast discharge of oxygen into the system can cause dangerous heating, which could result in fire or explosion of combustibles within the system. A relief valve is installed in both high- and low-pressure systems to safely relieve excessive pressure, which might be caused by overcharging.

To test and inspect the oxygen system, first remove all oil, grease, and dirt from hands, clothing, and tools. Inspect tubing and mechanisms for corrosion, moisture, dirt, or grease. Check tubing to ensure that there is at least a 2-inch clearance between the oxygen tubing and any flexible control cable or other flexible moving parts of the aircraft. There should be at least a ½-inch clearance between oxygen tubing and ridge control tubes or other rigid components. Check for at least a 6-inch separation between oxygen tubing and the flight and engine control cables and electrical lines. If electrical conduit is used, this separation can be reduced to 2 inches.

Check that the tubing, fittings, and other oxygen equipment is a safe distance from hot ducts and any equipment that generates heat. If routing of the tubing near heat-generating components cannot be avoided, be sure the oxygen tubing is insulated. If insulation is already in place, check for any signs of deterioration or chafing.

Components of the oxygen system, particularly the tubing, should be free of chafing or vibration. Oxygen supply valves should be located in such a manner that permits operation by the pilot during flight. The shutoff valve should also be easily accessible during flight and should be as close to the oxygen cylinder as practical to prevent excess loss of oxygen.

Inspect the oxygen cylinder for damage caused by vibration, baggage, or other cargo (Fig. 5-33). If necessary, install a guard or shield to protect the cylinder. There should be at least a ½-inch clearance between the cylinder and a firewall or shroud isolating a designated fire zone. The oxygen cylinder will need to be hydrostatically tested periodically. Check the maintenance manuals for time intervals between testing, since this can vary depending on the size and type of cylinder. This tests the cylinder's structural integrity by filling with water under pressure to look for cracks. Look at the exterior of the cylinder near the shutoff valve, since test dates are stamped into the cylinder. Some cylinders have a maximum service life, which means after a certain number of years, the cylinder is scrapped. Inspect masks for cracks or other defects, and check that straps are in place and operable.

Periodically perform a function test to make sure the system is ready to go when you need it. Open the cylinder valve slowly and watch the pressure gauge. Open the supply valve and remove one of the mask tubes and bayonet fittings

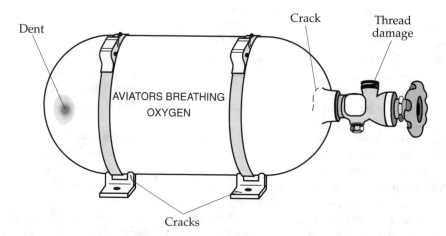

Fig. 5-33. Check the oxygen cylinder for any indications that it has been rubbing against anything during transport. Brackets should be secure and free of corrosion. Any marks on the cylinder itself should be brought to the attention of your mechanic.

from one of the masks in the kit. Plug the bayonet into each of the oxygen outlets. A small flow should be detected from each outlet. You can check this by holding the tube up to your lips while the bayonet is plugged in.

Now check the complete system for any leaks. Use a soap solution made from a mild soap or with a commercial leak check solution, and lightly coat every junction, assembly, and fitting. If bubbles are formed, there is a leak, and you need to get to a mechanic. If there are leaks, close the cylinder shutoff valve and reduce the pressure in the system by plugging a mask tube into one of the outlets or by loosening one of the connections in the system slowly until the pressure gauge reads zero.

Examine the system to determine that the flow of oxygen through each outlet is at least equal to the minimum required by the manufacturer at all altitudes at which the aircraft will be operated. The check should be made at the point at which the system is most likely to lose pressure. The most accurate check will require the use of a gas meter or some other device that your mechanic might be willing to loan you. A continuous-flow system that uses a manually adjusted regulator can be checked at sea level, but a continuous-flow system that uses an automatic regulator might have to be checked at maximum altitude, which will be encountered during the normal operation of the aircraft. Follow the instructions provided by the manufacturer.

In the diluter-demand and straight-demand systems, it is not necessary to check the amount of flow through the various outlets, since the flow characteristics of the particular regulator being used can be obtained from the manufacturer of the regulator. However, in such systems, the availability of the oxygen to each regulator should be checked by turning the lever of the diluter-demand regulator to the 100 percent oxygen position and inhaling through the tube via the mask to determine whether the regulator valve and the flow indicator are operating.

You can ensure that each user of the system will receive adequate flow by listening for an audible indication of oxygen flow, watching for inflation of the reservoir bag, or installing a flow indicator.

Make sure that operating instructions for the particular type of oxygen system is printed legibly on a placard and is easily accessible by the pilot. The instructions should include a graph or table that shows the duration of the oxygen supply at various cylinder pressures and altitudes. An example is given in Fig. 5-34. This chart is not a substitute for data provided by the manufacturer.

Actual duration in hours at various altitudes

No. of persons	8,000 ft	10,000 ft	12,000 ft	15,000 ft
Pilot only	7.6 hrs	7.1 hrs	6.7 hrs	6.35 hrs
Pilot and 1 pass	5.07 hrs	4.74 hrs	4.47 hrs	4.24 hrs
Pilot and 2 pass	3.8 hrs	3.55 hrs	3.36 hrs	3.18 hrs
Pilot and 3 pass	3.04 hrs	2.84 hrs	2.68 hrs	2.54 hrs
Pilot and 4 pass	2.53 hrs	2.37 hrs	2.24 hrs	2.12 hrs

Fig. 5-34. Be sure you have selected the proper size oxygen cylinder for your make and model aircraft and your flight characteristics.

6

Saving on your annual

IF YOU HAVE BEEN FLYING FOR VERY LONG, YOU HAVE PROBABLY HAD that heart-stopping experience of going to pick up the plane after annual and being presented with a repair bill you hadn't expected. Owners like to blame these on the mechanics, who are accused of everything from fixing things that weren't broken to trying to pay off their kids' orthodontist with one bill.

It isn't nice to accuse your mechanic of such foul deeds. How do you think he or she is going to feel when you want a problem fixed that you found? An angry mechanic is not a pretty sight. You can avoid all this unpleasantness by doing a preannual yourself so you are alerted to any problems that might add to your repair bill. One owner of a Cessna 182 thought the 16 hours allowed for an annual of his plane was excessive, so he persuaded his mechanic to let him do an owner-assisted annual. It took him 62 hours.

Like any other profession, there are some A&Ps who are better than others. They might have better training, more experience, or just better mechanical aptitude. How do you find them? What do you do if they do improper or substandard work?

Start by asking other pilots and aircraft owners who they use and what they like about the A&P. Do they feel that all necessary work is being done? Do they feel unnecessary work is being done? How long has the mechanic been certificated and what is his or her experience with your make and model? Ask about the mechanic's background and training. While many of the mechanics who have been around for a long time learned the trade on the job, a lot of younger mechanics have just as much knowledge and skill as a result of education. There are many fine aviation colleges and universities that teach aircraft maintenance, including hands-on training. In fact, if you live near one of these schools, you could get some information from them. Even some community colleges are teaching aircraft maintenance, so check with your local school.

Another source of information, particularly if you are looking for an avionics shop, is the manufacturer. Call and ask who in your area is authorized to perform maintenance on the manufacturer's equipment. Don't hesitate to ask what they know about the quality of the shop's work, what their turnaround time is like, etc.

Then visit the repair station yourself. Look to see if there is adequate protection of your equipment while it is being worked on. Repair stations aren't going to be spic and span, but they should be reasonably tidy, given the type of work that goes on there. Talk to the manager, IA, or head A&P and ask about their experience and the experience of their employees. And don't feel bashful about asking to see certificates. It is your responsibility as much as the repair station's to ensure that approved people perform the work on your plane. Not all personnel at the repair station need to be certificated (see chapter 1), but someone in the shop must have the appropriate rating.

Also, don't be bashful about asking to see manuals and paperwork such as airworthiness directives, type certificate data sheets, or other documents that might be necessary to perform the work on your airplane.

Ask about shop rates. How much an annual will cost, how long it might take, and what is included in the price are all things you should have a clear understanding of ahead of time.

When you make your final choice, remember that cheapest is not always best. Repair stations, particularly avionics shops, are required to make considerable investments in manuals and equipment in order to get their certificates and properly attend to your equipment. Like most things, you get what you pay for. A low shop rate might indicate they do not have all the necessary equipment or manuals. And you probably need to know how you are going to settle up. Ask if you can use your credit cards, check, or good old American money. If you are the type who wishes to be involved in the annual or repairs to some degree, ask if the shop permits this.

An important consideration when choosing a repair station is what type of warranty is offered. Does the warranty cover parts and labor or parts only? And since warranties might vary on different components of the system, make sure you get the warranty in writing.

If you have not been referred to the repair station by someone you know and trust, ask for references. It sounds silly because who is going to give you the name of someone who won't give them a good reference, but you might be surprised what you hear. The repair station operator might think Joe Smith didn't mind getting his plane back two weeks late, but Joe might tell you a completely different story. You will also want to know how much lead time the repair station requires. What kinds of problems can they handle on a drop-in basis, and what requires an appointment?

In general, the people who work on airplanes do so because they love their jobs. They are truly interested in doing the job right and not cutting corners. However, there might come a time when you have a problem with the work that was performed. Start by giving the repair station the opportunity to correct the problem or to explain why the work was done the way it was. In all likelihood, the situation will end there.

The only governmental agency that oversees the work of aircraft maintenance personnel is the FAA. They have a prescribed course of action they must follow whenever they receive a complaint, which can be more trouble than it's worth. Save contacting them until you have exhausted all other avenues of recourse. Try the Better Business Bureau or your state's consumer protection agency first, for example.

A word about owner-assisted annuals. Not all mechanics are willing to put themselves through this. One shop we know of has a sign that states: "Shop Rate—$45/hour. If you help—$55/hour." Arguments can be made both for and against this type of annual.

From the owner's standpoint, it will save money, even if all you do is take things out and open inspection panels. It also shows you a lot about the condition of your plane and how it operates. You might just learn something that makes you a better, safer pilot.

Mechanics look at owners quite differently. Yes, they are the customer and they are always right. But we have had cases where owners thought they wanted to help because "it can't be that difficult." Then when they get into the messy, difficult stuff, they suddenly remember an appointment across town. The plane is left partially disassembled, and the mechanic doesn't know if the owner intends to finish the job or not. It isn't unheard of for owners to misrepresent their level of mechanical ability, also. It can take a trained mechanic twice as long as it should to show an untrained person how to perform a task. So if you're going to ask for an owner-assisted annual, be fair about how much you can and want to do.

Annuals come in all shapes and sizes, both in terms of the work that gets done and the requirements. Not that we figure you forgot, but...an aircraft is due for annual inspection every 12 calendar months. If you have one done on the first of the month, the next annual isn't due until the end of that same month one year hence, so you might squeeze 13 months out, but no more. Additionally, if the aircraft is used for hire and reward, an inspection each 100 hours is required.

The scope of both the annual and the 100-hour inspections is identical. The only difference is who is permitted to sign each one off. An IA can signoff either inspection, while an A&P is only permitted to perform 100-hour inspections. You might want to have the 100-hour inspection signed off as an annual by the IA so that you don't get caught having to have an annual done when a 100-hour inspection was done just a month or two earlier.

Now we'll do a sort of miniannual to try to detect any problems. Start by doing the ground runup as discussed in chapter 3.

And though we doubt you are skipping any steps during your preflight, just to be safe, go through the whole magilla again. Make a list of anything that you think is not operating properly or that you have questions about.

Next go for a flight (sorry, but somebody has to do it). Keep an eye on the things on the squawk list you made during the ground inspection. Notice if those items are affected by such things as altitude change, engine rpm, or ambient temperature. Add to the list anything that shows up during the flight that you have questions about. During the flight, operate all the systems, especially those you don't use very often. Equipment suffers from lack of use as much as from use, maybe more. So check everything.

Back on the ground, it's time to do as thorough an inspection as you can without any major disassembly. You can also do some things to prepare your plane for annual that will cut down on the bill.

If you have a copy of the maintenance manual, you will find in it a copy of the recommended inspection checklist. It's a good guide for your inspection and will keep you from missing things. If you don't have the maintenance manual (and why not, if you're doing repairs?) ask your mechanic for a copy of the checklist he or she uses. Before you begin, ask the mechanic who will perform the annual and which things are included in the basic price. If it includes changing oil, for example, there is no point in your doing it. But you can do some things he or she might charge extra for. As you work your way through the checklist, here are some additional things to look for and do.

Check the tires and if you think they should be replaced, do it. If you have any questions you can always ask the mechanic if the tires need replacing and do it later. Pull the air filter off and have a look at it. If it is clogged with dirt, rap it on a flat surface to knock out as much dirt as possible, but leave the air gun alone. Blasting a paper filter with compressed air will only damage it. Your mechanic might decide to change the air filter during the annual anyway, but this way, you will know for sure what kind of condition it is in. Before you put the filter back, run your finger inside the induction system to check for dirt. There shouldn't be any. If there is, dirt is getting in someplace, and you need to find out where.

While you're in the area, check the engine compartment for any indications of leaks, corrosion, loose fittings, etc. It will help if you steam clean the engine and take it for a flight or two before the annual. Any leaks will be readily apparent and not hidden by buildup of dirt. And your mechanic will love working on a clean engine. Many mechanics are recommending changing all hoses in an airplane every 10 years. In some areas of the country like the desert southwest, it might need to be done more frequently. Check your hoses and belts for signs of cracks or weather checking. If they are hoses you are not permitted to change, add them to your squawk list.

Check the carburetor heat controls. The controls should be easy to operate with no binding. When the control is moved, the door inside the carb air box should move from one extreme to the other. There should be no loose screws, rivets, or other fasteners inside or out. Sometimes there is a material similar to baffling material around the door to better seal and direct airflow inside. Make sure this material is not about to come loose and be ingested by the engine. The door should be tightly closed before the control knob inside the cockpit hits the instrument panel. Also by checking the bottom of the carburetor air box, you can see if the engine is running either too rich or is overprimed regularly by looking for fuel stains in this area. This can also point to the float in the carburetor sticking when the airplane is at rest, allowing fuel to drain out the venturi and down into the carb air box. Manually operated alternate air doors can be checked the same way, but automatic ones aren't so easy. In fact, they are all but impossible, so leave that to your mechanic.

Inspect the engine area for any signs of ominous fluid leaks and for blistered or discolored paint. An engine paint job going bad could mean overtemping or normal wearing, but it is worth checking out further. Flake away the bad paint and check the metal underneath. If the metal is discolored, that portion of the engine is getting too hot for some reason. Bring it to your mechanic's attention.

Now check the exhaust system from stem to stern. Look for anything loose, cracked, or discolored. Stains from the exhaust are a quick giveaway to any problems with the system. Exhaust leaks generally leave a whitish-grey powder in the vicinity of the leak. If you can find the leaks when they're very small, hopefully they can be corrected by simple tightening of the fittings. If the leak is allowed to worsen, you will need repairs, possibly expensive ones. In a severe case, an exhaust leak can actually act as a blow torch, cutting away parts of the airplane you really do need.

While you're looking over the exhaust system, you can look on the inside of the exhaust stack as well as the exterior of the airplane downwind of the exhaust stack. The exhaust stain and soot buildup can tell you a lot about how well the engine is running. Heavy carbon caking can be an indication of possible oil burning in the cylinders. A darker soot buildup can be an indication the engine is running too rich. For those of you running auto gas, this darker buildup is an indication that the mixture setting is correct. Do not lean anymore if you are running auto gas.

Pull the spark plugs for an inspection. Clean, regap, and reinstall or replace as necessary. (Again, check to see if this is part of the base price of the annual before you do it. No sense in spending time if you aren't going to save money.)

Some mechanics recommend rotating spark plugs at each oil change to extend their life. If your mechanic is of this ilk, you can save yourself some money by doing it yourself (and noting it in the maintenance records, of course). All the spark plugs should look about the same. If they don't, you might have a misfiring cylinder or some other insidious problem that deserves attention. If the electrodes are white to gray, it could indicate overleaning, which could be a matter of how you lean or a plugged injector (assuming you have injectors).

Soot on the electrodes is just the opposite problem—too rich a mixture. Again, it might be your operating style or an indication of some other problem. Tell your mechanic about it. If you find oil on the spark plugs on the bottom, don't worry about it. It's normal.

If your plane is turbocharged, inspect as much of it as you can get to. If the turbo has a blanket around it, it should be secure, with no signs of serious heat damage. Turbocharged engines generally have more external oil lines. These need to be inspected for items such as leaks, dried out or stiff hoses, loose or missing supports, or clamps and chafed areas. People love to use nylon tie wraps to tie things up, but beware. Nylon can actually cut through the hoses. While you're looking around the turbo area, inspect everything nearby for overheating due to the tremendous heat found in that area. This is definitely an area where you do not want oil or fuel leaks of any kind. It would certainly give the fire fighters a reason to break out the hot dogs and marshmallows. Fuel injectors also should be inspected for security and integrity. Clamps should be tight, and there should be no indications of leakage except around the air bleeds.

Now take a mirror and a flashlight and try to see as much of the engine as you can. You're looking for anything unusual that you should bring to the mechanic's attention. Inspect for cracks, loose bolts, or anything else that appears to be abnormal. Induction hoses should be flexible and free of any cracks or holes. If the induction hose is leaking, you will usually find either fuel stains on the induction tubes, or you might even find that the hose is actually wet with fuel. At first glance this wetness might look like oil. However, if you wipe your finger through it, you will notice a bluish or greenish tint to it when you smear it. It might also have an avgas odor to it. Something else to look for while inspecting the engine are homesteaders. As we mentioned in the preflight chapter, mice, birds, and other critters can be very persistent and don't like being evicted.

Inspect the battery and its cables for signs of spilled fluid or corrosion. And speaking of batteries, don't forget the ELT battery, which now has a required inspection time as we spoke of earlier.

Inspect emergency exits, if so equipped, and all hardware for deterioration, wear, and security of attachment. If you have not actuated the emergency exit before, wait until the annual and let your mechanic show you how to work it and put it back together. Doors should have no wrinkles in the skin, dents, scratches, loose rivets, or corrosion. The door should be easy to operate through its full range of travel, and the warning light, if so equipped, should be operational. Examine rubber seals for cuts, tears, excessive wear, contact with the door frame, and general deterioration. Inspect bearings, hinges, latches, springs, and pins for general condition.

Actuate the emergency exit and check for ease of removal and proper functioning of the release mechanism at all angles of pull. The emergency exit should be free of cracks, dents, deep scratches, and loose rivets or bolts. Make sure it is properly aligned. Check rubber seals for wear, deterioration, cuts, and tears. Operating mechanisms should also be properly aligned and free of any damage. Also inspect any external release mechanisms for ease of operation and general condition.

Crew compartment sliding windows can be examined for cracks, dents, scratches, loose rivets, and corrosion. The extrusion seal should be making good contact with the fuselage canopy and be in good condition. Check the window mechanism for corrosion, wear, or other damage.

Check to make sure all placards and markings are legible and not covered by curtains, clothes racks, etc. Any interior modification that you might have done could obscure the placards as well, so check for visibility. Determine that seats, tables, and other furnishings do not block accessibility to the emergency exit. Check that safety wire on any emergency exit mechanisms is of the type recommended by the manufacturer. Do not use stainless steel or other types of stiff wire. Copper or aluminum wire is preferable.

There is one more job you can perform that will make you welcome at any repair facility while saving you some money at the same time. That job is unfastening all access panels. If you are going to do an owner-assisted annual, you will also be glad you did this ahead of time. This gives you the opportunity to spend time unsticking all those stuck screws that make everyone crazy. You'll have plenty of time to drill out any that just don't want to come out if you schedule this job for a week or so before the annual. Open every access panel and replace any screws that gave you grief. If you want to be terribly efficient, you can dip the screws in an antiseize compound before reinstalling them. (You can overdo it with this stuff, so in case you haven't heard us say this before, follow the instructions.)

If you have been thorough about your preflight during the previous year, you will have noticed, and taken care of, any obvious damage or deterioration. However, you might want to take time to more closely inspect places you usually glance at during your preflight. Also at this time take a look at areas you don't usually look at during preflight, areas such as the belly of the airplane. Just crawl right under and really give it a look-see. When fluid leaks from your airplane during a flight, it could end up almost anywhere on the plane. Don't limit your inspection to just those areas around filler ports or vents. Check the belly, under the wings, and the tail. Look for any evidence of new fluid leaks, corrosion, and rock damage from takeoffs and landings. If you own a high-wing aircraft, go get a ladder and give the top of the wing and fuselage a good, close look. Placards near the fuel caps should be legible. There should be no obvious damage, and the antenna should all be in one piece.

Before you take your airplane into your friendly neighborhood maintenance facility for an annual inspection, take the time to gather all of the aircraft's paperwork together. Are all the required documents in the airplane? Pop quiz: What are the required documents? Give up?

- Airworthiness certificate.
- Registration.
- Radio station license.
- Operation limitations in the form of placards, markings on the instruments, and the appropriate pilot operation handbook.
- Weight and balance (current would be preferable).
- Equipment list (a lot of times this is part of the weight and balance).

Other paperwork that would be nice to have in one spot is all of the maintenance records. Some people will only bring the most current logbooks. However, when the mechanic is researching airworthiness directives, a previous logbook might show compliance that the current logbook doesn't show thus eliminating any unnecessary inspections.

Yes, it all takes valuable time you could use building your hours, but if the plane doesn't run properly, you won't be able to fly anyway. By planning ahead, you can perform this work over the course of a few weekends before or after a flight. And not only will you save yourself the shock of unexpected repairs, but also you will know your aircraft better.

7

Troubleshooting

YOU'VE HAD IT HAPPEN AND IT MAKES YOU FEEL FOOLISH. YOU TAKE your airplane—or car or VCR—into the repair shop and start explaining what the problem is. Then you try to demonstrate to the mechanic what you are talking about, and the thing won't do what you just said it always does. No funny noises, no inoperable components. Sheepishly, you go away. Maybe we can help.

WHERE TO BEGIN

When you first notice a problem, ask anyone else in the plane if they have touched anything. How many times has someone gotten in your car and adjusted the air conditioning or changed radio stations? One would think people would be more careful in an airplane, but old habits die hard. Even another pilot might have changed some setting thinking he or she was helping.

If everything is set the way you think it should be, look for another source of your problem. These things will help the mechanic isolate the problem. Observe flight conditions at the time the problem appears. Is it on taxi, runup, or during flight? Does it happen only during ascent or descent? Ascent and descent? Level flight?

What other systems or gauges are operative at the time the problem occurs? Static in the radio or intercom might be coming from another instrument. Note CHT and EGT readings, engine power setting, altitude, and altimeter setting. What atmospheric conditions prevail? Extreme heat or cold or moisture from rain or snow cause certain problems to occur. Now for some more specifics.

AVIONICS

One common problem with avionics is a lack of understanding of the capabilities of the equipment. You lay out a lot of dollars for a piece of equipment thinking it will provide you with certain data, only to learn later that if you want it to do that, you need to have something else to go along with it. Or it isn't compatible with other avionics you already have installed. This especially becomes a problem when you start mixing and matching brands. As much as possible, stick with one brand throughout the system. If it is necessary to switch brands, ask an avionics technician or the manufacturer if it will work with what you already have.

Many of the problems with these systems manifest themselves as noise in the headsets or over the speakers. Much of the time, the radios are just picking up and amplifying noise generated by something else in the airplane (no, it's probably not your weird cousin Freddie, so you can't use this as an excuse to leave him home.) The chore, then, is to identify the source of the noise and eliminate it.

Radio noise is one of the most aggravating and elusive of all problems. You put the headset on, and all you hear is something that reminds you of that noisy breakfast cereal. Worse, you can't hear or transmit. Problems with the radios can be very expensive and as difficult to isolate as electrical problems. Anything you can do to zero in on the problem before you visit the avionics shop is bound to save you time and money.

Intermittent problems pose obstacles of their own. Trying to locate the cause of the difficulty will require you to make careful observations so the technician can try to duplicate the problem. Notice how long into the flight the failure happens, at what altitude, and what the ambient temperature is. Are other radios on at the time of the failure?

A big problem for the technician with intermittent conditions is trying to recreate the failure. The technician can't fix it if it ain't broke. When these things behave as so often happens—i.e., it won't act up when the technician is around—make arrangements ahead of time to take the technician flying, or tell the technician you are going for a flight to try to recreate the problem. Then if the system fails while you are flying, take the airplane back to the avionics shop. Do not shut anything down. Get somebody's attention who will send out the technician so he or she can look at the failed system. When doing this, exercise extreme caution since you still have a giant meat slicer spinning out front. And you will park in such a way that you aren't filling the shop with dust, won't you? That is, if you want them to fix your airplane.

You can save a lot of time and money by trying to isolate the problem yourself. Inspect the system as much as possible without disassembling anything. Look for obvious things that can lead to failure of electronics. These things include damaged or overheated equipment, connections, or wiring; poor electrical bonding; improper support of wiring or conduit; dirty or loose equipment and connections; failed fuses, circuit breakers, and electric lamps; and broken or missing antenna insulation, springs, or safety wires. While you're doing the inspection, clean anything that has an accumulation of dust or corrosion that does not require disassembly. Cleaning can be accomplished with a blast of dry air, or contact cleaners that are made for the purpose. Not all contact cleaners are good for all surfaces so read and follow instructions. During the inspection, check for any indications of moisture in the system. Water that might have seeped in around the windshield could have caused some damage to the radios.

All wires and cables involved in the radios or other electronics need to be in good condition, as well as any conduit they are trained through. If they are rubbing together or against the airframe, they could be causing your problem. Inspect any open wiring for fraying, damage, or distortion. Fluids and electronics do not mix so make sure any lines carrying oil, hydraulic fluids, or other moisture-producing materials are separate and there is no indication of a leak. If possible, make sure the wires are above the fluid-carrying lines so any leak that might develop will not soak the wiring, causing the insulation to break down and possibly resulting in shorts and fire.

Clamps holding wires and cables in place should be tight enough to perform that function but not so tight they break the wires. In places where the cables pass through structure or bulkheads, inspect for proper clamping or grommets. The wires should have enough slack in them to prevent being pulled taut and pulling on the terminals.

Conduit can be either metallic or nonmetallic, rigid, or flexible. It's used to protect the wires. Check the conduit to make sure the end fittings and clamps are not distorted and that drain points are free of dirt, grease, and critters. The conduits should be free of abrasion caused by anything rubbing against them. Any plastic wire sleeves should be checked for similar damage.

You might be tempted to use electrical tape to repair any minor damage or abrasion you find. You should know that standard electrical or PVC tape is not approved for use in aircraft since it is not flame resistant. In recent years, however, some manufacturers have begun making fire-resistant tape that is approved for use in aircraft. This tape will have the Fire Underwriter's Laboratory approval (UL) on the wrapping. Flame resistant or not, PVC will decompose at temperatures above 221°F (105°C) with rapid loss of insulating qualities. It is not recommended for use in areas that might approach those temperatures.

Poorly soldered or loose terminal connections, missing safety wire, and loose quick-disconnects can also cause problems with the system, so keep an eye out for any of these things during your inspection. Also look to make sure there is enough clearance between exposed current-carrying parts and ground.

One of the easiest items to check out and repair is the grounding of the radios. Corrosion buildup between access panels can prevent a good ground, as can dust and dirt. If the plane has recently been painted, it might be that the paint is preventing panels from coming into close enough contact to get a good ground. Poor bonding between static wicks and the airframe might also prevent adequate grounding, resulting in hissing and popping.

If you have recently had work done on the plane that involved removal of access panels, try turning the radio on while someone sits inside and listens and you give those panels a smack. If the radios struggle to come to life, you have found your problem.

Electrical noise generated from various pieces of equipment in the plane is more likely the source of your problem rather than the radios themselves. First check to be sure the proper voltage is being used in the system, particularly if you have newer equipment. On electrical systems with a 12-volt battery, the alternator or generator will actually put out about 14 volts. If the voltage drops to 10, the radios won't function properly. The same is true of a 24-volt system. The alternator or generator will be producing in the neighborhood of 28 volts. A drop to 20 volts will affect the radios.

Next check the ignition system and the alternator or generator, particularly if you have just had work done on one of these items and had no noise before the repair. Noise caused by the alternator or generator makes a unique sound: a high-pitched whine that sounds a bit like a siren. The noise will change with engine speed. At low rpms, it might sound like bacon frying. You might also hear clicking and popping noises.

A simple check involves using a cheap AM radio. Turn it on loud, then with the engine running and everything else turned off, listen for any pops on the radio. The noise probably comes from the ignition leads. Try scraping the outer shielding of the ignition leads where they join the magneto harness. If the AM radio is picking up a nearly continuous stream of static, the noise could be the result of poor grounding between a mag and the engine case. Poor bonding between the engine and the airframe can also cause the noise. You might want to ask your A&P about installing a metallic-braid covering and special end connections for ignition wires between the magneto and spark plugs. Replacing the spark plugs might also eliminate the noise. Another test to help isolate the noise source is to add throttle or go from both mags to one or the other. If the noise goes away, in all likelihood, the magnetos or ignition leads are the problem.

Installation of a filter on the alternator might clear up the noise. However, the new solid-state regulators can be next to impossible to be made completely quiet. This has to do with the way they regulate voltage. Another troublemaker could be the alternator itself. Alternators are generating ac current and then diodes in the alternator convert it to dc current. When one or more of the diodes fail, ac current enters the electrical system and the radios will receive and transmit this noise. Overhauling the alternator will help correct this problem.

One type of static even has its own name—precipitation static. As the name implies, it could be caused by ice, rain, or snow, but it also can be caused by dust, sand, and airborne particles. As a result of precipitation static charging, the electrical potential of the aircraft rises until it reaches the corona threshold. (*Corona* is the discharge of electric current from an object into the surrounding air.) This creates a noise that can be coupled into the aircraft antennae. Static dischargers can be installed on the aircraft to eliminate precipitation static and are normally mounted on the control surfaces and other extremities of the aircraft. Inspect these static dischargers for secure mounting, wear, abrasion, or any other damage.

Problems coming from the generator are often found in the commutator. As the generator spins and the commutator makes and breaks contact with the generator poles, arcing occurs. It is almost impossible to completely eliminate this situation, but cleaning the commutator contacts will help reduce it. You can also mount a radio frequency filter near the generator to help resolve the problem. Grounding the generator frame is another possible solution.

Alternators tend to be less of a problem, but defective diodes in the solid-state rectifiers might send clicking noises through your headset. Ground the alternator, install a filter, or replace the diodes.

Then there are electric motors, of which you might have several, sending their own noises out. One indication that one of these motors is the source of the problem is that the noise will not change with engine speed.

To determine which one is the problem, fire up the motors one at a time. You might have to get a little creative with this step, though, because the noise could be caused by a certain combination of two or more motors. Isolating this problem will help you while away for an otherwise dull weekend or two. Be sure to check the rotating beacon during this step since it can also generate noise. Check to make sure that the unit is adequately grounded. The problem might also be internal, such as worn brushes and/or commutator.

The battery is another possible culprit for producing noise and sending little messages through your radios. If you have recently had a hard landing or the battery got knocked around while you were transporting it, internal connections might have come loose. Corroded terminals can also cause unwanted radio noise.

Check the battery casing for any sign of damage and gently shake it back and forth while listening for anything loose rattling around inside. Cleaning the terminals is the obvious solution to corrosion, but if you hear rattling sounds, invest in a new battery.

Gyro flywheels and shafts on motors are other possible culprits for radio noise. As with the electric motors, turn off one gyro at a time to attempt to determine which one is causing the problem. You might have to use the circuit breakers to shutdown groups of gyros, which will make finding the problem a greater test of your ingenuity.

Nonelectrical gyros can also generate noise, which will be obvious if the noise only occurs when the vacuum pump is running. After the engine is shutdown and while the gyros are winding down, listen to the radios. If the noise disappears as the instruments wind down, you might have found the problem. Bonding straps on control surfaces that are not in top condition or that have come loose is another place to check for the source of any radio noise.

Lorans are notorious for causing interference with radios, which shows itself as a ticking noise, and so do other microprocessor-based avionics. As with other equipment, try turning off one at a time to see if you can determine which one is causing trouble.

Sometimes wiring placed too close together can cause interference on the radios. Check for transmitter cables that are too close to speaker leads or intercom wiring. While you're checking the wiring, look for poor shielding as well.

Switches and relays on audio panels are another possibility worth checking out. Try placing the various switches in different positions. Anything that is loose or that has poor connections should be repaired by the appropriately rated technician.

A word about the transponder and encoding altimeter static checks that are required every two years. These are typically not done during an annual. You must keep separate records and make sure that they are done on schedule.

New inspection requirements on emergency locator transmitters require that the system must be checked every 12 months. That means inspection of the mounting, a function test, and inspection for any signs of indication. The function test requires more than just getting in the airplane and turning on the ELT. You must check the G-switch, which will test how well the ELT will operate under sudden deceleration conditions. You must also check the broadcast strength of ELT. Coordinate this test with flight service or the control tower to determine if they are able to pick up your signal.

And finally, (we think) notice if the noise you hear is relative to the flashing of the strobe light. Turn the strobes off as a final check. You might be able to resolve the problem by having the light moved so that it is more than 5 feet from the avionics and intercom wiring.

After going through all this and finding nothing, it might be that the instrument is just dead. But before you rush out and replace it, try a couple more things to confirm whether or not it is terminal.

If all your vacuum instruments croak at the same time, the problem is more likely the vacuum pump than the instruments, so start checking there. However, if only one instrument appears to be gone, you can perform a few simple tests on the ground to try to figure out if you need to start shopping for new equipment.

Vacuum instruments need air to work. No air supply, no readings. Throttle up while looking at the suction gauge. You should get a normal reading that stays steady. Wavering of the reading indicates that air supply is being inhibited somewhere along the line. If the reading changes as engine rpm changes, the problem might be a sticky relief valve. While the suction gauge is reading steady, look at the instrument that you are having problems with and see if it is still misbehaving.

Avionics and static instruments can be checked without a runup. Some problems might be obvious, such as loose pointers, or, if you have LED displays, a blank display. The more high-tech the equipment, the more you should rely on your avionics specialist. You might want to lie upside down and backwards under the dashboard to see if you can spot any broken wires that might be the source of the problem. Beyond that, you should leave it alone.

Gyros could have similar under-the-dash problems. Take it from one who has been there. Give yourself plenty of room. Either move the seats as far back as possible, or better yet, take them out. Make sure you have a bright, working flashlight before you start crawling around. Checking the flashlight first might save you at least one bump on the head.

Examine everything you can get to without disassembling anything. Check vacuum lines for kinks, cuts, or twists that might inhibit air flow. Check wiring for breaks or loose connections. Inspect connectors for corrosion and security. There isn't anything you are permitted to repair, but once you identify it, you will make your mechanic's job easier (and cheaper).

If all these steps don't reveal any problems, the instrument you are having trouble with is probably terminal. An avionics specialist can confirm this. Tell the specialist all the things you have checked. Before giving you the bad news, he or she will likely recheck them in case you missed something.

HEADSETS AND INTERCOMS

Headsets and intercoms are becoming more popular, and sometimes they can be the cause of problems with the avionics. Portable intercoms might have a separate battery pack or might be of the type that plugs into the cigarette lighter. Both types have caused headaches for pilots and avionics repair stations alike. Any loose connection anywhere in the system will not only prevent the intercom from working, but also could affect other radios. A loose connection at the cigarette lighter or battery pack, damage to any wires in the system itself, or headsets with improper connections all could cause problems.

If you wish to have an intercom in your plane, we strongly recommend you have a panel-mounted unit, which costs about the same as a portable one but is much more dependable. Once the intercom is "hardwired" into the system, many of the problems with loose connections are automatically eliminated.

Cheap headsets can also raise havoc with the system. The less expensive headsets might not have adequate shielding around the wires. The shielding is designed to block out random radio signals drifting through your space. Without the shielding, you could get lots of interference, loud squeals, very poor reception or transmission, and other noises that could drown out the person trying to talk.

Microphones in the headsets can be either electric or dynamic each of which works on different principles. Mixing and matching equipment between manufacturers or types of microphones will result in a system that generates yet more headaches. You can see that buying a cheap intercom is a foolish economy. Ideally, your system will be a panel-mounted intercom with the same make and model of headset for each seat in the plane.

Once you get the headphones on, you will hear all sorts of things you never heard your airplane do before. This is because you are actually amplifying those sounds while blocking out a lot of peripheral noise. You'll hear the strobe doing its thing, the pinging of flashing beacons or anticollision lights. You might hear the alternator whine, which changes in pitch with changes in engine rpms. A bad ground in the intercom system can result in more noise. Check all the wiring for proper shielding and grounding. High-quality headsets have a control on the ear piece, which can help eliminate a lot of the noise.

Also check your speakers. Older ones with paper cones are subject to damage. It might be worth replacing the speakers with newer technology.

If you have examined everything in the aircraft and still have not found the cause of the noise, move outside to check exterior equipment. You have had the experience of damaging the antenna on your car by driving through your favorite fast food emporium, then as you drive out, you remember your French fries and back up to get them. Your antenna becomes a pretzel, and you can't listen to anything. In all likelihood, you haven't damaged your airplane's antenna in quite the same manner, but other kinds of abuse can cause problems.

Poor connections or corrosion at the base will cause noise, or possibly even inoperable radios. Wiggling the antenna while the radio is on can reveal this problem quickly, as can an inspection of the mounting both inside and outside.

Whether your antenna is of the fixed or trailing wire variety, begin inspecting any antennae by checking for cracked or broken insulators, broken tension springs, and missing end thimbles. If insulated wire is used in the antenna, inspect the insulation for cracks, overheating, or abrasion. Even pinholes could cause trouble so look carefully. Look at the fixed antenna mast and ensure that it is tightly mounted and there is no damage to the mount. The sealant of whip or blade antennae should be checked for any signs of damage or distortion.

High-performance aircraft use flush-mounted antennae that are recessed into the fuselage or other portions of the aircraft. The recesses are covered with Fiberglas or some other material that allows the passage of radio frequency energy. If the covers are painted, they should be painted with a type of paint that will not interfere with the passage of radio frequency energy.

Connectors on coaxial cable antenna should be checked for proper fastening. Some connectors rely on the position of the center pin by its physical connection to the center conductor of the cable. If this pin is often connected or disconnected, it might eventually fail to make the proper connection altogether. Cable connectors can be clamped or safetyed so they don't separate.

Loop antennae are designed to work with a particular receiver. These loops have directional sensitivity, which makes them accurate navigational devices. Connecting wires between the loops and receivers are also designed for the specific equipment. Only components that meet the manufacturer's specifications should be used.

Occasionally the metal in the aircraft might distort the electromagnetic field of an incoming signal and result in reading inaccuracies. This is called *loop quadrantal error* and can only be corrected by trained technicians who have appropriate equipment.

Radar antennae are covered with a radome to protect them from the elements. Part of the airframe, the radome must have certain electrical and physical properties to work properly. It must permit the passage of radar signals and return echoes with minimum distortion and absorption. In order to do this, it must have a certain electrical thickness. Any variation in this thickness can result in a reduction of radar range, distorted displays, inaccurate directions, and false targets. You might like being able to blame the equipment next time you get lost, but it's better not to get lost in the first place.

Weather radar equipment, including the radome, should be inspected visually for signs of damage such as holes, cracks, chipping and peeling of paint. Fittings and fasteners should be snug and free of corrosion. Check neoprene erosion caps and lightning strips for any indication of deterioration.

Scuff marks on the radomes usually indicate impact damage from birds, foreign objects, or hangar or ramp equipment. If you see any of these marks, check closer for any damage that might have been caused on impact.

Damage to the paint on the radome might be an indicator of further damage and warrants closer inspection. Look for scuff marks or signs of lightning strikes, such as burn marks. Of course, damage to the paint could be simply a matter of a poor paint job. A closer inspection both internally and externally is necessary to determine if further damage has occurred. Location and identification of damage in its early stages means proper corrective action will be taken to prevent further damage. Damage to the paint will permit moisture to get trapped underneath. If the moisture freezes during flight, the efficiency of your radar is drastically reduced.

Neoprene erosion caps are used to protect the equipment from rain. These little guys can conceal a certain amount of damage to the radome and make impact damage difficult to detect. If there is any question about the degree of damage you find in the radome, hie thee to an avionics shop to have it removed for closer inspection and repair as needed. Neoprene erosion caps can also have air bubbles, surface fraying, and loose edges around the cap, so look for these items. They shouldn't be there.

Lightning diverter strips are used to protect the radome from damage from lightning strikes. They also are designed to prevent radio interference from static charge buildup on the radome. Proper grounding of these strips to the aircraft structure should be assured each time a radome is inspected or repaired. Damaged or burned strips should be replaced for maximum protection of your equipment.

Plastic nose caps should not be installed over a radome unless the manufacturer has recommended it. They might cause distortion of the radar beam, weak signals, poor definition, and radar display clutter. If moisture collects under the cap, it can further block or distort the signal. The caps also could mask certain types of damage or problems with the radome. Any other coverings or coatings such as paint should be of a type that is approved by the manufacturer to prevent interference with signals. For example, metallic based paints or undercoatings might set up reflections that can damage the equipment.

Any solvents or paint strippers used to clean or repair the equipment should be used judiciously. They might weaken any bonding points, or the neoprene erosion cap, attack the resins used in construction and in general weaken the structural integrity.

ENGINE PROBLEMS

A lot of things can go wrong with the engine, and with so many components involved, the trouble can be difficult to diagnose. Any help you can give the mechanic will be appreciated. As mentioned earlier, try to determine what is going on at the time of the problem. Check rpms, note altitude, ambient temperature, and what accessories or other components are on at the same time.

A rough-running engine could be caused by improper leaning techniques. Have you changed the way or under what conditions you lean the engine? If the plane or engine is new, it could be you need a new technique as well. Bad fuel can also be the cause of a rough-running engine. Consider whether you have purchased fuel someplace new or whether the possibility exists that the incorrect fuel was used.

Difficulties with oil pressure readings can be caused by a number of things, as can changes in oil consumption. Are you using a new type or grade of oil? It could be the wrong one and might result in higher oil consumption. Low oil pressure could simply be a matter of insufficient oil. Check the oil level before you go to the repair station if you have noticed low oil pressure.

It is often thought that failure to achieve redline rpms is caused by the engine not putting out enough power. While that possibility exists, other things can result in the same problem. If your airplane is equipped with a constant-speed prop, the problem might be that the governor is holding back the propeller. Adjustment of the governor might be what is called for rather than engine repairs.

The tachometer is an important indicator of the work the engine is doing, but if rpms don't seem to be reading appropriately, based on your experience with the plane, the problem might be the tach. Some need to be oiled occasionally. Leave this task to the A&P, though, who will know what oil and how much to use. If your tach is getting rather old, it could be time to replace it or have it overhauled. There are portable electronic tachs that can be used to test the accuracy of the tach in the airplane. Perform this test before you condemn the old tach and spend money you might not have to.

The throttle might be the guilty party if you are having trouble reaching full power. Corrosion or loose connections might be preventing the throttle from traveling its full arc, thereby limiting engine power.

Leaks or blockage in the induction or exhaust systems can also limit engine power by essentially altering the mixture to leaner or richer than you think you are getting. On turbocharged engines, induction leaks redirect manifold pressure overboard rather than into the cylinders. The turbo relies on exhaust for energy, so leaks in the exhaust system will limit the ability of the turbo to do its thing. Broken baffles in the muffler might be the source of an exhaust system problem. This type of inspection should be done by your mechanic. Carbureted engines could show signs of reduced power if the carb heat door is leaking. Inspect it for any signs of deterioration.

Engine knock is difficult to hear in an airplane, but if you detect unusual noises coming from the engine compartment, refer the matter to your mechanic. To help determine the problem, make a note about power settings before you go.

Recent work performed on the engine might have been done improperly. Be sure you inform the A&P of any work you have had done or did yourself. (Yes, it's okay to tell him about work you did but shouldn't have done. He's not going to turn you in, and it might help resolve the trouble.)

Sudden stoppage of the powerplant or even a brief slowdown could be caused by several things. The propeller might have struck something, foreign objects might be interrupting fuel, oil or electrical flow, or any of a variety of other problems. To determine the source of the problem, a thorough inspection is necessary.

Begin by removing the cowling and inspecting the engine for any visible damage or audible internal damage. Slowly rotate the propeller shaft to check for abnormal binding or sounds. Inspect the crankshaft flange or splines for signs of twisting, cracks, or other deformation. Rotate the shaft slowly in 90 degree increments and check for concentricity of the shaft.

Remove the oil sump drain plug and check for metal chips or any other foreign materials. Also check the oil screens for metal particles and contamination. Check the engine case exterior for signs of oil leakage and cracks. Inspect cylinders and cylinder hold-down areas for any signs of oil leakage. Check the mounting flanges of accessories such as the magneto, generator, and pumps for any sign of damage or leakage.

Engine mounts should be examined for looseness, distortion, or signs of wear, and check the engine mount structure for bent, cracked, or buckled tubes. The airframe around the mounts should also be inspected for damage. If the source of the stoppage was the propeller striking a foreign object, the propeller needs to be thoroughly inspected prior to the next flight using the manufacturer's instructions.

One of the more serious problems that can develop with the engine is piston rings that stick. It's an expensive problem to repair, so you want to make sure that is truly the problem before you tell the mechanic to start taking the whole thing apart.

One of the first indications you can have of a piston ring problem is a sudden rise in oil consumption. Of course, this could be the symptom of a number of things that need to be eliminated (see the section on lubricating systems in chapter 7).

Most of those things will result in a gradual increase in oil consumption whereas a piston ring problem probably will cause a sudden increase in the engine's use of oil. If you have had your plane for a while, you know what kind of consumption is normal.

Oil analysis might turn up sticking piston rings as well. Rising levels of iron and chrome means the rings and the upper cylinder are doing rude things to each other, resulting in these metals beings deposited in the oil. This is a prime example of why an oil analysis should be done regularly. One reading wouldn't tell you if levels are rising. Several analyses will show these changes.

Another indication of sticking piston rings is crankcase pressurization. Engine manufacturers provide data for what is acceptable crankcase pressure. However, they don't give that information in terms we commoners can understand simply. The specifications are given in inches of water. This is because engineers like to develop things in such a way that makes them feel more clever than the rest of us. Naturally, a special tool had to be developed in order to take this reading. It's called a *water manometer,* and it isn't likely to be found in the everyday toolbox. For the most accurate readings or determination about crankcase pressurization, this gauge is best. But you can do a couple of things to give you some indication of what's happening with the crankcase.

For those planes equipped without an oil-air separator on the case breather, there will be indications of oil on the breather and on the belly of the airplane. If your plane does have a separator, you need to conduct another test. Disconnect the separator and check the oil level. Top it off, if necessary, and then take a flight. Afterwards, check the oil level again to see if it has seriously diminished. Also check the belly of the fuselage for any signs of oil. These are the two indicators of crankcase pressurization that, in turn, mean the piston rings are sticking.

A cylinder compression check will also turn up sticking piston rings, but since you have been spending all your spare cash on your plane, you probably don't have the equipment to perform this check. That is why there are A&Ps in the world.

There are products that are available that can be added to the fuel to help loosen up sticking piston rings. Ask your mechanic for a recommendation, then read the instructions and follow them exactly for best results.

COOLING SYSTEM

A thorough preflight is your best diagnostic tool in locating trouble with the cooling system. Improper seal on the cowling baffles will show up during your inspection, as will any plugged air inlets.

Have you changed any of your flight techniques? Are you remembering to always face the plane into the wind during runup? Shifting too quickly from cruise to idle during descent could also be preventing the engine from cooling properly. Shutting down the engine too quickly at the end of the flight could also be part of the problem.

LUBRICATING SYSTEM

Problems with the lubricating system could appear to be a problem with the engine because insufficient oil can result in an overheated engine. A serious, fast leak might show up first through unusual engine noise.

As mentioned earlier, low oil pressure could be simply the result of low oil level. It could also be that you are using the wrong grade oil. Compare what was last put in with the manufacturer's recommendations. Check the condition of the oil filter. A clogged filter could be the source of high oil temperature or reduced pressure.

FUEL SYSTEM

Checking the fuel for contamination before each flight will quickly alert you to one of the most common causes of problems in the fuel system. If you detect bad fuel, drain the tanks and refill with fresh fuel. Machines need to run fairly regularly to be in tiptop shape. If the plane hasn't been flown in a while, it's a good idea to drain the fuel and start fresh.

Failure of the engine to start or keep running could be as a result of failure in the fuel system. Clogged lines or an inoperative fuel pump might be the culprit. You can change the lines, but you must visit an A&P for the fuel pump.

TURBOCHARGER

Note readings of instruments and gauges such as the altimeter, CHT, and EGT. You might want to add the cowl flap position as well. Complete failure of the turbocharger will be reflected in a sudden loss of manifold pressure, so make a note of that reading, also. Often, turbocharger problems are related to oil, so also tell the mechanic what oil you use and when it was last changed.

Describe what the turbocharger is doing that you think it shouldn't be doing. It might be surging, bootstrapping, slowing, or losing and gaining power. The more you can tell the mechanic, the quicker—and perhaps, cheaper—he or she can fix the problem.

Clogged air inlets and gas leaks in the exhaust manifold or the turbine inlet could affect the operation of the turbocharger, so start by checking these areas. While you're checking, watch for any indication of leaks, bad gaskets and loose or deteriorated connections. Start with the induction side, then move to the exhaust side, including the cylinder exhaust stacks. Inspect oil lines for damage, kinks, or pinches. Occasionally the overboost relief valve gets gunked up with foreign matter, causing it to stay ever-so-slightly open and resulting in a reduced critical altitude. Check the crankcase breather to be sure it is also operational.

If you have not identified the problem so far, it might be with the wastegate or the turbo itself. Diagnosing these problems requires removing the turbo and partially disassembling it. The cure is overhaul or replacement, so it's best to leave this to your mechanic.

If you are flying at the time of the failure, fly as though you have a normally aspirated engine. Keep a close eye on the instruments, and if anything starts to look out of place, land at the next airport and have the system checked.

ELECTRICAL SYSTEM

Failures in the electrical system are very difficult to locate, even for the most experienced mechanic. There are a few things you can check before going to the repair station, however.

Check to make sure the master switch was not inadvertently turned off. If the gauges indicate the battery is not charging, first be sure all connections are tight at the battery and that they are free of corrosion. Also check the alternator belt for cracks or looseness. And we're sure you also checked to be sure the light bulbs were good.

Broken wires can cause problems, of course, as can wires that are rubbing together, but finding these problems might involve more extensive disassembly than you are permitted to do. Even if you locate the problem, you'll have to have a mechanic fix it, but locating it first can save you some money. Anything you can tell the mechanic to help isolate the problem will help. An unexplained dimming of lights or the smell of something burning should be reported.

HYDRAULICS

Reduced pressure in the hydraulic lines could be as simple to resolve as topping up the fluid level. Check the reservoir to make sure it's full. If a leak in the lines is the source of the problem, you might very well see indications of the leak during your preflight. Any sign of hydraulic fluid—or any other fluid, for that matter—should be investigated prior to flight.

Reduced hydraulic pressure can also be caused by trouble with the pump. This is a job for your mechanic. Air might have gotten into the lines, causing the brakes to feel spongy when you apply them, or causing a bouncing needle on the gauge. The problem can be easily resolved by bleeding the lines. This also is a job for your mechanic.

If you recently had the fluid changed, there is also a chance that the wrong replacement fluid was used. This will show up as the system overheating or simply ceasing to function. And if the fluid hasn't been changed in a while, it could be dirty. Changing it might clear up the problem.

PNEUMATICS

Clogged filters, leaks in hoses, or loose components can cause problems with the pneumatics of your plane. Most of this system is not accessible without substantial disassembly, so it's best left to the mechanic. But do note conditions under which the failure occurs, i.e., as engine rpm changes, etc. If you find you need to have the pump changed often, bring this to your mechanic's attention so it can be checked out further.

INSTRUMENTS

Excessive drift in the heading instruments or slow response to changes in attitude during flight indicates a problem with the gyro system. Most often, it is a failure of the bearings as a result of friction. All gyro instruments make a whining sound as they slow down after shutdown. Bearing failure will manifest itself by a loud whine in the gyros after the engine is shutdown. Another indication of worn bearings is a quick spooldown. If you shutdown the airplane and less than a minute later your gyros are quiet, expect to replace or overhaul them in the near future.

The instruments will also either fail to operate or operate incorrectly if power is not getting to them. This could be caused by blockage of the venturi, leaking lines or fittings, dirty filters, or an inoperative pump.

Inspect instruments for secure mounting, broken or loose knobs, bent or missing pointers, and improper operation. Apply power and check for excessive mechanical noise, erratic or intermittent operation, failure to indicate, sluggishness, or indication of excessive friction. Check that warmup time is not excessive and caging functions are normal. Warning flags, indicating lights, and test circuits must be operable.

During engine runup, look to see if instruments are indicating normally and are not affected by engine rpm. Periodically check tubing connections and airframe mounts for security and condition. Inspect pneumatic tubing for leaks, corrosion, erosion, cracks, bends, and pinching, as well as any evidence of chafing. Make sure all instrument lights are working and controls are operational. As much as possible without disassembly, check fuses, fuse clips, and connections for security and corrosion or dirt. Wires should have no bends, chafing, excessive tension, improper support, or broken lacing and ties. Indications of overheating or contamination of foreign matter should be brought to the attention of the avionics shop. Check ventilation openings to be sure they are open and free of dirt and bugs.

SHOCK STRUTS

Problems with the struts will manifest themselves readily as a bumpy ride or insufficient shock absorption when you touch down. Another indication is if the plane is sitting askew or too low when on the ground. It could be tipped to one side or trying to get its nose on the ground. Most problems are an indication that either the air or fluid is low.

First, how much of the shock strut is exposed? We're talking here about the part of the strut that slides inside the outer tube. Is the strut inflated properly? Some manufacturers will give a dimension for strut extended with the aircraft on the ground, while others will give a pressure for the air or nitrogen in the strut with the aircraft on jacks. Insufficient pressure will allow the strut to "bottom out" and allow internal parts to come in contact with each other, resulting in damaged or broken pieces. Overextended struts result in less shock dampening. Damage can occur not only to parts of the landing gear, but also to parts of the airframe.

There is a way of determining which needs to be replenished. If you can, take hold of something on the low side of the plane, raise it, and let go. If it rides to the ground rather smoothly while the strut returns to its compressed position, you need air. Most of the time, its air has leaked out due to such causes as changes in the seasons and minor leaks past O-rings or valve stems. This is normal and you just need to give the struts a little shot of air or nitrogen. If it bounces around as it returns to the compressed position, you need fluid.

After you replenish whichever one is needed, you would be well advised to try to find out what caused the shortage. Leaking fluid will have left a trail wherever it is leaking, so that should be pretty easy to isolate. A common place for this leak to occur is at the O-ring sealing between the inner and outer tubes of the shock strut. Dirt will get between the strut and the O-ring, damaging it, and allowing the fluid to leak past. If the damage to the O-ring is severe enough, the air under pressure will blow the fluid out all over the strut and wheel. The pressure will go to nothing also resulting in a totally collapsed strut. Fixing this requires an overhaul of the strut, which is usually a simple replacement of all O-rings and seals. This is another job for your mechanic. If the leak is internal, though, it won't be noticeable by this type of inspection. Open the air valve. If fluid and/or foam spray out, you can be pretty sure the leak is inside. This also requires an overhaul of the strut.

Air leaks aren't as simple to track down since they don't leave any telltale signs behind. Slow air leaks are even more aggravating to try to locate. The only practical solution is to add air and see if the low-strut condition returns.

If you have been flying off dirt strips, the problem with the struts might just be an accumulation of dirt inside, which prevents the hydraulic fluid from moving back and forth between the chambers. The solution is to drain the fluid, clean the chambers, and put in all new fluid. If you haven't been in dirty locations, you might have some mechanical failure, and you need to see your mechanic. There might be a lack of lubrication, overtightened bolts, or some other situation that requires identifying and repairing.

A

AIM/FAR Part 43— Maintenance, preventive maintenance, rebuilding, and alteration

Appendix A—Major alterations, major repairs, and preventive maintenance

Appendix B—Recording of major repairs and major alterations

Appendix C—[Reserved]

Appendix D—Scope and detail of items (as applicable to the particular aircraft) to be included in annual and 100-hour inspections

Appendix E—Altimeter system test and inspection

Appendix F—ATC transponder tests and inspections

Source: Docket No. 1993 (29 FR 5451, 4/23/64) effective 7/6/64 unless otherwise noted.

§ 43.1 Applicability.

(a) Except as provided in paragraph (b) of this section, this part prescribes rules governing the maintenance, preventive maintenance, rebuilding, and alteration of any—

(1) Aircraft having a U.S. airworthiness certificate;

(2) Foreign-registered civil aircraft used in common carriage or carriage of mail under the provisions of Part 121, 127, or 135 of this chapter; and

(3) Airframe, aircraft engines, propellers, appliances, and component parts of such aircraft.

(b) This part does not apply to any aircraft for which an experimental airworthiness certificate has been issued, unless a different kind of airworthiness certificate had previously been issued for that aircraft.

(Amdt. 43-23, Eff. 10/15/82)

§ 43.2 Records of overhaul and rebuilding.

(a) No person may describe in any required maintenance entry or form an aircraft, airframe, aircraft engine, propeller, appliance, or component part as being overhauled unless—

(1) Using methods, techniques, and practices acceptable to the Administrator, it has been disassembled, cleaned, inspected, repaired as necessary, and reassembled; and

(2) It has been tested in accordance with approved standards and technical data, or in accordance with current standards and technical data acceptable to the Administrator, which have been developed and documented by the holder of the type certificate, supplemental type certificate, or a material, part, process, or appliance approval under § 21.305 of this chapter.

(b) No person may describe in any required maintenance entry or form an aircraft, airframe, aircraft engine, propeller, appliance, or component part as being rebuilt unless it has been disassembled, cleaned, inspected, repaired as necessary, reassembled, and tested to the same tolerances and limits as a new item, using either new parts or used parts that either conform to new part tolerances and limits or to approved oversized or undersized dimensions.

Docket No. 21071 (47 FR 41076, 9/16/82)
(Amdt. 43-23, Eff. 10/15/82)

§ 43.3 Persons authorized to perform maintenance, preventive maintenance, rebuilding, and alterations.

(a) Except as provided in this section and § 43.17, no person may maintain, rebuild, alter, or perform preventive maintenance on an aircraft, airframe, aircraft engine, propeller, appliance, or component part to which this part applies. Those items, the performance of which is a major alteration, a major repair, or preventive maintenance, are listed in Appendix A.

(b) The holder of a mechanic certificate may perform maintenance, preventive maintenance, and alterations as provided in Part 65 of this chapter.

(c) The holder of a repairman certificate may perform maintenance and preventive maintenance as provided in Part 65 of this chapter.

(d) A person working under the supervision of a holder of a mechanic or repairman certificate may perform the maintenance, preventive maintenance, and alterations that his supervisor is authorized to perform, if the supervisor personally observes the work being done to the extent necessary to ensure that it is being done properly and if the supervisor is readily available, in person, for consultation. However, this paragraph does not authorize the performance of any inspection required by Part 91 or Part 125 of this chapter or any inspection performed after a major repair or alteration.

(e) The holder of a repair station certificate may perform maintenance, preventive maintenance, and alterations as provided in Part 145 of this chapter.

(f) The holder of an air carrier operating certificate or an operating certificate issued under Part 121, 127, or 135, may perform maintenance, preventive maintenance, and alterations as provided in Part 121, 127, or 135.

(g) The holder of a pilot certificate issued under Part 61 may perform preventive maintenance on any aircraft owned or operated by that pilot which is not used under Part 121, 127, 129, or 135.

(h) Notwithstanding the provisions of paragraph (g) of this section, the Administrator may approve a certificate holder under Part 135 of this chapter, operating rotorcraft in a remote area, to allow a pilot to perform specific preventive maintenance items provided—

(1) The items of preventive maintenance are a result of a known or suspected mechanical difficulty or malfunction that occurred en route to or in a remote area;

(2) The pilot has satisfactorily completed an approved training program and is authorized in writing by the certificate holder for each item of preventive maintenance that the pilot is authorized to perform;

(3) There is no certificated mechanic available to perform preventive maintenance;

(4) The certificate holder has procedures to evaluate the accomplishment of a preventive maintenance item that requires a decision concerning the airworthiness of the rotorcraft; and

(5) The items of preventive maintenance authorized by this section are those listed in paragraph (c) of Appendix A of this part.

(i) A manufacturer may—

(1) Rebuild or alter any aircraft, aircraft engine, propeller, or appliance manufactured by him under a type or production certificate;

(2) Rebuild or alter any appliance or part of aircraft, aircraft engines, propellers, or appliances manufactured by him under a Technical Standard Order Authorization, an FAA-Parts Manufacturer Approval, or Product and Process Specification issued by the Administrator; and

(3) Perform any inspection required by Part 91 or Part 125 of this chapter on aircraft it manufactures, while currently operating under a production certificate or under a currently approved production inspection system for such aircraft.

(Amdt. 43-3, Eff. 4/2/66); (Amdt. 43-4, Eff. 10/1/66); (Amdt. 43-12, Eff. 11/15/69); (Amdt. 43-23, Eff. 10/15/82); (Amdt. 43-25, Eff. 1/6/87)

§ 43.5 Approval for return to service after maintenance, preventive maintenance, rebuilding, or alteration.

No person may approve for return to service any aircraft, airframe, aircraft engine, propeller, or appliance, that has undergone maintenance, preventive maintenance, rebuilding, or alteration unless—

(a) The maintenance record entry required by § 43.9 or § 43.11, as appropriate, has been made;

(b) The repair or alteration form authorized by or furnished by the Administrator has been executed in a manner prescribed by the Administrator; and

(c) If a repair or an alteration results in any change in the aircraft operating limitations or flight data contained in the approved aircraft flight manual, those operating limitations or flight data are appropriately revised and set forth as prescribed in § 91.9 of this chapter.

(Amdt. 43-23, Eff. 10/15/82); (Amdt. 43-31, Eff. 8/18/90)

§ 43.7 Persons authorized to approve aircraft, airframes, aircraft engines, propellers, appliances, or component parts for return to service after maintenance, preventive maintenance, rebuilding, or alteration.

(a) Except as provided in this section and § 43.17, no person, other than the Administrator, may approve an aircraft, airframe, aircraft engine, propeller, appliance, or component part for return to service after it has undergone maintenance, preventive maintenance, rebuilding, or alteration.

(b) The holder of a mechanic certificate or an inspection authorization may approve an aircraft, airframe, aircraft engine, propeller, appliance, or component part for return to service as provided in Part 65 of this chapter.

(c) The holder of a repair station certificate may approve an aircraft, airframe, aircraft engine, propeller, appliance, or component part for return to service as provided in Part 145 of this chapter.

(d) A manufacturer may approve for return to service any aircraft, airframe, aircraft engine, propeller, appliance, or component part which that manufacturer has worked on under § 43.3(h). However, except for minor alterations, the work must have been done in accordance with technical data approved by the Administrator.

(e) The holder of an air carrier operating certificate or an operating certificate issued under Part 121, 127, or 135, may approve an aircraft, airframe, aircraft engine, propeller, appliance, or component part for return to service as provided in Part 121, 127, or 135 of this chapter, as applicable.

(f) A person holding at least a private pilot certificate may approve an aircraft for return to service after performing preventive maintenance under the provisions of § 43.3(g).

(Amdt. 43-6, Eff. 7/6/66); (Amdt. 43-12, Eff. 11/15/69); (Amdt. 43-23, Eff. 10/15/82)

§ 43.9 Content, form, and disposition of maintenance, preventive maintenance, rebuilding, and alteration records (except inspections performed in accordance with Part 91, Part 123, Part 125, § 135.411(a)(1), and § 135.419 of this chapter).

(a) *Maintenance record entries.* Except as provided in paragraphs (b) and (c) of this section, each person who maintains, performs preventive maintenance, rebuilds, or alters an aircraft, airframe, aircraft engine, propeller, appliance, or component part shall make an entry in the maintenance record of that equipment containing the following information:

(1) A description (or reference to data acceptable to the Administrator) of work performed.

(2) The date of completion of the work performed.

(3) The name of the person performing the work if other than the person specified in paragraph (a)(4) of this section.

(4) If the work performed on the aircraft, airframe, aircraft engine, propeller, appliance, or component part has been performed satisfactorily, the signature, certificate number, and kind of certificate held by the person approving the work. The signature constitutes the approval for return to service only for the work performed.

In addition to the entry required by this paragraph, major repairs and major alterations shall be entered on a form, and the form disposed of, in the manner prescribed in Appendix B, by the person performing the work.

(b) Each holder of an air carrier operating certificate or an operating certificate issued under Part 121, 127, or 135, that is required by its approved operations specifications to provide for a continuous airworthiness maintenance program, shall make a record of the maintenance, preventive maintenance, rebuilding, and alteration, on aircraft, airframes, aircraft engines, propellers, appliances, or component parts which it operates in accordance with the applicable provisions of Part 121, 127, or 135 of this chapter, as appropriate.

(c) This section does not apply to persons performing inspections in accordance with Part 91, 123, 125, § 135.411(a)(1), or § 135.419 of this chapter.

(Amdt. 43-1, Eff. 4/1/65); (Amdt. 43-3, Eff. 4/2/66); (Amdt. 43-11, Eff. 10/16/69); (Amdt. 43-15, Eff. 10/23/72); (Amdt. 43-16, Eff. 9/8/72); (Amdt. 43-23, Eff. 10/15/82)

§ 43.11 Content, form, and disposition of records for inspections conducted under Parts 91 and 125 and §§ 135.411(a)(1) and 135.419 of this chapter.

(a) *Maintenance record entries.* The person approving or disapproving for return to service an aircraft, airframe, aircraft engine, propeller, appliance, or component part after any inspection performed in accordance with Part 91, 123, 125, § 135.411(a)(1), or § 135.419 shall make an entry in the maintenance record of that equipment containing the following information:

(1) The type of inspection and a brief description of the extent of the inspection.

(2) The date of the inspection and aircraft total time in service.

(3) The signature, the certificate number, and kind of certificate held by the person approving or disapproving for return to service the aircraft, airframe, aircraft engine, propeller, appliance, component part, or portions thereof.

(4) Except for progressive inspections, if the aircraft is found to be airworthy and approved for return to service, the following or a similarly worded statement—"I certify that this aircraft has been inspected in accordance with (insert type) inspection and was determined to be in airworthy condition."

(5) Except for progressive inspections, if the aircraft is not approved for return to service because of needed maintenance, noncompliance with applicable specifications, airworthiness directives, or other approved data, the following or a similarly worded statement—"I certify that this aircraft has been inspected in accordance with (insert type) inspection and a list of discrepancies and unairworthy items dated (date) has been provided for the aircraft owner or operator."

(6) For progressive inspections, the following or a similarly worded statement—"I certify that in accordance with a progressive inspection program, a routine inspection of (identify whether aircraft or components) and a detailed inspection of (identify components) were performed and the (aircraft or components) are (approved or disapproved) for return to service." If disapproved, the entry will further state "and a list of discrepancies and unairworthy items dated (date) has been provided to the aircraft owner or operator."

(7) If an inspection is conducted under an inspection program provided for in Part 91, 123, 125, or § 135.411(a)(1), the entry must identify the inspection program, that part of the inspection program accomplished, and contain a statement that the inspection was performed in accordance with the inspections and procedures for that particular program.

(b) *Listing of discrepancies and placards.* If the person performing any inspection required by Part 91 or 125 or § 135.411(a)(1) of this chapter finds that the aircraft is unairworthy or does not meet the applicable type certificate data, airworthiness directives, or other approved data upon which its airworthiness depends, that person must give the owner or lessee a signed and dated list of those discrepancies. For those items permitted to be inoperative under § 91.30(d)(2), that person shall place a placard, that meets the aircraft's airworthiness certification regulations, on each inoperative instrument and the cockpit control of each item of inoperative equipment, marking it "Inoperative," and shall add the items to the signed and dated list of discrepancies given to the owner or lessee.

(Amdt. 43-3, Eff. 4/2/66); (Amdt. 43-13, Eff. 6/15/70); (Amdt. 43-16, Eff. 9/8/72); (Amdt. 43-23, Eff. 10/15/82); (Amdt. 43-30, Eff. 12/13/88)

§ 43.12 Maintenance records: Falsification, reproduction, or alteration.

(a) No person may make or cause to be made:

(1) Any fraudulent or intentionally false entry in any record or report that is required to be made, kept, or used to show compliance with any requirement under this part;

(2) Any reproduction, for fraudulent purpose, of any record or report under this part; or

(3) Any alteration, for fraudulent purpose, of any record or report under this part.

(b) The commission by any person of an act prohibited under paragraph (a) of this section is a basis for suspending or revoking the applicable airman, operator, or production certificate, Technical Standard Order Authorization, FAA-Parts Manufacturer Approval, or Product and Process Specification issued by the Administrator and held by that person.

Docket No. 16383 (43 FR 22636)

(Amdt. 43-19, Eff. 6/26/78); (Amdt. 43-23, Eff. 10/15/82)

§ 43.13 Performance rules (general).

(a) Each person performing maintenance, alteration, or preventive maintenance on an aircraft, engine, propeller, or appliance shall use the methods, techniques, and practices prescribed in the current manufacturer's maintenance manual or Instructions for Continued Airworthiness prepared by its manufacturer, or other methods, techniques, and practices acceptable to the Administrator, except as noted in § 43.16. He shall use the tools, equipment, and test apparatus necessary to assure completion of the work in accordance with accepted industry practices. If special equipment or test apparatus is recommended by the manufacturer involved, he must use that equipment or apparatus or its equivalent acceptable to the Administrator.

(b) Each person maintaining or altering, or performing preventive maintenance, shall do that work in such a manner and use materials of such a quality, that the condition of the aircraft, airframe, aircraft engine, propeller, or appliance worked on will be at least equal to its original or properly altered condition (with regard to aerodynamic function, structural strength, resistance to vibration and deterioration, and other qualities affecting airworthiness).

(c) *Special provisions for holders of air carrier operating certificates and operating certificates issued under the provisions of Part 121, 127, or 135 and Part 129 operators holding operations specifications.* Unless otherwise notified by the administrator, the methods, techniques, and practices contained in the maintenance manual or the maintenance part of the manual of the holder of an air carrier operating certificate or an operating certificate under Part 121, 127, or 135 and Part 129 operators holding operations specifications (that is required by its operating specifications to provide a continuous airworthiness maintenance and inspection program) constitute acceptable means of compliance with this section.

(Amdt. 43-15, Eff. 10/23/72); (Amdt. 43-20, Eff. 10/14/80); (Amdt. 43-23, Eff. 10/15/82); (Amdt. 43-28, Eff. 8/25/87)

§ 43.15 Additional performance rules for inspections.

(a) *General.* Each person performing an inspection required by Part 91, 123, 125, or 135 of this chapter, shall—

(1) Perform the inspection so as to determine whether the aircraft, or portion(s) thereof under inspection, meets all applicable airworthiness requirements; and

(2) If the inspection is one provided for in Part 123, 125, 135, or § 91.409(e) of this chapter, perform the inspection in accordance with the instructions and procedures set forth in the inspection program for the aircraft being inspected.

(b) *Rotorcraft.* Each person performing an inspection required by Part 91 on a rotorcraft shall inspect the following systems in accordance with the maintenance manual or Instructions for Continued Airworthiness of the manufacturer concerned:

(1) The drive shafts or similar systems.

(2) The main rotor transmission gear box for obvious defects.

(3) The main rotor and center section (or the equivalent area).

(4) The auxiliary rotor on helicopters.

(c) *Annual and 100-hour inspections.* (1) Each person performing an annual or 100-hour inspection shall use a checklist while performing the inspection. The checklist may be of the person's own design, one provided by the manufacturer of the equipment being inspected or one obtained from another source. This checklist must include the scope and detail of the items contained in Appendix D to this part and paragraph (b) of this section.

(2) Each person approving a reciprocating-engine-powered aircraft for return to service after an annual or 100-hour inspection shall, before that approval, run the aircraft engine or engines to determine satisfactory performance in accordance with the manufacturer's recommendations of—

(i) Power output (static and idle r.p.m.);

(ii) Magnetos;

(iii) Fuel and oil pressure; and

(iv) Cylinder and oil temperature.

(3) Each person approving a turbine-engine-powered aircraft for return to service after an annual, 100-hour, or progressive inspection shall, before that approval, run the aircraft engine or engines to determine satisfactory performance in accordance with the manufacturer's recommendations.

(d) *Progressive inspection.* (1) Each person performing a progressive inspection shall, at the start of a progressive inspection system, inspect the aircraft completely. After this initial inspection, routine and detailed inspections must be conducted as prescribed in the progressive inspection schedule. Routine inspections consist of visual examination or check of the appliances, the aircraft, and its components and systems, insofar as practicable without disassembly. Detailed inspections consist of a thorough examination of the appliances, the aircraft, and its components and systems, with such disassembly as is necessary. For the purposes of this subparagraph, the overhaul of a component or system is considered to be a detailed inspection.

(2) If the aircraft is away from the station where inspections are normally conducted, an appropriately rated mechanic, a certificated repair station, or the manufacturer of the aircraft may perform inspections in accordance with the procedures and using the forms of the person who would otherwise perform the inspection.

(Amdt. 43-3, Eff. 4/2/66); (Amdt. 43-8, Eff. 10/14/68); (Amdt. 43-21, Eff. 2/1/81); (Amdt. 43-22, Eff. 4/1/81); (Amdt. 43-22A, Eff. 2/3/81); (Amdt. 43-23, Eff. 10/15/82); (Amdt. 43-25, Eff. 1/6/87); (Amdt. 43-31, Eff. 8/18/90)

§ 43.16 Airworthiness limitations.

Each person performing an inspection or other maintenance specified in an Airworthiness Limitations section of a manufacturer's maintenance manual or Instructions for Continued Airworthiness shall perform the inspection or other maintenance in accordance with that section, or in accordance with operations specifications approved by the Administrator under Parts 121, 123, 127, or 135, or an inspection program approved under § 91.409(e).

Docket No. 8444 (33 FR 14104, 9/18/68)

(Amdt. 43-9, Eff. 10/17/68); (Amdt. 43-20, Eff. 10/14/80); (Amdt. 43-23, Eff. 10/15/82); (Amdt. 43-31, Eff. 8/18/90)

§ 43.17 [Maintenance, preventive maintenance, and alterations performed on U.S. aeronautical products by certain Canadian persons.

[(a) *Definitions.* For purposes of this section:

[Aeronautical product means any civil aircraft or airframe, aircraft engine, propeller, appliance, component, or part to be installed thereon.

[Canadian aeronautical product means any civil aircraft or airframe, aircraft engine, propeller, or appliance under airworthiness regulation by the Canadian Department of Transport, or component or part to be installed thereon.

[U.S. aeronautical product means any civil aircraft or airframe, aircraft engine, propeller, or appliance under airworthiness regulation by the FAA or component or part to be installed thereon.

[(b) *Applicability.* This section does not apply to any U.S. aeronautical products maintained or altered under any bilateral agreement made between Canada and any other than the United States.

[(c) *Authorized persons.*

[(1) A person holding a valid Canadian Department of Transport license (Aircraft Maintenance Engineer) and appropriate ratings may, with respect to a U.S.-registered aircraft located in Canada, perform maintenance, preventive maintenance, and alterations in accordance with the requirements of paragraph (d) of this section and approve the affected aircraft for return to service in accordance with the requirements of paragraph (e) of this section.

[(2) A company (Approved Maintenance Organization) (AMO) whose system of quality control for the maintenance, alteration, and inspection of aeronautical products has been approved by the Canadian Department of Transport, or a person who is an authorized employee performing work for such a company may, with respect to a U.S.-registered aircraft located in Canada or other U.S. aeronautical products transported to Canada from the United States, perform maintenance, preventive maintenance, and alterations in accordance with the requirements of paragraph (d) of this section and approve the affected products for return to service in accordance with the requirements of paragraph (e) of this section.

[(d) *Performance requirements.* A person authorized in paragraph (c) of this section may perform maintenance (including any inspection required by § 91.409 of this chapter, except an annual inspection), preventive maintenance, and alterations, provided:

[(1) The person performing the work is authorized by the Canadian Department of Transport to perform the same type of work respect to Canadian aeronautical products;

[(2) The work is performed in accordance with §§ 43.13, 43.15, 43.16 of this chapter, as applicable;

[(3) The work is performed such that the affected product complies with the applicable requirements of Part 36 of this chapter; and

[(4) The work is recorded in accordance with §§ 43.2(a), 43.9, and 43.11 of this chapter, as applicable.

[(e) *Approval requirements.*

[(1) To return an affected product to service, a person authorized in paragraph (c) of this section must approve (certify) maintenance, preventive maintenance, and alterations performed under this section, except that an Aircraft Maintenance Engineer may not approve a major repair or major alteration.

[(2) An AMO whose system of quality control for the maintenance, preventive maintenance, alteration, and inspection of aeronautical products has been approved by the Canadian Department of Transport, or an authorized employee performing work for such an AMO, may approve (certify) a major repair or major alteration performed under this section if the work was performed in accordance with technical data approved by the Administrator.

[(f) No person may operate in air commerce an aircraft, airframe, aircraft engine, propeller, or appliance on which maintenance, preventive maintenance, or alteration has been performed under this section unless it has been approved for return to service by a person authorized in this section.]

Docket No. 6992 (31 FR 5948, 4/19/66)

(Amdt. 43-5, Eff. 5/2/66); (Amdt. 43-10, Eff. 11/29/68); (Amdt. 43-23, Eff. 10/15/82); (Amdt. 43-31, Eff. 8/18/90); [(Amdt. 43-33, Eff. 2/10/92)]

APPENDIX A—MAJOR ALTERATIONS, MAJOR REPAIRS, AND PREVENTIVE MAINTENANCE

(a) *Major alterations—(1) Airframe major alterations.* Alterations of the following parts and alterations of the following types, when not listed in the aircraft specifications issued by the FAA, are airframe major alterations:

(i) Wings.

(ii) Tail surfaces.

(iii) Fuselage.

(iv) Engine mounts.

(v) Control system.

(vi) Landing gear.

(vii) Hull or floats.

(viii) Elements of an airframe including spars, ribs, fittings, shock absorbers, bracing, cowling, fairings, and balance weights.

(ix) Hydraulic and electrical actuating system of components.

(x) Rotor blades.

(xi) Changes to the empty weight or empty balance which result in an increase in the maximum certificated weight or center of gravity limits of the aircraft.

(xii) Changes to the basic design of the fuel, oil, cooling, heating, cabin pressurization, electrical, hydraulic, de-icing, or exhaust systems.

(xiii) Changes to the wing or to fixed or movable control surfaces which affect flutter and vibration characteristics.

(2) *Powerplant major alterations.* The following alterations of a powerplant when not listed in the engine specifications issued by the FAA, are powerplant major alterations.

(i) Conversion of an aircraft engine from one approved model to another, involving any changes in compression ratio, propeller reduction gear, impeller gear ratios or the substitution of major engine parts which requires extensive rework and testing of the engine.

(ii) Changes to the engine by replacing aircraft engine structural parts with parts not supplied by the original manufacturer or parts not specifically approved by the Administrator.

(iii) Installation of an accessory which is not approved for the engine.

(iv) Removal of accessories that are listed as required equipment on the aircraft or engine specification.

(v) Installation of structural parts other than the type of parts approved for the installation.

(vi) Conversions of any sort for the purpose of using fuel of a rating or grade other than that listed in the engine specifications.

(3) *Propeller major alterations.* The following alterations of a propeller when not authorized in the propeller specifications issued by the FAA are propeller major alterations:

(i) Changes in blade design.

(ii) Changes in hub design.

(iii) Changes in the governor or control design.

(iv) Installation of a propeller governor or feathering system.

(v) Installation of propeller de-icing system.

(vi) Installation of parts not approved for the propeller.

(4) *Appliance major alterations.* Alterations of the basic design not made in accordance with recommendations of the appliance manufacturer or in accordance with

an FAA Airworthiness Directive are appliance major alterations. In addition, changes in the basic design of radio communication and navigation equipment approved under type certification or a Technical Standard Order that have an effect on frequency stability, noise level, sensitivity, selectivity, distortion, spurious radiation, AVC characteristics, or ability to meet environmental test conditions and other changes that have an effect on the performance of the equipment are also major alterations.

(b) *Major repairs—(1) Airframe major repairs.* Repairs to the following parts of an airframe and repairs of the following types, involving the strengthening, reinforcing, splicing, and manufacturing of primary structural members or their replacement, when replacement is by fabrication such as riveting or welding, are airframe major repairs.

(i) Box beams.

(ii) Monocoque or semimonocoque wings or control surfaces.

(iii) Wing stringers or chord members.

(iv) Spars.

(v) Spar flanges.

(vi) Members of truss-type beams.

(vii) Thin sheet webs of beams.

(viii) Keel and chine members of boat hulls or floats.

(ix) Corrugated sheet compression members which act as flange material of wings or tail surfaces.

(x) Wing main ribs and compression members.

(xi) Wing or tail surface brace struts.

(xii) Engine mounts.

(xiii) Fuselage longerons.

(xiv) Members of the side truss, horizontal truss, or bulkheads.

(xv) Main seat support braces and brackets.

(xvi) Landing gear brace struts.

(xvii) Axles.

(xviii) Wheels.

(xix) Skis, and ski pedestals.

(xx) Parts of the control system such as control columns, pedals, shafts, brackets, or horns.

(xxi) Repairs involving the substitution of material.

(xxii) The repair of damaged areas in metal or plywood stressed covering exceeding six inches in any direction.

(xxiii) The repair of portions of skin sheets by making additional seams.

(xxiv) The splicing of skin sheets.

(xxv) The repair of three or more adjacent wing or control surface ribs or the leading edge of wings and control surfaces, between such adjacent ribs.

(xxvi) Repair of fabric covering involving an area greater than that required to repair two adjacent ribs.

(xxvii) Replacement of fabric on fabric covered parts such as wings, fuselages, stabilizers, and control surfaces.

(xxviii) Repairing, including rebottoming, of removable or integral fuel tanks and oil tanks.

(2) *Powerplant major repairs.* Repairs of the following parts of an engine and repairs of the following types, are powerplant major repairs:

(i) Separation or disassembly of a crankcase or crankshaft of a reciprocating engine equipped with an integral supercharger.

(ii) Separation or disassembly of a crankcase or crankshaft of a reciprocating engine equipped with other than spur-type propeller reduction gearing.

(iii) Special repairs to structural engine parts by welding, plating, metalizing, or other methods.

(3) *Propeller major repairs.* Repairs of the following types to a propeller are propeller major repairs:

(i) Any repairs to, or straightening of steel blades.

(ii) Repairing or machining of steel hubs.

(iii) Shortening of blades.

(iv) Retipping of wood propellers.

(v) Replacement of outer laminations on fixed pitch wood propellers.

(vi) Repairing elongated bolt holes in the hub of fixed pitch wood propellers.

(vii) Inlay work on wood blades.

(viii) Repairs to composition blades.

(ix) Replacement of tip fabric.

(x) Replacement of plastic covering.

(xi) Repair of propeller governors.

(xii) Overhaul of controllable pitch propellers.

(xiii) Repairs to deep dents, cuts, scars, nicks, etc., and straightening of aluminum blades.

(xiv) The repair or replacement of internal elements of blades.

(4) *Appliance major repairs.* Repairs of the following types to appliances are appliance major repairs:

(i) Calibration and repair of instruments.

(ii) Calibration of radio equipment.

(iii) Rewinding the field coil of an electrical accessory.

(iv) Complete disassembly of complex hydraulic power valves.

(v) Overhaul of pressure type carburetors, and pressure type fuel, oil and hydraulic pumps.

(c) *Preventive maintenance.* Preventive maintenance is limited to the following work, provided it does not involve complex assembly operations: (1) Removal, installation, and repair of landing gear tires.

(2) Replacing elastic shock absorber cords on landing gear.

(3) Servicing landing gear shock struts by adding oil, air, or both.

(4) Servicing landing gear wheel bearings, such as cleaning and greasing.

(5) Replacing defective safety wiring or cotter keys.

(6) Lubrication not requiring disassembly other than removal of nonstructural items such as cover plates, cowlings, and fairings.

(7) Making simple fabric patches not requiring rib stitching or the removal of structural parts or control surfaces. In the case of balloons, the making of small fabric repairs to envelopes (as defined in, and in accordance with, the balloon manufacturers' instructions) not requiring load tape repair or replacement.

(8) Replenishing hydraulic fluid in the hydraulic reservoir.

(9) Refinishing decorative coating of fuselage, balloon baskets, wings tail group surfaces (excluding balanced control surfaces), fairings, cowlings, landing gear, cabin, or cockpit interior when removal or disassembly of any primary structure or operating system is not required.

(10) Applying preservative or protective material to components where no disassembly of any primary structure or operating system is involved and where such coating is not prohibited or is not contrary to good practices.

(11) Repairing upholstery and decorative furnishings of the cabin, cockpit, or balloon basket interior when the repairing does not require disassembly of any primary structure or operating system or interfere with an operating system or affect the primary structure of the aircraft.

(12) Making small simple repairs to fairings, nonstructural cover plates, cowlings, and small patches and reinforcements not changing the contour so as to interfere with proper air flow.

(13) Replacing side windows where that work does not interfere with the structure or any operating system such as controls, electrical equipment, etc.

(14) Replacing safety belts.

(15) Replacing seats or seat parts with replacement parts approved for the aircraft, not involving disassembly of any primary structure or operating system.

(16) Troubleshooting and repairing broken circuits in landing light wiring circuits.

(17) Replacing bulbs, reflectors, and lenses of position and landing lights.

(18) Replacing wheels and skis where no weight and balance computation is involved.

(19) Replacing any cowling not requiring removal of the propeller or disconnection of flight controls.

(20) Replacing or cleaning spark plugs and setting of spark plug gap clearance.

(21) Replacing any hose connection except hydraulic connections.

(22) Replacing prefabricated fuel lines.

(23) Cleaning or replacing fuel and oil strainers or filter elements.

(24) Replacing and servicing batteries.

(25) Cleaning of balloon burner pilot and main nozzles in accordance with the balloon manufacturer's instructions.

(26) Replacement or adjustment of nonstructural standard fasteners incidental to operations.

(27) The interchange of balloon baskets and burners on envelopes when the basket or burner is designated as interchangeable in the balloon type certificate data and the baskets and burners are specifically designed for quick removal and installation.

(28) The installations of anti-misfueling devices to reduce the diameter of fuel tank filler openings provided the specific device has been made a part of the aircraft type certificate data by the aircraft manufacturer, the aircraft manufacturer has provided FAA-approved instructions for installation of the specific device, and installation does not involve the disassembly of the existing tank filler opening.

(29) Removing, checking, and replacing magnetic chip detectors.

[(30) The inspection and maintenance tasks prescribed and specifically identified as preventive maintenance in a primary category aircraft type certificate or supplemental type certificate holder's approved special inspection and preventive maintenance program when accomplished on a primary category aircraft provided:

[(i) They are performed by the holder of at least a private pilot certificate issued under part 61 who is the registered owner (including co-owners) of the affected aircraft and who holds a certificate of competency for the affected aircraft (1) issued by a school approved under § 147.21(f) of this chapter; (2) issued by the holder of the production certificate for that primary category aircraft that has a special training program approved under § 21.24 of this subchapter; or (3) issued by another entity that has a course approved by the Administrator; and

[(ii) The inspections and maintenance tasks are performed in accordance with instructions contained in the special inspection and preventive maintenance program approved as part of the aircraft's type design or supplemental type design.]

(Amdt. 43-14, Eff. 8/18/72); (Amdt. 43-23, Eff. 10/15/82); (Amdt. 43-24, Eff. 11/7/84); (Amdt. 43-25, Eff. 1/6/87); (Amdt. 43-27, Eff. 6/5/87); [(Admt. 43-34, Eff. 12/31/92)]

APPENDIX B—RECORDING OF MAJOR REPAIRS AND MAJOR ALTERATIONS

(a) Except as provided in paragraphs (b), (c), and (d) of this appendix, each person performing a major repair or major alteration shall—

(1) Execute FAA Form 337 at least in duplicate;

(2) Give a signed copy of that form to the aircraft owner; and

(3) Forward a copy of that form to the local Flight Standards District Office within 48 hours after the aircraft, airframe, aircraft engine, propeller, or appliance is approved for return to service.

(b) For major repairs made in accordance with a manual or specifications acceptable to the Administrator, a certificated repair station may, in place of the requirements of paragraph (a)—

(1) Use the customer's work order upon which the repair is recorded;

(2) Give the aircraft owner a signed copy of the work order and retain a duplicate copy for at least two years from the date of approval for return to service of the aircraft, airframe, aircraft engine, propeller, or appliance;

(3) Give the aircraft owner a maintenance release signed by an authorized representative of the repair station and incorporating the following information:

(i) Identity of the aircraft, airframe, aircraft engine, propeller or appliance.

(ii) If an aircraft, the make, model, serial number, nationality and registration marks, and location of the repaired area.

(iii) If an airframe, aircraft engine, propeller, or appliance, give the manufacturer's name, name of the part, model, and serial numbers (if any); and

(4) Include the following or a similarly worded statement—

"The aircraft, airframe, aircraft engine, propeller, or appliance identified above was repaired and inspected in accordance with current Regulations of the Federal Aviation Agency and is approved for return to service.

Pertinent details of the repair are on file at this repair station under Order No._____,

No._____ Date_____

Signed _____ for
     (signature of authorized representative)

_____   _____
     (repair station name)   (certificate number)

_____."
     (address)

(c) For a major repair or major alteration made by a person authorized in § 43.17, the person who performs the major repair or major alteration and the person authorized by § 43.17 to approve that work shall execute an FAA Form 337 at least in duplicate. A completed copy of that form shall be—

(1) Given to the aircraft owner; and

(2) Forwarded to the Federal Aviation Administration, Aircraft Registration Branch, Post Office Box 25082, Oklahoma City, Okla. 73125, within 48 hours after the work is inspected.

(d) For extended-range fuel tanks installed within the passenger compartment or a baggage compartment, the person who performs the work and the person authorized to approve the work by § 43.7 of this part shall execute an FAA Form 337 in at least triplicate. One (1) copy of the FAA Form 337 shall be placed on board the aircraft as specified in § 91.417 of this chapter. The remaining forms shall be distributed as required by paragraph (a) (2) and (3) or (c) (1) and (2) of this paragraph as appropriate.

(Amdt. 43-10, Eff. 11/29/68); (Amdt. 43-29, Eff. 12/8/87); (Amdt. 43-31, Eff. 8/18/90)

APPENDIX C —[RESERVED]

(Amdt. 43-3, Eff. 4/2/66); (Amdt. 43-13, Eff. 6/15/70)

APPENDIX D—SCOPE AND DETAIL OF ITEMS(AS APPLICABLE TO THE PARTICULAR AIRCRAFT) TO BE INCLUDED IN ANNUAL AND 100-HOUR INSPECTIONS

(a) Each person performing an annual or 100-hour inspection shall, before that inspection, remove or open all necessary inspection plates, access doors, fairing, and cowling. He shall thoroughly clean the aircraft and aircraft engine.

(b) Each person performing an annual or 100-hour inspection shall inspect (where applicable) the following components of the fuselage and hull group:

(1) Fabric and skin—for deterioration, distortion, other evidence of failure, and defective or insecure attachment of fittings.

(2) Systems and component—for improper installation, apparent defects, and unsatisfactory operation.

(3) Envelope, gas bags, ballast tanks, and related parts—for poor condition.

(c) Each person performing an annual or 100-hour inspection shall inspect (where applicable) the following components of the cabin and cockpit group:

(1) Generally—for uncleanliness and loose equipment that might foul the controls.

(2) Seats and safety belts—for poor condition and apparent defects.

(3) Windows and windshields—for deterioration and breakage.

(4) Instruments—for poor condition, mounting, marking, and (where practicable) improper operation.

(5) Flight and engine controls—for improper installation and improper operation.

(6) Batteries—for improper installation and improper charge.

(7) All systems—for improper installation, poor general condition, apparent and obvious defects, and insecurity of attachment.

(d) Each person performing an annual or 100-hour inspection shall inspect (where applicable) components of the engine and nacelle group as follows:

(1) Engine section—for visual evidence of excessive oil, fuel, or hydraulic leaks, and sources of such leaks.

(2) Studs and nuts—for improper torquing and obvious defects.

(3) Internal engine—for cylinder compression and for metal particles or foreign matter on screens and sump drain plugs. If there is weak cylinder compression, for improper internal condition and improper internal tolerances.

(4) Engine mount—for cracks, looseness of mounting, and looseness of engine to mount.

(5) Flexible vibration dampeners—for poor condition and deterioration.

(6) Engine controls—for defects, improper travel, and improper safetying.

(7) Lines, hoses, and clamps—for leaks, improper condition and looseness.

(8) Exhaust stacks—for cracks, defects, and improper attachment.

(9) Accessories—for apparent defects in security of mounting.

(10) All systems—for improper installation, poor general condition, defects, and insecure attachment.

(11) Cowling—for cracks, and defects.

(e) Each person performing an annual or 100-hour inspection shall inspect (where applicable) the following components of the landing gear group:

(1) All units—for poor condition and insecurity of attachment.

(2) Shock absorbing devices—for improper oleo fluid level.

(3) Linkages, trusses, and members—for undue or excessive wear fatigue, and distortion.

(4) Retracting and locking mechanism—for improper operation.

(5) Hydraulic lines—for leakage.

(6) Electrical system—for chafing and improper operation of switches.

(7) Wheels—for cracks, defects, and condition of bearings.

(8) Tires—for wear and cuts.

(9) Brakes—for improper adjustment.

(10) Floats and skis—for insecure attachment and obvious or apparent defects.

(f) Each person performing an annual or 100-hour inspection shall inspect (where applicable) all components of the wing and center section assembly for poor general condition, fabric or skin deterioration, distortion, evidence of failure, and insecurity of attachment.

(g) Each person performing an annual or 100-hour inspection shall inspect (where applicable) all components and systems that make up the complete empennage assembly for poor general condition, fabric or skin deterioration, distortion, evidence of failure, insecure attachment, improper component installation, and improper component operation.

(h) Each person performing an annual or 100-hour inspection shall inspect (where applicable) the following components of the propeller group:

(1) Propeller assembly—for cracks, nicks, binds, and oil leakage.

(2) Bolts—for improper torquing and lack of safetying.

(3) Anti-icing devices—for improper operations and obvious defects.

(4) Control mechanisms—for improper operation, insecure mounting, and restricted travel.

(i) Each person performing an annual or 100-hour inspection shall inspect (where applicable) the following components of the radio group:

(1) Radio and electronic equipment—for improper installation and insecure mounting.

(2) Wiring and conduits—for improper routing, insecure mounting, and obvious defects.

(3) Bonding and shielding—for improper installation and poor condition.

(4) Antenna including trailing antenna—for poor condition, insecure mounting, and improper operation.

(j) Each person performing an annual or 100-hour inspection shall inspect (where applicable) each installed miscellaneous item that is not otherwise covered by this listing for improper installation and improper operation.

(Amdt. 43-3, Eff. 4/2/66)

APPENDIX E—ALTIMETER SYSTEM TEST AND INSPECTION

Each person performing the altimeter system tests and inspections required by § 91.411 shall comply with the following:

(a) Static pressure system:

(1) Ensure freedom from entrapped moisture and restrictions.

(2) Determine that leakage is within the tolerances established in § 23.1325 or § 25.1325, whichever is applicable.

(3) Determine that the static port heater, if installed, is operative.

(4) Ensure that no alterations or deformations of the airframe surface have been made that would affect the relationship between air pressure in the static pressure system and true ambient static air pressure for any flight condition.

(b) Altimeter:

(1) Test by an appropriately rated repair facility in accordance with the following subparagraphs. Unless otherwise specified, each test for performance may be conducted with the instrument subjected to vibration. When tests are conducted with the temperature substantially different from ambient temperature of approximately 25 degrees C., allowance shall be made for the variation from the specified condition.

(i) *Scale error*. With the barometric pressure scale at 29.92 inches of mercury, the altimeter shall be subjected successively to pressures corresponding to the altitude specified in Table I up to the maximum normally expected operating altitude of the airplane in which the altimeter is to be installed. The reduction in pressure shall be made at a rate not in excess of 20,000 feet per minute to within approximately 2,000 feet of the test point. The test point shall be approached at a rate compatible with the test equipment. The altimeter shall be kept at the pressure corresponding to each test point for at least 1 minute, but not more than 10 minutes, before a reading is taken. The error at all test points must not exceed the tolerances specified in Table I.

(ii) *Hysteresis*. The hysteresis test shall begin not more than 15 minutes after the altimeter's initial exposure to the pressure corresponding to the upper limit of the scale error test prescribed in subparagraph (i); and while the altimeter is at this pressure, the hysteresis test shall commence. Pressure shall be increased at a rate simulating a descent in altitude at the rate of 5,000 to 20,000 feet per minute until within 3,000 feet of the first test point (50 percent of maximum altitude). The test point shall then be approached at a rate of approximately 3,000 feet per minute. The altimeter shall be kept at this pressure for at least 5 minutes, but not more than 15 minutes, before the test reading is taken. After the reading has been taken, the pressure shall be increased further, in the same manner as before, until the pressure corresponding to the second test point (40 percent of maximum altitude) is reached. The altimeter shall be kept at this pressure for at least 1 minute, but not more than 10 minutes, before the test reading is taken. After the reading has been taken, the pressure shall be increased further, in the same manner as before, until atmospheric pressure is reached. The reading of the altimeter at either of the two test points shall not differ by more than the tolerance specified in Table II from the reading of the altimeter for the corresponding altitude recorded during the scale error test prescribed in paragraph (b)(i).

(iii) *After effect*. Not more than 5 minutes after the completion of the hysteresis test prescribed in paragraph (b)(ii), the reading of the altimeter (corrected for any change in atmospheric pressure) shall not differ from the original atmospheric pressure reading by more than the tolerance specified in Table II.

(iv) *Friction*. The altimeter shall be subjected to a steady rate of decrease of pressure approximating 750 feet per minute. At each altitude listed in Table III, the change in reading of the pointers after vibration shall not exceed the corresponding tolerance listed in Table III.

(v) *Case leak*. The leakage of the altimeter case, when the pressure within it corresponds to an altitude of 18,000 feet, shall not change the altimeter reading by more than the tolerance shown in Table II during an interval of 1 minute.

(vi) *Barometric scale error.* At constant atmospheric pressure, the barometric pressure scale shall be set at each of the pressures (falling within its range of adjustment) that are listed in Table IV, and shall cause the pointer to indicate the equivalent altitude difference shown in Table IV with a tolerance of 25 feet.

(2) Altimeters which are the air data computer type with associated computing systems, or which incorporate air data correction internally, may be tested in a manner and to specifications developed by the manufacturer which are acceptable to the Administrator.

(c) Automatic Pressure Altitude Reporting Equipment and ATC Transponder System Integration Test. The test must be conducted by an appropriately rated person under the conditions specified in paragraph (a). Measure the automatic pressure altitude at the output of the installed ATC transponder when interrogated on Mode C at a sufficient number of test points to ensure that the altitude reporting equipment, altimeters, and ATC transponders perform their intended functions as installed in the aircraft. The difference between the automatic reporting output and the altitude displayed at the altimeter shall not exceed 125 feet.

(d) Records: Comply with the provisions of § 43.9 of this chapter as to content, form, and disposition of the records. The person performing the altimeter tests shall record on the altimeter the date and maximum altitude to which the altimeter has been tested and the persons approving the airplane for return to service shall enter that data in the airplane log or other permanent record.

TABLE I

Altitude	Equivalent pressure (inches of mercury)	Tolerance ± (feet)
−1,000	31.018	20
0	29.921	20
500	29.385	20
1,000	28.856	20
1,500	28.335	25
2,000	27.821	30
3,000	26.817	30
4,000	25.842	35
6,000	23.978	40
8,000	22.225	60
10,000	20.577	80
12,000	19.029	90
14,000	17.577	100
16,000	16.216	110
18,000	14.942	120
20,000	13.750	130
22,000	12.636	140
25,000	11.104	155
30,000	8.885	180
35,000	7.041	205
40,000	5.538	230
45,000	4.355	255
50,000	3.425	280

TABLE II—TEST TOLERANCES

Test	Tolerance (feet)
Case Leak Test	±100
Hysteresis Test:	
First Test Point (50 percent of maximum altitude)	75
Second Test Point (40 percent of maximum altitude)	75
After Effect Test	30

TABLE III—FRICTION

Altitude (feet)	Tolerance (feet)
1,000	±70
2,000	70
3,000	70
5,000	70
10,000	80
15,000	90
20,000	100
25,000	120
30,000	140
35,000	160
40,000	180
50,000	250

TABLE IV—PRESSURE-ALTITUDE DIFFERENCE

Pressure (inches of Hg)	Altitude difference (feet)
28.10	−1,727
28.50	−1,340
29.00	−863
29.50	−392
29.92	0
30.50	+531
30.90	+893
30.99	+974

(Amdt. 43-2, Eff. 7/29/65); (Amdt. 43-7, Eff. 8/1/67); (Amdt. 43-19, Eff. 6/26/78); (Amdt. 43-23, Eff. 10/15/82); (Amdt. 43-31, Eff. 8/18/90)

APPENDIX F—ATC TRANSPONDER TESTS AND INSPECTIONS

The ATC transponder tests required by § 91.413 of this chapter may be conducted using a bench check or portable test equipment and must meet the requirements prescribed in paragraphs (a) through (j) of this appendix. If portable test equipment with appropriate coupling to the aircraft antenna system is used, operate the test equipment for ATCRBS transponders at a nominal rate of 235 interrogations per second to avoid possible ATCRBS interference. Operate the test equipment at a nominal rate of 50 Mode S interrogations per second for Mode S. An additional 3 dB loss is allowed to compensate for antenna coupling errors during receiver sensitivity measurements conducted in accordance with paragraph (c)(1) when using portable test equipment.

(a) Radio Reply Frequency:

(1) For all classes of ATCRBS transponders, interrogate the transponder and verify that the reply frequency is 1090±3 Megahertz (MHz).

(2) For classes 1B, 2B, and 3B Mode S transponders, interrogate the transponder and verify that the reply frequency is 1090±3 MHz.

(3) For classes 1B, 2B, and 3B Mode S transponders that incorporate the optional 1090±1 MHz reply frequency, interrogate the transponder and verify that the reply frequency is correct.

(4) For classes 1A, 2A, 3A, and 4 Mode S transponders, interrogate the transponder and verify that the reply frequency is 1090±1 MHz.

(b) Suppression: When Classes 1B and 2B ATCRBS Transponders, or Classes 1B, 2B, and 3B Mode S transponders are interrogated Mode 3/A at an interrogation rate between 230 and 1,000 interrogations per second; or when Classes 1A and 2A ATCRBS Transponders, or Classes 1B, 2A, 3A, and 4 Mode S transponders are interrogated at a rate between 230 and 1,200 Mode 3/A interrogations per second:

(1) Verify that the transponder does not respond to more than 1 percent of ATCRBS interrogations when the amplitude of P_2 pulse is equal to the P_1 pulse.

(2) Verify that the transponder replies to at least 90 percent of ATCRBS interrogations when the amplitude of the P_2 pulse is 9 dB less than the P_1 pulse. If the test is conducted with a radiated test signal, the interrogation rate shall be 235±5 interrogations per second unless a higher rate has been approved for the test equipment used at that location.

(c) Receiver Sensitivity:

(1) Verify that for any class of ATCRBS Transponder, the receiver minimum triggering level (MTL) of the system is –73±4 dBm, or that for any class of Mode S transponder the receiver MTL for Mode S format (P6 type) interrogations is –74±3 dBm by use of a test set either:

(i) Connected to the antenna end of the transmission line;

(ii) Connected to the antenna terminal of the transponder with a correction for transmission line loss; or

(iii) Utilized radiated signal.

(2) Verify that the difference in Mode 3/A and Mode C receiver sensitivity does not exceed 1 dB for either any class of ATCRBS transponder or any class of Mode S transponder.

(d) Radio Frequency (RF) Peak Output Power:

(1) Verify that the transponder RF output power is within specifications for the class of transponder. Use the same conditions as described in (c)(1) (i), (ii), and (iii) above.

(i) For Class 1A and 2A ATCRBS transponders, verify that the minimum RF peak output power is at least 21.0 dBw (125 watts).

(ii) For Class 1B and 2B ATCRBS Transponders, verify that the minimum RF peak output power is at least 18.5 dBw (70 watts).

(iii) For Class 1A, 2A, 3A, and 4 and those Class 1B, 2B, and 3B Mode S transponders that include the optional high RF peak output power, verify that the minimum RF peak output power is at least 21.0 dBw (125 watts).

(iv) For Classes 1B, 2B, and 3B Mode S transponders, verify that the minimum RF peak output power is at least 18.5 dBw (70 watts).

(v) For any class of ATCRBS or any class of Mode S transponders, verify that the maximum RF peak output power does not exceed 27.0 dBw (500 watts).

Note: The tests in (e) through (j) apply only to Mode S transponders.

(e) Mode S Diversity Transmission Channel Isolation: For any class of Mode S transponder that incorporates diversity operation, verify that the RF peak output power transmitted from the selected antenna exceeds the power transmitted from the nonselected antenna by at least 20 dB.

(f) Mode S Address: Interrogate the Mode S transponder and verify that it replies only to its assigned address. Use the correct address and at least two incorrect addresses. The interrogations should be made at a nominal rate of 50 interrogations per second.

(g) Mode S Formats: Interrogate the Mode S transponder with uplink formats (UF) for which it is equipped and verify that the replies are made in the correct format. Use the surveillance formats UF = 4 and 5. Verify that the altitude reported in the replies to UF = 4 are the same as that reported in a valid ATCRBS Mode C reply. Verify that the identity reported in the replies to UF = 5 are the same as that reported in a valid ATCRBS Mode 3/A reply. If the transponder is so equipped, use the communication formats UF = 20, 21, and 24.

(h) Mode S All-Call Interrogations: Interrogate the Mode S transponder with the Mode S only all-call format UF = 11, and the ATCRBS/Mode S all-call formats (1.6 microsecond P_4 pulse) and verify that the correct address and capability are reported in the replies (downlink format DF = 11).

(i) ATCRBS-Only All-Call Interrogation: Interrogate the Mode S transponder with the ATCRBS-only all-call interrogation (0.8 microsecond P_4 pulse) and verify that no reply is generated.

(j) Squitter: Verify that the Mode S transponder generates a correct squitter approximately once per second.

(k) Records: Comply with the provisions of § 43.9 of this chapter as to content, form, and disposition of the records.

(Amdt. 43-17, Eff. 1/26/73); (Amdt. 43-18, Eff. 12/31/73); (Amdt. 43-19, Eff. 6/26/78); (Amdt. 43-26, Eff. 4/6/87); (Amdt. 43-31, Eff. 8/18/90)

B

Recommended tools

THE FOLLOWING LIST OF TOOLS WILL BE INDISPENSABLE IN ALLOWING you to maintain your airplane. While it is possible to use a wrench for a hammer, and a screwdriver for a pin punch, you'll find your work goes easier with the right tools. It isn't necessary to spend a fortune on your tools, but for things like screwdrivers, which get a lot of use, you might want to spend a little extra and buy brand names that carry a warranty. For the more expensive items like a torque wrench, you might want to identify it in some way such as engraving it or coloring the handle so when it gets borrowed, you can easily retrieve it.

You might find it beneficial to have a separate set of tools that you can keep at the airport. If you don't have a hangar, leave the toolbox in your airplane, then move it to the driver's seat of your car when you go flying. That way you won't forgret to put it back in the plane before you go back home. Or you might want to build a weatherproof storage bin that can be left at the tiedown. Build it so you can run one of the tiedown chains through the box to keep it in place.

A word about a very important item on the following list—the torque wrench. This is one of the most misused tools in the workshop. Long ago, manufacturers of items that require the general public to eventually work on them learned that the same general public falls into two categories. There are those who are afraid of overtightening a nut or bolt, so they don't tighten enough and the thing falls apart. Then there are those who feel that each nut and bolt they encounter in their lives is something to be brought into submission with a good, solid turn of the wrench. The torque wrench was developed to help make the fastening process more consistent, particularly in those areas that are most crucial.

This handy little device is of no use, however, if used improperly. Learn the difference between foot-pounds and inch-pounds if you don't already know. And make sure the torque wrench is calibrated regularly and stored "unsprung." Leaving it set at any reading while stored will weaken the mechanism and eventually give you false readings.

One other tool bears special mention here. It's the spark plug socket, used, oddly enough, to remove and install spark plugs. It's tempting to use any deep socket that will fit, but the one specifically designed for the purpose will protect the plugs (Fig. B-1).

Fig. B-1. This photo shows the inside of an aircraft spark plug socket. Notice that the hex shape only goes partially into the interior, then the socket becomes round. This will help prevent damage to the spark plug threads where the ignition harness attaches.

Here is our suggested beginning tool list. Your collection of tools will grow as your work on the plane increases.

- Maintenance and parts manuals for your plane.
- Flashlight.
- Screwdrivers (use a name brand that carries a warranty):
  ~#1 Phillips, #2 Phillips of various lengths.
  ~Slot: ¼", ³⁄₁₆", ⅛", also of various lengths.

- Scribe/ice pick.
- Combination wrenches:
  ~$\frac{1}{4}$, $\frac{5}{16}$, $\frac{11}{32}$, $\frac{3}{8}$, $\frac{7}{16}$, $\frac{1}{2}$, $\frac{9}{16}$, $\frac{5}{8}$, $\frac{11}{16}$, $\frac{3}{4}$, $\frac{13}{16}$, $\frac{7}{8}$, $\frac{15}{16}$. (These might all be available as a set, except $\frac{11}{32}$. You might have to buy it separately.)
- 1 adjustable wrench.
- Pliers:
  ~Needle nose, slip joint, arc joint, diagonal cutting.
- Socket sets:
  ~$\frac{1}{4}$ drive and $\frac{3}{8}$ drive.
  ~$\frac{7}{8}$ deep spark plug. (Don't substitute a deep throat wrench. The fluting can damage threads.)
- Torque wrench, 10–75 ft/lb range.
- Hammers:
  ~1 softface/plastic tip/ nonmarring.
  ~Selection of ball peen (1 light, 1 heavier).
- Multimeter.
- Toolbox to keep everything in one place.
- Nice to have: electric drill/driver with torque clutch.

Index

Illustration page numbers are in **boldface**.

ABOUT THE AUTHORS

Mary Woodhouse is the business and aviation reporter at *The Daily Courier* in Prescott, Arizona and has written extensively on a variety of aviation matters. She holds a commercial license for hot air balloons and operated a balloon repair station in Phoenix, Arizona for 13 years.

Scott Gifford is an aviation mechanic and holds an Airframe and Powerplant certificate and Inspection Authorization. He is also a pilot and certified multi-engine flight instructor, a sailplane pilot, and owner of a Cessna 140. He has been actively involved in the Experimental Aircraft Association and is currently rebuilding a 1920s Ryan B-1.